OXFORD MODERN LANGUAGES
AND LITERATURE MONOGRAPHS

Editorial Committee

M. M. BOWIE   D. J. CONSTANTINE
E. M. JEFFREYS   I. W. F. MACLEAN
R. A. G. PEARSON   R. W. TRUMAN   J. R. WOODHOUSE

Postcolonial Paradoxes in French Caribbean Writing

Césaire, Glissant, Condé

JEANNIE SUK

CLARENDON PRESS · OXFORD

OXFORD
UNIVERSITY PRESS

Great Clarendon Street, Oxford, OX2 6DP

Oxford University Press is a department of the University of Oxford.
It furthers the University's objective of excellence in research, scholarship,
and education by publishing worldwide in

Oxford New York

Athens Auckland Bangkok Bogotá Buenos Aires Cape Town
Chennai Dar es Salaam Delhi Florence Hong Kong Istanbul Karachi
Kolkata Kuala Lumpur Madrid Melbourne Mexico City Mumbai
Nairobi Paris São Paulo Shanghai Singapore Taipei Tokyo Toronto Warsaw

and associated companies in Berlin Ibadan

Oxford is a registered trade mark of Oxford University Press
in the UK and certain other countries

Published in the United States
by Oxford University Press Inc., New York

© Jeannie Suk 2001

The moral rights of the author have been asserted
Database right Oxford University Press (maker)

First published 2001

All rights reserved. No part of this publication may be reproduced,
stored in a retrieval system, or transmitted, in any form or by any means,
without the prior permission in writing of Oxford University Press,
or as expressly permitted by law, or under terms agreed with the appropriate
reprographics rights organization. Enquiries concerning reproduction
outside the scope of the above should be sent to the Rights Department,
Oxford University Press, at the address above

You must not circulate this book in any other binding or cover
and you must impose the same condition on any acquirer

British Library Cataloguing in Publication Data
Data available

Library of Congress Cataloging in Publication Data
Data available
ISBN 0-19-816018-6

1 3 5 7 9 10 8 6 4 2

Typeset by Regent Typesetting, London
Printed in Great Britain
on acid-free paper by
T J International Ltd,
Padstow, Cornwall

ACKNOWLEDGEMENTS

First, I would like to thank Malcolm Bowie, who nurtured this project as a book from the start. Without his wisdom and guidance, there would be no book. My warm thanks to Colin Davis and Celia Britton for their sympathetic reading of the text before it became a manuscript. At Oxford, Belinda Jack and Robert Young were very helpful to me at key stages.

My debts to past teachers are enormous: Lynne Huffer, Claudine Kahan, Susan Blood, Cathy Caruth, and Caroline Rody. Special thanks to Christopher L. Miller and Vera Kutzinski for their encouragement and their kindness in reading the manuscript.

The Marshall Commission funded my graduate study and made this book possible. Wadham College and St Hugh's College also generously supported my research and travel. I am also indebted to the Columbia University Center for Pyschoanalytic Training and Research, where I was an Affiliate Scholar during 1998–99. Thanks also to my seminar students at Yale during the spring of 1999 for engaging energetically with the ideas in this book.

I also wish to thank Lani Guinier for her generosity as a mentor and for enabling me to reinvent myself.

I appreciate the help of Matthew Hollis, my editor at OUP.

The loyalty and friendship of Deborah Wexler, Mira Seo, Janna Wagner, Tricia Harmon, Lucille Wood, Paras Mehta, and Bert Huang continue to touch me deeply.

Julie Chi-hye Suk discussed all the ideas in this book with me and read every word. To have a sister who is also a colleague is a rare privilege. Christine Suk has been humorous, tolerant, even indulgent. My parents have given me extraordinary, unconditional support in all my endeavours.

Finally, I thank Noah Feldman, without whom this project would neither have begun nor been completed. I owe him everything.

CONTENTS

1. INTRODUCTION: POSTCOLONIALITY, ALLEGORY, AND THE FRENCH CARIBBEAN   1

2. CROSSINGS, RETURNS: CÉSAIRE'S *CAHIER D'UN RETOUR AU PAYS NATAL*   24

3. GLISSANT, *DÉTOUR*, AND HISTORY   56

4. ARCHETYPAL RETURNS: *HÉRÉMAKHONON* AND *UNE SAISON À RIHATA*   84

5. ALLEGORY, SORCERY, AND HISTORICAL REWRITING: *MOI, TITUBA, SORCIÈRE . . . NOIRE DE SALEM*   117

6. REPRESENTING CARIBBEAN CROSSINGS: *TRAVERSÉE DE LA MANGROVE*   149

EPILOGUE   181

Bibliography   187

Index   201

I

INTRODUCTION: POSTCOLONIALITY, ALLEGORY, AND THE FRENCH CARIBBEAN

The rise of postcolonial studies has produced the commonplace that the term 'postcolonial' is problematic: it possesses an uneasily defined temporality, politics, and institutional location. That 'postcolonial' has myriad possible designations—among them a historical period, a political status, a geographical area, a critical stance, an intellectual development—contributes to the difficulty of its definition even in the face of its increasing adoption and usage. This difficulty may have the effect of eroding the term's specificity and force. It is thus not surprising that theorists of the still-emerging field of postcolonial studies have devoted much of their writing to contesting the definition of the term.

Rather than engaging this debate directly, this book explores postcoloniality at one of its margins through the paradoxes that emerge in the literature and theory of the francophone Antilles.[1] Bending to our purposes Homi Bhabha's imperative to focus on the 'in-between' space of encounter and contact between self and other in the formation of identity, we could say that the concept of postcoloniality might itself benefit from attention to in-between spaces.[2] The Antilles, geographically, culturally, and politically situated in between, provide rich terrain on which to reflect on the concept. Through the paradigm of its literature, and its literary culture, which are indeed not literally postcolonial in the political sense, this book attempts an indirect series of approaches to the concept of the postcolonial.

The paradigmatic status of the Antilles in this book may perhaps appear to be at odds with the concept of marginality that is equally

---

[1] This book is primarily about the literature of Martinique and Guadeloupe, which I often refer to as the Antilles, rather than the French West Indies or the French Caribbean, more familiar to English-speaking readers, simply for convenience and because it is the francophone designation.
[2] Bhabha writes of the 'need to think beyond narratives of originary and initial subjectivities and to focus on those moments or processes that are produced in the articulation of cultural differences'. See *The Location of Culture* (London: Routledge, 1994), 1–2.

important to it. This tension is inevitable, for the central paradox that motivates this book is the way in which the postcolonial has come to 'represent' the idea of the margin made familiar by poststructuralism. How is this a paradox? That the abstract signs of theory could find grounding referents in the plight and people of the postcolonial world seems at once a somewhat anti-climactic relief and a disappointment. The 'dangerous supplementarity' of the in-between doesn't seem so dangerous when revealed to have been an allegory of a concrete situation. This book explores the ways in which Antillean literature bears multiple allegorical burdens, unveiling paradoxes of postcoloniality and poststructuralism while recounting the failure of such referential relationships. I focus on the metaphorical overlay and interplay of three spaces—geographical, tropological, psychic—in which the relationship between Antillean and postcolonial problematics can be illuminated: the space of the ocean that must be crossed, the breaks and discontinuities of allegorical signification, and the traumatic gap in historical consciousness. I show the ways in which these marginal spaces specific to Caribbean, deconstructive, and psychoanalytic modes of thought cross, allegorize, and repeat each other in the interface between them.

The 'interstitial perspective' has become paramount in our time, whose characteristic spatio-temporal disjunctures and displacements are signalled by the proliferation of 'posts-'—postmodern, poststructural, post-war.[3] On the level of descriptive periodization, however, there is concern in some quarters that the term postcolonial is 'not only a fiction, but a most pernicious fiction, a cover-up of a dangerous period in our peoples' lives'.[4] That the term may falsely suggest an end to colonialism and ignore continuing neo-colonial global inequality suggests that there may in fact be nothing 'post-' about postcolonial. Despite the emergence of independence and nationhood in some formerly colonized areas of the world during the second part of the twentieth century, the designation of postcolonial for our present may be premature. The state that postcoloniality designates may not yet exist.

The 'after' implied by the term is de-emphasized, however, by Ashcroft, Griffiths, and Tiffin, who take the term to 'to cover all the culture affected by the imperial process from the moment of coloni-

[3] *Location of Culture*, 1–2.
[4] Ama Ata Aidoo, 'That Capacious Topic: Gender Politics', in Phil Mariani (ed.), *Critical Fictions*, (Seattle: Bay Press, 1991), 151–4: 152.

zation to the present day. This is because there is a continuity of preoccupations throughout the historical process initiated by European imperial aggression.'[5] Similarly refusing the temporal break of the post-, Stephen Slemon locates 'a specifically anti- or *post*-colonial *discursive* purchase in culture, one which begins in the moment that colonial power inscribes itself onto the body and space of its Others and which continues as an often occulted tradition into the modern theatre of neo-colonialist international relations'.[6] These theorists emphasize the unbroken 'continuity of preoccupations' and the continuity of anticolonial resistance, stretching from the beginning of colonialism into the present. The post- indicates a movement beyond colonialism. This 'beyond' extends back through history across the temporal break that the post- designates.

These definitions and contestations exhibit and confront the anxiety about a break with the past that seems to be occasioned by the term 'postcolonial'. The term's disavowal by some and its justification by others work to establish continuity in the face of the term's implied discontinuity. In the debate over whether postcolonial describes the present or a state not yet achieved, includes or excludes the past, the interplay between past, present, and future points us to a paradox. The anticolonial process of getting beyond colonialism that is crucial to some definitions of postcoloniality implies a progress: the resistance to colonialism as moving beyond it. On the other hand, the extension of the beyond across the temporal break that the post- implies links the past and the present in a state that is continuously postcolonial to the very extent that it is still colonial, not beyond it. Forward-looking progress and backward-looking regress, discontinuity and continuity, depend upon each other. If the term 'postcolonial' signals 'a widespread, epochal crisis in the idea of linear, historical "progress"',[7] the paradox perhaps has to do with

---

[5] *The Empire writes back: Theory and Practice in Post-Colonial Literatures* (London: Routledge, 1989), 2.

[6] 'Modernism's Last Post', in Ian Adam and Helen Tiffin (eds.), *Past the Last Post: Theorising Post-Colonialism and Post-Modernism* (Hemel Hempstead: Harvester Wheatsheaf, 1991), 1–12: 3.

[7] Postcolonialism, along with other posts- like postmodernism and post-structuralism, entails a critique of Enlightenment narratives of progress. However, as McClintock points out, 'the *term* "post-colonial".... is haunted by the very figure of linear "development" that it sets out to dismantle.... Metaphorically poised on the border between old and new, end and beginning, the term heralds the end of a world era, but within the same trope of linear progress that animated that era.' Anne McClintock, 'The Angel of Progress: Pitfalls of the Term "Post-Colonialism"', *Social Text*, 31–2 (1992), 84–98: 85.

recapitulating a narrative of progress in the effort to move beyond that narrative. Bhabha articulates the paradoxical interplay of present, past, and future thus:

'Beyond' signifies spatial distance, marks progress, promises the future; but our intimations of exceeding the barrier or boundary—the very act of going beyond—are unknowable, unrepresentable, without a return to the present which, in the process of repetition, becomes disjunct and displaced. . . . The present can no longer be simply envisioned as a break or a bonding with the past and the future, no longer a synchronic presence.[8]

The present of postcoloniality can be formulated as a moment of going beyond through a return to the present. Interstitiality can be understood as a temporal paradox in which looking to the future necessarily entails a *return*. The present, the past, and the future do not keep to their proper places, whether in continuum or rupture, but haunt each other, making for what Bhabha calls 'the "unhomely" condition of the modern world'.[9] Bhabha's gloss of the post- as signalling a need for a return to the present proposes a useful strategy for this book, which, in looking to spatial, rhetorical, and psychic intimations of beyond, investigates various forms of return that occur within the distances that promise the future.

Debates about chronology, periodization, and temporality go hand in hand with debates about history. Ashcroft, Griffiths, and Tiffin suggest the complicity of historical discourse and European colonialism, arguing that 'the emergence of history in European thought is coterminous with the rise of modern colonialism', and that history was 'a prominent, if not the prominent instrument for the control of subject peoples'.[10] Whether or not history was empirically an effective tool for subjugation, it appears that the concept of history becomes a site of struggle in postcolonial discourse in part because of a notion that 'historicism projected the West as History', and that its Others were peripheral, ignored, or repressed in the writing of history.[11] Thus various postcolonial theorists have stressed the importance of doing history in a way that decentres the sovereign

---

[8] *Location of Culture*, 4.
[9] Ibid.
[10] *The Post-Colonial Studies Reader* (London: Routledge, 1995), 355.
[11] Gyan Prakash, 'Subaltern Studies as Postcolonial Criticism', *American Historical Review*, 99/5 (1994), 1475–90: 1475 n.

INTRODUCTION 5

subjectivity of the colonizer.[12] Aijaz Ahmad alleges that postcolonialism has failed to meet this challenge:

In periodising our history in the triadic terms of pre-colonial, colonial and post-colonial, the conceptual apparatus of 'postcolonial criticism' privileges as primary the role of colonialism as the principle of structuration in that history, so that all that came before colonialism becomes its own prehistory and whatever comes after can only be lived as infinite aftermath.[13]

Ahmad observes that, within the concept of postcoloniality, the very representability of the colonized depends upon a referential struc-ture of centre and periphery, in which the 'pre-' and 'post-' are by definition peripheral histories to the authorizing centre of colonialism.

In its efforts to uncover previously unknown histories, the Subaltern Studies Group relies, in another way, on a centre-periphery model in which the authentic, veiled, core of the subaltern voice is retrieved; Gayatri Spivak's famous critique of the group's approach inspires reflection on the relationship between history and unrepresentability.[14] Spivak draws attention to the problem of absence and discontinuity that makes the project of representing the colonized far more complex than a model of giving voice to previously untold, authentic experience. This book is concerned with what happens to the possibility of representation not only when the centrality of the colonizer's history is destabilized, but when a recoupable counter-history is absent.

ALLEGORY

The relationship between history and representation comes to the fore in the paradoxical movement of allegory. Theoretical treatment of the structure of allegory resonates with the paradoxes in the concept of postcoloniality. Traditionally, the structure of allegory has been formulated according to a centre-periphery model, in

[12] In making reference to the term 'history' throughout, this book takes as one point of departure the line of enquiry exemplified by Robert Young's work in *White Mythologies: Writing History and the West* (London and New York: Routledge, 1990), where he argues, through a discussion of the concept of history in several western, especially Marxist, traditions, that history takes shape as a totalizing and Eurocentric discourse.
[13] 'The Politics of Literary Postcoloniality', *Race and Class*, 36/3 (1995), 1–20: 9.
[14] 'Can the Subaltern Speak?' in Cary Nelson and Lawrence Grossberg (eds.), *Marxism and the Interpretation of Culture* (Basingstoke: Macmillan Education, 1988), 271–313: 308.

which interpretation removes a veil to reveal the underlying meaning. Dante's account of the 'allegory of poets' as a sense that 'hides itself under the cloak', and 'a truth hidden under the beautiful lie', holds out the possibility of both hiding and revealing.[15] On the one hand, allegory seems to offer the possibility of access to meaning, and literary interpretation becomes the project of unveiling the truth that is cloaked by a figure. On the other hand, that very cloak, the beautiful lie, can be the hallmark of the unreadability of allegory. Allegory has discontinuity at its heart, an explicit break between sign and referent that highlights difference, arbitrariness, and inaccessibility. Paul de Man writes, 'Allegorical narratives tell the story of the failure to read.... Allegories are always allegories of metaphor and, as such, they are always allegories of the impossibility of reading.'[16]

Allegory has received renewed attention in recent years, in part because it has become a rich site of entanglement for the problems of representation and history raised by postcolonial writing and post-structuralism. Stephen Slemon privileges allegory as a mode of interpretation in postcolonial discourse.[17] However, he distinguishes allegory in postcolonial discourse from the versions of allegory 'now in critical currency' in post-structuralist discourse, in which allegory stands for 'the valorisation of textuality, irony, and the arbitrary in the theory of meaning'.[18] In postcolonial allegory rather, the referent is history, which becomes 'transformed' through its allegorization: 'The common pursuit is to proceed beyond a "determinist view of history" by revising, reappropriating, or reinterpreting history as a concept.'[19] The binocular lens of allegory refocuses our concept of history as fixed monument into a concept of history as the creation of a discursive practice, and in doing so it opens history, fiction's 'other', to the possibility of transformation.[20]

Thus, on the one hand, allegory implies a set of external historical referents that ground the interpretation of texts; on the other hand, allegory offers the possibility of liberation from determinate narratives of history. Even while Slemon rejects the textual liberation

[15] *Il Convivio*, ed. by G. Busnelli and Giuseppe Vandelli, 2 vols. (Florence: F. Le Monnier, 1934–7), ii. 97. John MacQueen writes of allegories: 'something far different from their apparent subject is concealed beneath the veil', in *Allegory* (London: Methuen, 1971), 48.
[16] *Allegories of Reading* (New Haven: Yale University Press, 1979), 205.
[17] 'Post-Colonial Allegory and the Transformation of History', *Journal of Commonwealth Literature*, 23/1 (1988), 157–68: 159.
[18] Ibid.
[19] Ibid.
[20] Ibid.

INTRODUCTION 7

valorized in the post-structural incarnation of allegory, he relies on it to define the transformative function of allegory in postcolonial literature. Paradoxically, through the de-emphasis of textuality, irony, and arbitrariness, history becomes highlighted as a discursive practice. Allegory both anchors and unmoors at the same time.

The tension between arbitrariness and determinacy tends to riddle discourses about allegory. This is due to the discontinuity at the heart of allegory that implicates questions of the past. In Paul de Man's 'rhetoric of temporality', the passage of time is constitutive of the allegorical sign, which always refers to an anterior sign.[21] Debates about allegory display contradictory notions of its relationship to the past. By some accounts allegory allows access to a history that is in danger of being erased, while on others it effects a forgetting.[22] These coexisting contradictory properties of allegory map the paradoxes of postcoloniality, which is marked by discontinuity with the past as well as by a desire for return. Preoccupied as it is with anteriority and with the gaps that constitute its function, allegory gives us cause to reflect on the relationship of fictionality to questions of history and historylessness. Fineman's juxtaposition of allegory, distance, and the relationship between the past and the present is suggestive: 'It is as though allegory were precisely that mode that makes up for distance, or heals the gap, between the present and a disappearing past, which, without interpretation, would be otherwise irretrievable and foreclosed.'[23] I would suggest that the connection and importance of allegory to postcolonial writing lies in the nostalgic longing associated with the allegorical mode.

In 'The Rhetoric of Temporality', however, Paul de Man argues that the renunciation of nostalgia informs the allegorical mode:

Whereas the symbol postulates the possibility of an identity or identification, allegory designates primarily a distance in relation to its own origin, and, renouncing the nostalgia and the desire to coincide, it establishes its language in the void of this temporal difference. In doing so, it prevents the self from an illusory identification with the non-self, which is now fully, though painfully, recognized as a non-self.[24]

[21] 'The Rhetoric of Temporality', in Charles Singleton (ed.), *Interpretation: Theory and Practice* (Baltimore: Johns Hopkins University Press, 1969), 173–209.
[22] See Craig Owens, 'The Allegorical Impulse: Towards a Theory of Postmodernism', *October*, 19 (1981), 67–86: 68; Paul Smith, 'The Will to Allegory in Postmodernism', *Dalhousie Review*, 62/1 (1982), 105–22: 118.
[23] 'The Structure of Allegorical Desire', in Stephen J. Greenblatt (ed.), *Allegory and Representation* (Selected Papers from the English Institute, NS 5; Baltimore: Johns Hopkins University Press, 1981), 26–60: 29.   [24] p. 191.

But this does not seem quite right. It would seem, rather, that the recognition of a permanent break does not preclude nostalgia, but rather occasions it, precisely because the 'painful' recognition of the break between self and non-self is felt in the form of nostalgia in allegorical texts. In de Man's conception, allegory, standing in contrast to the Romantic symbol, has a referent that is other to it: 'Allegory appears as dryly rational and dogmatic in its reference to a meaning that it does not itself constitute, whereas the symbol is founded on an intimate unity between the image that rises up before the sense and the supersensory totality that the image suggests.'[25] Christopher Miller likens allegorical signification to a process of emptying the allegorical sign of a proper meaning and pointing elsewhere:

Each sign points to another that precedes it, imparts meaning to it, and yet shows it, the present sign, to be empty. The process of giving meaning to the present is the same as showing the present to be empty . . . Everything points to something else as its predetermination, excusing itself and acquiring a meaning for itself.[26]

This allegorical process of a sign's simultaneous acquisition of meaning and being emptied of meaning is structurally achieved by the sign's pointing away from itself, toward an *anterior* sign. The element of temporality is a version of the constitutive element of otherness. Allegory boasts

a relationship between signs in which the reference to their respective meanings has become of secondary importance. But this relationship between signs necessarily contains a constitutive temporal element; it remains necessary, if there is to be allegory, that the allegorical sign refers to another sign that precedes it. The meaning constituted by the allegorical sign can then consist only in repetition . . . of a previous sign with which it can never coincide, since it is of the essence of this previous sign to be pure anteriority.[27]

The break between the allegorical sign and referent can be understood as a temporal break between sign and previous sign, which itself is 'pure anteriority'.

The key, then, is to notice and appreciate the confluence of nostalgia, anteriority, and otherness within allegory. De Man claims

---

[25] *Allegory and Representation*, 174.
[26] *Blank Darkness: Africanist Discourse in French* (Chicago: University of Chicago Press, 1985), 130.
[27] De Man, 'Rhetoric of Temporality', 190.

that the allegorical sign can never coincide with the previous sign to which it refers, since 'it is of the essence of this previous sign to be pure anteriority'; the previous sign is not merely anterior, but is anteriority itself. Miller discerns in de Man's valorization of allegory a totalizing, almost religious belief that in effect becomes a fetish: 'If allegory is the realm of the "entirely good," perhaps the only "pure anteriority" is God or a world where God and matter are one';[28] 'By desiring allegory, one alters its differential purity.'[29] Walter Benjamin offers a suggestive similar definition:

Any person, any object, any relationship can mean absolutely anything else. ... All of the things which are used to signify derive, from the very fact of their pointing to something else, a power which makes them appear no longer commensurable with profane things, which raises them onto a higher plane, and which can, indeed, sanctify them.[30]

These observations are useful for formulating the questions why nostalgia so consistently accompanies allegory, and how we are to understand the nostalgia for an anteriority, which seems to extend seamlessly from the linguistic to the phenomenal level. For even as difference remains the hallmark of allegory, its repetitive pointing toward pure anteriority may be the expression of longing for the subordination of difference to a sanctified unity. Hence, the hunger of allegory for absolute heterogeneity resembles, in another light, a craving for a lost wholeness.

ABSOLUTE DIFFERENCES, ABSOLUTE UNITIES

Benjamin writes of Baudelaire's *Les Fleurs du mal:* 'If there really is a secret architecture to this book, ... the cycle of poems that opens the volume is probably devoted to something irretrievably lost'.[31] Benjamin names the nostalgic encounter with an earlier life as the key to *Les Fleurs du mal:* 'The murmur of the past may be heard in the correspondences, and the canonical experience of them has its place in a previous life.'[32] The poems that Benjamin takes to be exemplary of this nostalgic encounter are heavily saturated with an exotic

[28] Miller, *Blank Darkness*, 133.
[29] Ibid. 134.
[30] *The Origin of German Tragic Drama*, trans. John Osborne (London: NLB, 1977), 175.
[31] 'On Some Motifs in Baudelaire', in *Illuminations*, ed. Hannah Arendt, trans. Harry Zohn (London: Fontana Press, 1992), 152–195: 177.
[32] Ibid. 178.

theme. While he does not remark on this, the realm of the *correspondances* is an exotic realm, and the experience of the *correspondances* is closely associated with, and intensified by, otherness. Consider, for example, Baudelaire's 'La Vie antérieure', which I quote in its entirety:

> J'ai longtemps habité sous de vastes portiques
> Que les soleils marins teignaient de mille feux,
> Et que leurs grands piliers, droits et majesteux,
> Rendaient pareils, le soir, aux grottes basaltiques.
>
> Les houles, en roulant les images des cieux,
> Mêlaient d'une façon solennelle et mystique
> Les tout-puissants accords de leur riche musique
> Aux couleurs de couchant reflété par mes yeux.
>
> C'est là que j'ai vécu dans les voluptés calmes,
> Au milieu de l'azur, des vagues, des splendeurs
> Et des esclaves nus, tout imprégnés d'odeurs,
>
> Qui me rafraîchissaient le front avec des palmes,
> Et dont l'unique soin était d'approfondir
> Le secret douloureux qui me faisait languir.[33]
>
> I lived a long time under vast porticoes
> whose splendors altered with the sea all day;
> by evening their majestic pillars turned,
> row after row, into tall basalt caves.
>
> Solemn and magical the waves rolled in
> bearing images of heaven on the swell,
> blending the sovereign music that they made
> with sunset colors mirrored in my eyes.
>
> There I lived, in a rapture of repose,
> amid the glories of that sky, that sea,
> and I had naked slaves, perfumed with musk,
>
> to fan me by the hour with rustling fronds,
> and their one study was to diagnose
> the secret torment which had sickened me.[34]

The presence of the 'esclaves nus' serves as the speaker's means to a state of intensified being. The slaves have only one role: 'dont l'unique soin était d'approfondir | Le secret douloureux qui me faisait languir'. The objectification of the Other takes the form of

---

[33] Charles Baudelaire, *Œuvres complètes*, ed. Claude Pichois (Bibliothèque de la Pléiade, 1; Paris: Gallimard, 1961, 17.

[34] Id., *Les Fleurs du Mal*, trans. Richard Howard (Boston: David Godine, 1982), 21.

INTRODUCTION

sexualization and feminization: the slaves are impregnated with odours, which exist solely to benefit the speaker. The slaves' function is to be the pure means to an authenticity enjoyed in an earlier life. In this poem especially, the idiom of the *correspondances* depends upon alterity—the difference of the slave—to achieve the transport to an earlier life. The slave becomes a trope for the difference that is needed to effect this nostalgic return.

In this poem of placeless, timeless, sweet languor, the appearance of 'esclaves nus' shifts our orientation from an unspecified, unmotivated space somewhere in the imagination, to a colonial locale. Thus, posited as means to a primordial, placeless past, the 'esclaves nus', as colonial metonyms, also pose a momentary disruption to it. The use of the slave as a figural means to the speaker's deepened access to the *correspondances* suggests the exploitation and reification of persons for the most seemingly abstract features of poetry. More specifically, it puts in the foreground the necessity of difference for figuration, as the exotic becomes a trope for the difference that is needed to accomplish a desired poetic or figural transport. The slave in 'La Vie antérieure' provides the alterity needed for transport to a desired state, which is explicitly a state of anteriority as such.

What does it means for a person, as an embodiment of alterity, to function in a literary text as a pure means to a desired anteriority? On the question of persons serving as means, Miller writes: 'Africanist discourse has been from the beginning a specific series of means for saying something "else", for describing difference and otherness; allegory would logically be a privileged mode of expression within that discourse.'[35] Miller designates Africanist discourse as allegorical because it is characterized by an 'overextension and incongruity between the European utterance and the African object'.[36] Miller's tying together of allegory and Africanist discourse constitutes a rendering of allegory as a special bearer of the marks of distance and difference that become pronounced in discourses about Europe's others.

Frederic Jameson's much-criticized essay 'Third-World Literature in the Era of Multinational Capitalism' alleges the necessarily allegorical status of the third-world writer's discourse.[37] Jameson

---
[35] *Blank Darkness*, 132.
[36] Ibid. 136.
[37] 'Third-World Literature in the Era of Multinational Capitalism', *Social Text*, 15 (1986), 65–88. All further references will be given in the text.

insists on the absolute otherness of Third World texts from First World texts: 'All third world texts are necessarily, I want to argue, allegorical, and in a very specific way: they are to be read as what I will call *national allegories*'. This differentiating feature in Third World texts is to be found 'particularly when their forms develop out of predominantly western machineries of representation, such as the novel' (69). Notwithstanding the use by Third World writers of first-world forms, Jameson's 'national allegory' is not characterized by Miller's 'overextension and incongruity' between discourse and object but, on the contrary, by the *unity* of the Third World discourse and its collective object.

We have seen that the theme of travel to an exotic far away locale in Baudelaire's 'La Vie antérieure' serves as the means to the attainment of a primal wholeness of experience for the European subject. Jameson begins with a brief discussion of the issue of canon expansion, in which he urges, as an argument for reading texts outside the canon, a recognition that our First World existence in an 'unavoidably fragmented society' (67) entails a constant exposure to non-canonical forms of culture in addition to the 'great books'. The trope of travel makes an appearance here, albeit subtly: 'Why, returning to the question of the canon, *should* we only read certain kinds of books? No one is suggesting we should *not* read those, but why should we not also read other ones? We are not after all, being shipped to that "desert island" beloved of great books lists.' Jameson points out that we inevitably 'read' many alternative texts in the 'force field of mass culture' (66) whether we admit it or not. What draws me to this innocuous passage is the nagging implication that if we *were* being shipped to that desert island, we might in fact choose only from the 'great books' lists. In this passage, it is merely the condition—the inevitable condition—of living in the midst of an ever-present mass culture in which our exposure to the multiplicity of non-canonical texts is an 'unavoidable' fact, that gives prescriptive weight to reading outside the European canon. If the world we currently inhabit is 'fragmented', might the imagined desert island be a place of wholeness? The implicit contrast between First World fragmented existences/selves and the placeless desert island, where only great books might be read, flags the essay's familiar impulse to dramatize the expansion of our literary scope in terms of exotic travel. On the desert island, we have no need for the exoticism of Third World literature, but staying at home, we need to travel in our reading.

INTRODUCTION 13

The Third World in Jameson's essay exists in a less evolved past of the First World, characterized by 'its tendency to remind us of outmoded stages of our own first-world cultural development' (65). The absolute contrast between the Third and First Worlds is stated as the relationship between the lost past and the fallen present: acknowledging the 'present of postmodernism' in the First World, the essay 'calls for a reinvention of the radical difference of our own cultural past and its now seemingly old-fashioned situations and novelties' (66). The First World's past is to be found precisely in the present of the Third World, a repository of lost cultural values, and the Third World also becomes a means to a return to those values.

The absolute difference between Third and First World texts turns most importantly on a unity that is no longer available in the First World. First World capitalist culture is characterized by a 'radical split between public and private, between the poetic and the political, between . . . the domain of sexuality and the unconscious and that of the public world of classes, of the economic, and of secular power: in other words, Freud versus Marx'. By contrast, the Third World maintains a 'wholly different' relationship between these two spheres, in which any narrative of the private sphere necessarily refers to the public sphere:

> Third-world texts, even those which are seemingly private and invested with a properly libidinal dynamic—necessarily project a political dimension in the form of national allegory: *the story of the private individual destiny is always an allegory of the embattled situation of the public third-world culture and society*' (69).

A contradiction comes to the fore in Jameson's differentiation of First World allegory from Third World allegory. He claims that in the First World, allegory can refer in either direction:

> What is important to stress is . . . its optional nature: we can use it to convert the entire situation of the novel into an allegorical commentary on the destiny of Spain, but we are also free to reverse its priorities and to read the political analogy as metaphorical decoration for the individual drama, and as a mere figural intensification of this last. (78–9)

In contrast, an inflexible one-way referential relationship obtains in Third World culture: the private story refers primarily and directly to the public story, and so Jameson can, in his reading of Lu Xun, claim boldly, 'Ah Q is thus, allegorically, China itself' (74). The reversibility of the direction of allegorical reference in First World texts, as opposed to the unidirectionality of reference in Third World texts, corresponds to the fundamental separability of the private and the public:

> Here [in the First World] far from dramatizing the identity of the political and the individual or psychic, the allegorical structure tends essentially to separate these levels in some absolute way. We cannot feel its force unless we are convinced of the radical difference between politics and the libidinal: so that its operation reconfirms (rather than annuls) that split between public and private. (79)

Jameson acknowledges the inherently differentiating properties of allegory as such—self-conscious separation of levels, referential alterity—that operate in allegorical structures in First World texts. In the Third World, however, allegory effects the identity of levels, and the allegorical operation therefore 'annuls' the split between them.

Why should it be the case that the same rhetorical structure would reconfirm the break between sign and referent in one context and their unity in another? If, as Jameson acknowledges, the 'general poststructuralist assault on the so-called "centered subject"' discredits the notion of unity within individual and within collective subjectivities, how is it that in the Third World the unity of the individual and the collective, of the private and the public levels remains? Jameson's language about allegory reveals anxieties about the insights of poststructuralism and its epistemological and political implications.[38] The Third World in his essay serves as a useful far away terrain for remedying the anxiety-inducing fragmentation that post-structuralism has wrought, and brings back to the First World the recuperated benefits of this nostalgic return to an anterior state.[39]

Most illustrative of why Jameson should use allegory to such ends is the representative character of allegory itself. Joel Fineman points out that in recent critical discourse about allegory, 'Allegory rapidly acquires the status of trope of tropes, representative of the figurality of all language, of the distance between signifier and signified, and correlatively, the response to allegory becomes representative of

---

[38] On this point, see Robert Young, *White Mythologies*, 114–15.
[39] Rosemary Marangoly George argues that James establishes Third World literature as 'a site of nostalgia for the early days of theorizing on the novel as it was practiced by Western Marxists of the stature of Luckács and Benjamin'. See *The Politics of Home: Postcolonial Relocations and Twentieth-Century Fiction* (Cambridge: Cambridge University Press, 1996), 113.

critical activity *per se*.'⁴⁰ Allegory comes to represent both the success and failure of its own sense-making activity, and also to elicit responses that represent responses to the larger literary project of interpretation, translation, decoding. Hence there is much to be learned from Jameson's insistence that allegory must be the form that exemplifies the differential literary mode of the Third World. Where allegory might provoke anxiety about the unreadable break between levels, Jameson's claim that allegory operates differently in the Third World, to annul the fundamental split, constitutes a reappropriation of allegory for the purpose of recuperating a lost unity when it would typify disunity.⁴¹ The anxiety of indeterminacy can be put to rest when allegory, which can be seen as the ultimate trope of indeterminacy, can be tamed and made determinate. Allegory, an incongruent and yet apt choice, troubles the essay appropriately.

ALLEGORY AND HISTORY

We can understand the nostalgia expressed in Jameson's text as implicating three interrelated elements with which I began my reflection on allegory: authenticity, alterity, and anteriority. In the essay's rhetoric of otherness, the Third World is different from the First World by virtue of embodying a certain wholeness of experience that is lost to the First World. The Third World becomes a refuge from fragmentation and self-division. This suggests an intriguing similarity between a tendency found in the Baudelairean strand of exoticist discourse and the rhetoric of Jameson's essay on Third World literature. The essay can be understood as staging a nostalgic return of sorts, to an imaginary point prior to the deplorable poststructural split.

In this vein, the problem of one's relationship to history is central to Jameson's argument: the First World person is removed from material conditions, while the Third World person is in direct contact with the concrete matter of experience:

> These two contrasting realities are to be grasped, I think, in terms of a situational consciousness. . . . Only the slave knows what reality and the

⁴⁰ 'Structure of Allegorical Desire', 27.
⁴¹ Jameson's positing of allegory as a means to a lost wholeness is in tension with his own definition of allegory in *Marxism and Form* (Princeton: Princeton University Press, 1971), 60: 'Aura is thus in a sense the opposite of allegorical perception in that in it a mysterious wholeness of objects becomes visible.'

resistance of matter really are; only the slave can attain some true materialistic consciousness of his situation, since it is precisely to that that he is condemned. The Master, however, is condemned to idealism—to the luxury of a placeless freedom in which any consciousness of his own concrete situation fleets like a dream, like a word unremembered on the tip of the tongue, a nagging doubt which the puzzled mind is unable to formulate. (85)

This is an allegory of the discourse-object break at the heart of allegory. The Master is 'condemned' to the autonomy of language; and this implies the impossibility of formulating meaningful thoughts and an accurate notion of the self, and hence political and ethical paralysis. The slave by contrast, chained to matter, is assumed to retain the use of language in its direct referential function. By extension, the Master's remove from the concrete in effect destroys the capacity to remember: all he has is 'a word unremembered on the tip of the tongue'. The slave—the Third World alternative—is the object of nostalgia, not only for linguistic wholeness, but for the idea of historicity.

Jameson begins his essay with the question of why First World readers should read Third World texts, and ends with a specific diagnosis inspired by the Hegelian master-slave dialectic:

The view from the top is epistemologically crippling, and reduces its subjects to the illusion of a host of fragmented subjectivities, to the poverty of individual experience of isolated monads, to dying individual bodies without collective pasts or futures bereft of any possibility of grasping the social totality. This placeless individuality . . . offers a welcome from the 'nightmare of history', but . . . condemns our culture to psychologism and the 'projections' of private subjectivity. All of this is denied to third-world culture, which must be situational despite itself. And it is this, finally, which must account for the allegorical nature of third-world culture, where the telling of the individual story and the individual experience cannot but ultimately involve the whole laborious telling of the experience of the collectivity itself. (85–6)

This answer to the initial question about the distinct value of reading Third World texts arises from an implicit Marxist argument about history, in which colonialism has had real effects for both colonizer and colonized, determining their respective relationships to knowledge, history, and identity. Writing at a moment when the push for canon expansion is substantially beginning to affect university curricula in the USA, Jameson states that 'nothing is to be gained by passing over in silence the radical difference of non-canonical texts' (65). This, I think, is a challenge to a brand of multiculturalism that seeks canon expansion for diversity's sake. Responses to Jameson, while justified on the whole in criticizing the essay's totalizing tendency,[42] do not provide a satisfying alternative answer to the question of why it is important for people in the First World to read Third World texts. Arguments that point out that some of these texts are just as good as Western canonical books, or that these texts broaden one's vision, fall into the traps of tokenism and an empty multiculturalism that ultimately undermines the specific value of reading these books. Jameson claims that Third World texts implicate a collective life that is tied to the importance of history to identity. The bankruptcy of the Master's world is an allegory of the situation where history has been made irrelevant to the individual. The claim is that in the Third World history is a problem for the individual in a different way—one that is deeply relevant to the possibility of meaning. It is this different relationship to history, and by extension to the possibility of meaning, that Jameson offers to inspire a reading of Third World texts that is beyond the tokenism of the easy multicultural answer.

In *The Wake of Deconstruction*, Johnson also draws on allegory in a discussion of the politics of identity, to reach a somewhat different conclusion. She criticizes the idea that 'each person represents synecdochally' the collectivity.[43] Instead she argues for an allegorical view of identity that recognizes that identities are 'contractual' fictions rather than 'essential' truths, while still preserving the possibility of 'speaking "as a"'.[44] She argues for the recognition of *both* the fictionality of the labels and the real historical effects that they have had.[45] It is important for Johnson to retain both the unreadability *and* readability of people as signs, to endorse both the resistance to stereotypes *and* the ability to speak politically as a 'contractual' representative of a collectivity. A particular preoccupation with readable and unreadable pasts informs the readings in this book. Is it possible to read postcolonial literature as preoccupied with allegory, without neatly projecting its alterity on to a nostalgic annulment of post-structural discontinuity? That Jameson's text about allegory manifests this nostalgia in unexpected ways is symptomatic of the interaction in

---

[42] See George, *Politics of Home*, 102–13 for a thorough account of the criticism that Jameson's essay has garnered since its publication. Aijaz Ahmad's response in *In Theory: Classes, Nations, Literature* (London: Verso, 1992),. 95–122, is the most thoroughgoing critique.
[43] (Baltimore: Johns Hopkins University Press, 1987), p. 72.
[44] Ibid.
[45] Ibid.

postcolonial discourse between allegory, anteriority, and alterity. If Jameson locates in the First World a certain failure of representation (or failure to be representative), the Third World embodies a success that can only come with misrepresentation or misrecognition, and a 'speaking otherwise' about allegory as the refusal of the painful break between self and non-self.

CONTEXTS: ANTILLEAN, FRANCOPHONE, AND POSTCOLONIAL

This study accords a prominent place to works by the Guadeloupean writer Maryse Condé.[46] Since the 1960s, Condé has had a prolific career as a novelist, literary critic, and playwright, although she is best known for her novels. She has gained some notoriety for her tendency to react to and contest in her writing an array of contexts, traditions, and issues: for example, debates about Antillean literary culture (*négritude, antillanité, créolité*), feminism, race, identity, Africa, and postcolonial literature.

The term 'francophone', widely used in the context of literary groupings, is a remnant of the now unfashionable *francophonie*, which designates a global community of French speakers.[47] 'Francophone' is the only French analogue that has developed in parallel function to 'postcolonial' in the Anglo-American world. The study of postcolonial literature and francophone literature have been for the most part kept distinct in academic endeavours by the gap between English and French studies. The term postcolonial has not been prominent in the French context.[48] It is only recently that it has been used in relation to francophone literature; there is now a growing number of

[46] A critical book-length work exclusively on Maryse Condé has yet to appear. Special issues of journals devoted to Condé include: *Callaloo* 18/3, 'Maryse Condé: A Special Issue' (1995) and *World Literature Today* 67/4, 'Focus on Maryse Condé' (autumn 1993); a book of interviews: Françoise Pfaff, *Entretiens avec Maryse Condé* (Paris: Karthala, 1993); and a collection of essays drawn from the proceedings of a conference in Guadeloupe: Nara Araujo, (ed.), *L'Œuvre de Maryse Condé: À propos d'une écrivaine politiquement incorrecte* (Paris: L'Harmattan, 1996).

[47] For a useful discussion of *francophonie*, see Michel Tétu, *La Francophonie: Histoire, problématique et perspectives* (Paris: Hachette, 1988).

[48] In *Francophone Literatures: An Introductory Survey* (New York: Oxford University Press, 1996), 31 Belinda Jack points out that while nomenclature in the francophone debate continues to proliferate without consensus and 'militates against the genesis of a more homogeneous discipline, . . . American post-colonial studies . . . is rapidly gaining hegemony' in the anglophone debate. Her implication is that discussing francophone literature in light of the concept of postcoloniality contributes to this growing hegemony and homogeneity.

works on francophone literature and culture that make use of the term 'postcolonial'.[49] I locate this book within the project of exploring how francophone traditions pose the problems that currently trouble the concept of postcoloniality.

What complicates matters is the fact that the French Antilles are not classically postcolonial; they have been *départements d'outre-mer* since 1946. This has important resonance in light of the heated contestation over the meaning of postcolonial that, from the beginning, has been a central concern of postcolonial discourse. According to Hargreaves and McKinney, 'The very limited presence of an explicitly "post-colonial" discourse in France is in many ways a reflection of lingering neo-colonial reflexes.'[50] The debate over whether the post- in postcolonial implies a periodization emphasizing an end to colonialism, and whether this implication is misleading given continuing struggles against economic and cultural neocolonialism, has special relevance for the Antilles, where a relationship of dependence upon the *métropole* persists officially.[51] I would suggest that in one sense the use of the term postcolonial to talk about a not—properly—postcolonial Antillean literature disarms the critique of the term's periodization and chronology. Rather than functioning as a 'dangerous cover-up', deployment of the term in reference to an area that has not been politically decolonized (in the sense of political independence) underscores the unevenness of the decolonization process, as well as the 'lie' of the term. 'Postcolonial' then, becomes a contractual indicator of a practice of reading that accentuates the commonality of the problems that arise from colonialism, its aftermath, and continuation, regardless of formal political status.

Criticisms of the postcolonial often take as their target postcolonial intellectuals, who are usually Western-educated elites in their country of origin and in their host country, and who sometimes hold

---

[49] Françoise Lionnet, *Postcolonial Representations: Woman, Literature, Identity* (Ithaca, NY: Cornell University Press, 1995); Mary Jean Green et al, (eds.), *Postcolonial Subjects: Francophone Women Writers* (Minneapolis: University of Minnesota Press, 1996); *Yale French Studies*, 82–3, 'Post/Colonial Conditions: Exiles, Migrations, and Nomadisms' (1993); Alec G. Hargreaves and Mark McKinney (eds.), *Post-Colonial Cultures in France* (London: Routledge, 1997); Celia Britton, *Édouard Glissant and Postcolonial Theory: Strategies of Language and Resistance* (Charlottesville, Va: University Press of Virginia, 1999); Dina Sherzer, ed., *Cinema, Colonialism, Postcolonialism: Perspectives from the French and Francophone World* (Austin: University of Texas Press, 1996).
[50] *Post-Colonial Cultures in France*, 18.
[51] See the informative, multi-disciplinary collection of essays on the French Antilles, Richard Burton and Fred Reno, (eds.), *French and West Indian* (Warwick: Macmillan, 1995).

academic posts in prestigious Western universities. They are charged with being insufficiently representative of their people, with parlaying their alterity in the West into academic stardom. Postcolonial theory is seen as another means of continuing and reinscribing neocolonial relations.[52] Ahmad schematizes a global division of labour in which the Third World provides the metropolitan centres with primary materials, which are turned by postcolonial intellectuals into products for consumption by the cultural elite.[53] Celia Britton shows that the marketing and academic criticism of Antillean literature continue the colonial relations of production that imagine the Antilles as producers of raw materials for oral consumption: 'the main exports to metropolitan France are now pineapples, avocadoes, rum, bananas—and more recently, *novels*'.[54]

The location of the postcolonial within the privileged and hypocritical space of the Western academy, from which intellectuals in exile set the Eurocentric standards by which Third World culture is valued, has an Antillean exemplar. It is possible to be suspicious of Condé along lines similar to the criticisms that have been made of the most prominent of postcolonial intellectuals (Salman Rushdie, Homi Bhabha, Edward Said), such as those marshalled by Aijaz Ahmad in his critique of the concept of the postcolonial.[55] The aforementioned discomfort about a Third World intellectual's role in First World academe might be intensified in light of Condé's crossing of the expected boundary between artist and academic. She generates creative work and also leads the discourse about the standards by which it will be appreciated.[56] One might see Condé's active participation in the dissemination of American criticism of Antillean literature as an uncomfortable marriage of Third World creativity and Western academe. Unsurprisingly, she has been accused of addressing her work to a primarily Western readership.[57] Martinican *créolistes*

---

[52] See e.g. Slemon and Tiffin's introd. to eid. (eds.), *After Europe: Critical Theory and Post-Colonial Writing*, (Sydney: Dangaroo, 1989), ix–xxiii.

[53] See *In Theory*, 68–71.

[54] 'Eating their Words: The Consumption of French Caribbean Literature', *Association for the Study of African and Caribbean Literature in French Yearbook*, 1 (1996), 15–22: 15.

[55] Ahmad, *In Theory*, 68–9, 123–220.

[56] In the last twenty years, Condé has taught at American universities including University of California at Berkeley, the University of Virginia, Harvard, and Columbia. In addition to her creative writing, she has edited two collections of criticism of Antillean literature, in which many of the articles are devoted to her work: Maryse Condé et al (eds.), *L'Héritage de Caliban* (Guadeloupe: Jasor, 1992); ead. and Madeleine Cottenet-Hage (eds.), *Penser la créolité* (Paris: Karthala, 1995).

[57] For example, fellow Antillean writer Patrick Chamoiseau points to her explanatory

Bernabé, Chamoiseau, and Confiant begin their manifesto *Éloge de la créolité* (1989) with the declaration that Antillean literature does not yet exist, because Antillean writers write with a foreign audience in mind rather than for their own people.[58] Of all the Antilleans currently writing, Condé is perhaps the best known, her books the most popular on the international literary scene. The *créolistes'* statement has therefore prompted a response by Condé herself, as I shall discuss in Chapter 6.[59]

That all the *créolistes'* (and Condé's) books, including *Éloge de la créolité*, are published by the big Parisian houses, is a situation characteristic of postcoloniality in which certain cultural products only reach the local population, if at all, through the mediation of the *métropole*'s stamp of approval. Whether this external perspective that is endemic to the writing of Antillean literature prevents the development of a literature that can be deemed truly Antillean is a question that I shall not attempt to answer. However, bypassing the question of whether Condé is a 'truly' Guadeloupean or Antillean writer, I would argue that she is a particular breed of writer that one could call postcolonial. Her position of ironic distance from the Antilles, her active role in American academic criticism of Antillean literature, her fluency with the theoretical stakes of contemporary literary criticism, and her extreme self-consciousness and self-distancing regarding all these matters, might bother those who hold a romantic view of the creative artist, and those who are concerned about the Third World artist 'selling out' to the West. These characteristics, however, are exemplary of the peculiar position of the postcolonial intellectual. In the spirit of Arif Dirlik's quip that postcoloniality is born with the arrival of Third World intellectuals in First World academe,[60] I would suggest that Condé's work provides an especially fitting occasion for an exploration of the discomforts and paradoxes of postcoloniality.

---

footnotes in *Traversée de la Mangrove* as tell-tale signs of an outsider's perspective: 'All the footnotes that explain what we already know make us think, dear Maryse, that you are not addressing us, but some other people.' See his 'Reflections on Maryse Condé's *Traversée de la Mangrove*', *Callaloo*, 14/2 (1991), 389-95: 394. I discuss this novel and its interaction with *créolité* movement in Ch. 6, below.

[58] (Paris: Gallimard, 1989), 13.
[59] Condé, 'Order, Disorder, Freedom, and the West Indian Writer', *Yale French Studies*, 83/2 (1993), 121-35.
[60] 'The Postcolonial Aura: Third World Criticism in the Age of Global Capitalism', *Critical Inquiry*, 20 (1994), 328-56: 329.

The focus on the positions and motivations of postcolonial intellectuals serves as a crucible for reflecting on the concept of the postcolonial. For these figures, marginality becomes a self-conscious position that paradoxically leads to recognition. Bhabha's privileging of postcolonial hybridity, migrancy, and exile—emblematic of the post-structural fracturing of the centred subject—has been criticized as a self-justifying way to exalt the elite migrant intellectual, and as a political cop-out preventing the formation of efficacious identities for political struggle.[61] In these criticisms, it is possible to discern a playing-out of the complicated relationship between postcolonialism, its supposed political goals, Western forms of knowledge, and expectations of representativeness. In the now irrevocable state of cultural contact that is one effect of colonialism, there are pressing conflicts about the extent to which the formerly colonized ought to define themselves vis-à-vis Western influences, how this choice might affect the achievement of political goals, and the distance between the formerly colonized collectivity and the person who 'speaks for' it.

These types of conflicts are especially pronounced in the debates about French Antillean identity, whose development can broadly be traced in the three stages of Césaire's *négritude*, Glissant's *antillanité*, and Bernabé, Chamoiseau, and Confiant's *créolité*. The affirmation of an authentic blackness that gestured toward essentialism and formed the basis of *négritude*'s anti-colonialism is today re-evaluated in consideration of the mixture and creolization that has always been characteristic of Antillean life. In this revision, it seems that if there can be said to be an essential component to Antillean identity, it is this coexistence and intermingling of different influences, European and African among others.[62] Debates over the definition of *créolité* and over which writers are sufficiently Creole have, however, tended toward identitarian debates concerned with an authenticity that a Creole world-view seems to have the potential to debunk.[63] The political counterpart to these debates about Antillean identity is the

[61] See Ahmad, 'Politics of Literary Postcoloniality'; Slemon and Tiffin, *After Europe;* Ania Loomba and Suvir Kaul, 'Introduction: Location, Culture, Post-Coloniality', *Oxford Literary Review*, 16/1–2 (1994), 3–30; Benita Parry, 'Current Problems in the Study of Colonial Discourse', *Oxford Literary Review*, 9/1–2 (1987), 27–58.

[62] The focus on creolization in the francophone Caribbean follows the theorizing of anglophone Caribbean writers Edward Kamau Brathwaite, Wilson Harris, and Derek Walcott over the past thirty years.

[63] This is the line of the critique of *créolité* gently put forth by Édouard Glissant in *Poétique de la relation* (Paris: Gallimard, 1990), 103.

INTRODUCTION 23

debate about whether Martinique and Guadeloupe ought to attain independence or remain departments of France.[64] If contemporary Creole ideology embraces the French elements that contribute to the fabric of Antillean identity, does a struggle for independence become outdated? In these respects, the Antillean debates encapsulate conflicts central to postcoloniality, which are often played out upon the careers of a few 'representative' figures.

Into these debates, I read, sometimes more and sometimes less explicitly, self-conscious allegories of the postcolonial writer.[65] However, if postcoloniality is to take shape as more than a self-conscious reflection on the position of the postcolonial intellectual, the problems it raises must be generalizable. This book aims to articulate converging paradoxes of postcoloniality and Antilleanness through readings of instances of return, desired and undesired, voluntary and involuntary; through scenes of nostalgia, repetition, haunting, intertextuality, neurosis, rewriting, and homecoming. This book focuses on three related axes that I propose as loci of intersection between Antillean literature and postcolonial theory: crossing, allegory, and trauma. In putting into relation the trope of (re)crossing with rhetorical and psychoanalytic forms of return, I propose these juxtapositions and mutual interferences as heuristic rather than definitive, as models of mutual reference that are neither wholly self-conscious nor wholly unconscious.

[64] For an informative discussion of political and ideological positions in contemporary Martinique, see Richard D. E. Burton, 'Towards 1992: Political-Cultural Assimilation and Opposition in Contemporary Martinique', *French Cultural Studies*, 3 (1992), 61–86.

[65] Lydie Moudileno argues that the basis for the grouping of Antillean literature together is a common self-reflexivity: 'la majorité des auteurs "canoniques" antillais ont choisi de projeter dans leurs écrits un personnage écrivain qui devient leur dénominateur commun, confirmant une intuition de littérature antillaise, et la construisant comme telle à partir d'une loi de ressemblance'. *L'Écrivain antillais au miroir de sa littérature* (Paris: Karthala, 1997), 6.

2

CROSSINGS, RETURNS: CÉSAIRE'S *CAHIER D'UN RETOUR AU PAYS NATAL*

The grand dimensions of the voyage across the ocean provide the imagination with an endless expanse for literary inscription. Travel from one side of the oceanic expanse to another finds in its literary representation all the momentousness and anxiety of failure that it tends to lack in today's world of air travel. An ever-familiar trope in European literature of travel is the exotic voyage that puts the alienated traveller back in touch with his essential self, with an authenticity that is lost to Europe.[1]

This chapter focuses on the way the most potently influential text of anticolonial Antillean literature treats the consistently tight relation between the crossing of the ocean and the recovering of an original perfection. The founding text of *négritude* and francophone postcolonialism, Aimé Césaire's *Cahier d'un retour au pays natal* (1939), has as its lost object the colonized land.[2] The poem narrates a return, a process of reclaiming an identity and a people, and also responds to the literary voyages that preceded it. This chapter is primarily concerned with the poem's rewriting and reorienting of previous poetic voyages that are themselves already aware of crossing as a return that both constitutes a nostalgic quest for something lost and figures poetic activity.

The issue of rewriting and its motivation arises in the context of the seamless inheritance of nineteenth-century French exoticism by non-white Antillean poets in the late nineteenth and early twentieth centuries. The Antillean poetic tradition of imitating French models remained largely unchallenged until the 1930s. The dominant idea in this tradition was that the measure of the poet's skill was the extent to which the poet's race could not be guessed from reading the text.[3]

---

[1] This chapter is indebted to the language and insight of Christopher Miller's *Blank Darkness: Africanist Discourse in French* (Chicago: University of Chicago Press, 1985).

[2] Bilingual edn., trans. Mirelle Rosello with Annie Pritchard (Bloodaxe Contemporary French Poets, 4; Newcastle upon Tyne: Bloodaxe, 1995). All references are to this edn. and are given in the main text.

[3] Frantz Fanon writes, 'Le noir Antillais sera d'autant plus blanc, c'est-à-dire se rapprochera d'autant plus du véritable homme, qu'il aura fait sienne la langue française', in *Peau noire, masques blancs* (Paris: Seuil, 1995), 14.

Poets considered worthy of imitation included Baudelaire, Hugo, Verlaine, Leconte de Lisle, Hérédia, and Banville.[4] Antillean writers' imitation of the Romantics and Parnassians was not merely confined to a faithful copy of form, but also took on in particular the theme of exotic islands. As late as 1945, in the aftermath of World War II, the French Ministry of Colonies undertook to direct attention toward its overseas islands in a literary exhibition called *Les Antilles heureuses*.[5] It showcased side by side French and Antillean poets who had written about the islands, including Madame de Maintenon, Hérédia, Loti, Gilbert Gratiant, de Régnier, Francis James, Réné Maran, Saint-John Perse. It celebrated the continuation of the French literary tradition by Martinican and Guadeloupean poets. It is a hopeless task to distinguish among the poems collected there the French from the Antillean. The consistent theme is the evocation of a paradisiacal landscape, the languor and sweetness of life on the islands, an original perfection toward which poetic nostalgia tends. This exhibition is a case in point of the problem of motivation: both French poet and West Indian poet exploit the exoticism of a faraway paradise in the same manner. However, in the 'melancholia' of the West Indian poet, the loved object that is lost and to which the poem effects a wished-for return, is actually home.[6] In the inheritance of the use of the exotic as a trope for difference, the 'anxiety of influence' takes on a special valence.[7] How do this difference and this transport become complicated when the exotic landscape is one's home, when the difference invoked is one's own?

In Paris in the 1930s, Martinican students with surrealist and communist loyalties published *Légitime défense* (1932), a one-issue manifesto that violently denounced the assimilationism of the French West Indian bourgeoisie and reaffirmed black cultural values.[8] A decade

---

[4] See Lilyan Kesteloot's pioneering work *Les Écrivains noirs de langue française: Naissance d'une littérature* (7th edn. Brussels: Éditions de l'université de Bruxelles, 1977), 38–41.

[5] This exhibition took place in Paris, June–July 1945. Excerpts and discussion of poems from this exhibition are included in Kesteloot, *Écrivains noirs*, 38–41.

[6] Sigmund Freud, 'Mourning and Melancholia', in *Collected Papers*, trans. Joan Rivière, 5 vols. (New York: Basic, 1959), iv. 152–70.

[7] See Harold Bloom, *The Anxiety of Influence: A Theory of Poetry* (New York: Oxford University Press, 1973).

[8] However, Brent Edwards warns against the misperception, produced by Kesteloot's overemphasis of *Légitime défense*, that it was the first publication of its kind; he situates the journal among the wealth of black francophone material published in the 1920s and 1930s, in a range of journals including the important *La Revue du monde noir*. See his illuminating article, 'The Ethnics of Surrealism', *Transition*, 78 (1999), 84–135: 121–5.

later, Aimé and Suzanne Césaire, along with René Ménil, founded the journal *Tropiques* upon their return from Paris to their native Martinique. In both journals, articles denounced the mediocrity and lack of originality of literature being produced by Antillean black writers.[9] Attacking the poetry of one imitative Martinican poet, Suzanne Césaire famously writes in *Tropiques:* 'Littérature de sucre et de vanille. Tourisme littéraire. Guide bleu et C.G.T. Poésie, non pas. . . . Allons, la vraie poésie est ailleurs. Loin des rimes, des complaintes, des alizés, des perroquets.'[10]

Consider Suzanne Césaire's telling conclusion, '*la vraie poésie est ailleurs*'. Although her meaning here is that true poetry should not engage in literary tourism, her statement repeats the association of artistic creativity and an elsewhere. Baudelaire had written: 'Si je prends un homme du monde, un intelligent, et si je le transporte dans une contrée lointaine, je suis sûr . . . qu'elle créera en lui un monde nouveau d'idées.'[11] The French poet needs difference for creativity, as is suggested by the importance of uncanny phenomena for artistic inspiration in *Curiosités esthétiques*.[12] Perhaps unwittingly, Suzanne Césaire acknowledges this need for difference, for an elsewhere in poetry. She pithily articulates Antillean poetry's need for an original idiom as the need for a *different* elsewhere. On one level, her insistence that '*la vraie poésie est ailleurs*' is simply a distancing of European exoticism and the assimilationist exoticism of Antillean poets. But on another level, it suggests that what is necessary for a truly original Antillean poetry is precisely an alterity, an externality, an approach from elsewhere.

The importance of the approach from a 'necessary elsewhere' is also given another dimension by the intertextual aspect of Suzanne Césaire's statement.[13] The statement echoes Rimbaud's words 'la

---

[9] Kesteloot attributes pre-Césairean poetic mediocrity to its lack of engagement with the plight of black people (Kesteloot, *Écrivains noirs*, 37). For August Viatte the mediocrity of the period is tied to its being insufficiently regionalist; see *Histoire littéraire de l'Amérique française* (Paris: Presses universitaires de France, 1954), 483. Jack Corzani, however, urges a 'more indigenist viewpoint' for re-estimating the value of pre-*négritude* literature, emphasizing the heterogeneous ways in which it prepared the way for *négritude*. See his 'Poetry before Negritude', in A. James Arnold (ed.), *A History of Literature in the Caribbean: Hispanic and Francophone Regions*, (Comparative History of Literatures in European Languages Series, 10; Amsterdam: John Benjamins, 1994), 465–77: 465.

[10] 'Misère d'une poésie: John Antoine-Nau', *Tropiques*, 4 (Jan. 1942), 48–50: 50.

[11] *Œuvres complètes*, 954.

[12] Ibid. See Miller's discussion in *Blank Darkness*, 91.

[13] Michael Seidel, *Exile and the Narrative Imagination* (New Haven: Yale University Press, 1986), 15: 'exile enters as allegory or alibi, a necessary *elsewhere*'.

vraie vie est absente' which he wrote shortly before leaving for his own *ailleurs*.[14] Her title, 'Misère d'une poésie', echoes André Breton's *Misère de la Poésie: 'L'Affaire Aragon' devant l'opinion publique*, a tract condemning the Aragon affair in which Breton discusses the political functions of poetry.[15] Furthermore, ten years prior to Suzanne Césaire's 'Misère d'une poésie', in the very year of Breton's tract, Antillean Étienne Léro had also borrowed Breton's title for his article 'Misère d'une poésie', published in *Légitime défense* (June 1932).[16] This *Légitime défense* in turn took its title from Louis Aragon's and Breton's 1926 surrealist pamphlet *Légitime défense*.[17] This continual series of overt borrowings and imitations is especially intriguing as a frame for the call for black literary originality. If the purpose of Suzanne Césaire's article is to denounce black writers' imitation of French writers and to urge originality, her own borrowings might appear to complicate this message rather obviously. However, we can read her statement '*la vraie poésie est ailleurs*' in its intertextual context as a play on the complex relationship of writing, originality, and intertextuality. The borrowed phrase '*la vraie poésie est ailleurs*' uses the trope of a spatio-temporal and imaginary elsewhere to designate the otherness of prior poets and influences. Using borrowed words, Suzanne Césaire's gloss on a complicated originality is enacted in the very intertextual form in which it is presented. This is suggestive of the way in which poetic originality must be wrested away through a productive, perhaps inevitable, encounter with influences and precursors.

Kesteloot argues that black writers became truly original only after they had become 'engagés'.[18] This view has led critics like Jacqueline Leiner and Ronnie Scharfman to emphasize poetic language as a site of political engagement, and consequently to perform formalist

[14] Rimbaud, 'Délire I', in *Une saison en enfer* (1873). See *Œuvres complètes*, ed. André Rolland de Renéville and Jules Mouquet (Bibliothèque de la Pléiade, 68; Paris: Gallimard, 1946), 228–32. Rimbaud's elsewhere is Africa, where he lived as a merchant in Ethiopia from 1880 to 1891. Comparing Rimbaud and Césaire, one critic sees Rimbaud's poetry as identifying with blacks 'au point d'anticiper les principaux thèmes de la littérature néo-africaine'. See Jonathan Ngaté, '"Mauvais sang" de Rimbaud et *Cahier d'un retour au pays natal* de Césaire: La Poésie au service de la révolution', *Cahiers Césairiens*, 3 (1971), 25–32: 29.
[15] *Misère de la Poésie: 'L'Affaire Aragon' devant l'opinion publique* (Paris: Éditions surréalistes, 1932).
[16] I am indebted to Julie Suk for pointing out these connections between Suzanne Césaire, Léro, and Breton during her work on 'Poetry of Flesh: Double Consciousness in the Harlem Renaissance and *Négritude*' (unpublished thesis, Harvard University, 1997).
[17] André Breton, *Légitime Défense* (Paris: Éditions surréalistes, 1926).
[18] *Écrivains noirs*, 21.

readings that shed light on the ideological content of Aimé Césaire's poetry.[19] The attribution of black writers' artistic originality to the extent of their political engagement, which can be traced to Jean-Paul Sartre's and André Breton's privileging of black poetry as important to revitalizing their own poetic projects, is related to what I have been suggesting is a difference of motivation.[20] I understand the valorization of black engagement as the expression of the desire for the motivation that is perceived as lost to European poetry but supposedly abundant in black poetry. For the colonized Antillean poet inheriting the exotic as a trope for difference, the unmotivated poetic landscape becomes motivated, and it is at this moment that poetic originality will depend upon how an inherited elsewhere that is also one's own is *made* different.

Commentators have considered the *Cahier* to be the first truly original West Indian literary achievement that constitutes a decisive and sudden break from the imitative poetry of the exotic.[21] However, the revolutionary *Cahier* is also self-consciously concerned with an elsewhere, which is now the native land to which it wants to effect return. The projection of an elsewhere as poetic inspiration is a familiar gesture that Césaire assumes and transforms. Indeed, an often-told story about Césaire's actual moment of inspiration for the *Cahier* may exemplify the paradox of Suzanne Césaire's statement that true poetry is elsewhere. Césaire had left Martinique to study in Paris in 1932. In 1935, while visiting Yugoslavia with his friend Petar Guberina, he saw an island called Martinska in the Aegean Sea, and was so strongly reminded of his homeland, Martinique, that he felt compelled to start writing his poem of return.[22] It is through the displaced metaphorical mediation of Martinska that Césaire comes back to his own Martinique. In keeping with my reading of

---

[19] Jacqueline Leiner, *Imaginaire langage, identité culturelle, négritude* (Paris: Jean-Michel Place, 1980); Ronnie Scharfman, *Engagement and the Language of the Subject in the Poetry of Aimé Césaire* (Gainesville, Fla.: University Press of Florida, 1980).

[20] Sartre claims that black poetry is 'la seule grande poésie révolutionnaire' in 'Orphée noir', preface to *Anthologie de la nouvelle poésie nègre et malgache de langue française* (Paris: Presses universitaires de France, 1948), pp. ix–xliv: xii. Breton calls the *Cahier* 'le plus grand monument lyrique de ce temps' in 'Un grand poète noir', which I shall discuss below (cited in n. 44).

[21] See, for example, Ronnie Scharfman, 'Surrealism and Negritude in Martinique', in Denis Hollier (ed.), *A New History of French Literature* (Cambridge, Mass.: Harvard University Press, 1989), 942–80.

[22] See Abiola Irele's ancedotal account in his introduction to Aimé Césaire, *Cahier d'un retour au pays natal*, ed. with commentary Abiola Irele (Ibadan: New Horn Press, 1994), xiii–lxix: xxvii.

Suzanne Césaire's elsewhere as an alterity of an intertextual nature, it is possible to read this story as an allegory of intertextuality. Intertextuality, according to Barbara Johnson, 'designates the multitude of ways a text has of not being self-contained, of being traversed by otherness'.[23] The rewriting of the voyage elsewhere in the *Cahier* can be read as an allegory of intertextuality, of the necessary but problematic alterity of precursors' influences, paradoxically when an anterior authenticity—poetic and identitarian—is being invoked.

The *Cahier* was completed in 1938 and first published in part in the Parisian literary revue *Volontés* in 1939, the year of Césaire's actual return to Martinique after eight years in Paris.[24] Césaire had left Martinique in 1932 to study at the Lycée Louis-le-Grand in preparation for the examination for the École normale supérieure.[25] In Paris, against the backdrop of the social and political turmoil of Europe of the 1930s, he absorbed the intellectual developments of surrealism and Marxism, and the heritage of his poetic predecessors Baudelaire, Lautréamont, Rimbaud, Apollinaire, and Mallarmé.[26] In Paris, he also discovered the writers of the Harlem Renaissance and came into contact with other black intellectuals, most notably Léopold Sédar Senghor and Léon Gontran Damas, who with Césaire became the founders of the *négritude* movement.[27] The three produced a journal that highlighted poetry and the exploration of African culture,

[23] *A World of Difference* (Baltimore: Johns Hopkins University Press, 1987), 116.

[24] *Volontés* (Oct. 1939) published excerpts of the *Cahier*. Versions would later appear in the journal *Tropiques* in 1942, a New York edn. and a Paris edn. in 1947, and a 'definitive edition' in 1956 by *Présence Africaine*. For an account of the publishing history of the *Cahier*, see Thomas Hale, 'Two Decades, Four Versions: The Evolution of Aimé Césaire's *Cahier d'un retour au pays natal*', in Carolyn Parker and Stephen Arnold (eds.), *When the Drumbeat Changes*, (Washington: Three Continents Press, 1981), 186–95.

[25] Although there is no authoritative, full-length biography of Césaire, I have consulted the following sources for basic information about his life: Daniel Delas, *Aimé Césaire* (Paris: Hachette, 1991); Lilyan Kesteloot, *Aimé Césaire* (Poètes d'aujourd'hui, 85; Paris: Seghers, 1962); M. a. M. Ngal, *Aimé Césaire: Un homme à la recherche d'une patrie* (Dakar: nouvelles éditions africaines, 1975); Roger Toumson and Simonne Henry-Valmore, *Aimé Césaire: Le Nègre inconsolé* (Fort-de-France: Vent des îles, 1993).

[26] Césaire discusses the influence of this French poetic canon in 'Poésie et connaissance', *Tropiques*, 12 (Jan. 1945), 157–70. For a thorough discussion of Césaire's poetry in relation to 19th- and 20th-cent. French poets, see Bernard Mouralis, 'Césaire et la poésie française', *Revue des sciences humaines*, 48/76 (1979), 125–52. Locating Césaire at the interface of modernism and black consciousness movements, Arnold's seminal *Modernism and Negritude* also provides a detailed discussion of French literary influences in Césaire's work.

[27] Césaire's article 'Introduction à la poésie nègre américaine' shows his early admiration of Harlem Renaissance poetry. See *Tropiques*, 2 (July 1941), 37–42. See Kesteloot's informative account of the influence of the Harlem Renaissance on young black students in 1930s Paris, in *Écrivains noirs*, 63–82.

L'Étudiant noir, which was published for two years (1935–6).[28] It was in Paris, not in Martinique, that Césaire became aware of belonging to a community of blacks of the African diaspora, and of the imaginative potential of Africa as an origin and a source of renewal.[29] Césaire crossed the ocean to return to Martinique in 1939 just as World War II was declared.

On the question of influence at the time of the writing of the *Cahier*, Césaire admits: 'Quand je suis rentré à la Martinique, qu'est-ce que je connaissais? La littérature française: Rimbaud, Claudel, Baudelaire. . . . C'était les lectures de ma génération; j'ai subi les mêmes influences que tous les étudiants *français*, plus ou moins cultivés, subirent à cette époque.'[30] The notion of a lost anteriority to be regained by travel to an *ailleurs* is one with which Césaire was certainly familiar, and which he did not abandon as a theme.

The *Cahier*, founding text of *négritude* and of francophone postcolonialism, stages a return to that which has been lost. The *Cahier* traces a trajectory from the departure from the troubled Antilles to its reclamation upon return from Europe:

Partir . . . j'arriverais lisse et jeune dans ce pays mien et je dirais à ce pays dont le limon entre dans la composition de ma chair: 'J'ai longtemps erré et je reviens vers la hideur désertée de vos plaies.' (86)
To leave . . . I would arrive smooth and youthful in this land of mine and I would say to this land whose clay has been incorporated into my flesh: 'I

---

[28] Arnold writes, 'In [*Étudiant noir*] Césaire took a firm stand against the cultural assimilation of blacks. It was in this context that he coined the neologism negritude, calling for a resurrection of black values' (*Modernism and Negritude: The Poetry and Poetics of Aimé Césaire* (Cambridge, Mass: Harvard University Press, 1981). 9). However, the word does not appear in the one surviving issue of *Étudiant noir*; rather, it appears that the first published appearance of the word was in the *Volontés* edn. of the *Cahier* in 1939 (Christopher Miller, personal communication). The term has also been used to refer to various African, black, and anticolonial movements beyond the French-speaking world. For a discussion of the term negritude in all these guises, see Abiola Irele, 'Négritude and Nationalism: What is Négritude?', in id., *The African Experience in Literature and Ideology* (Bloomington, Ind.: Indiana University Press, 1981), 67–116.

[29] Martinican novelist and *créolité* theorist Raphaël Confiant has recently taken Césaire to task for having neglected indigenous creole culture in favour of a mythic Africa in his writings and political actions. See his controversial *Aimé Césaire: Une traversée paradoxale du siècle* (Paris: Stock, 1993), 37. This has prompted Annie Le Brun's harsh critique of Confiant and the ideology of *créolité* in *Pour Aimé Césaire* (Paris: Jean-Michel Place, 1994), 14–24, and *Statue cou coupé* (Paris: Jean-Michel Place, 1996).

[30] Jacqueline Leiner, 'Entretien avec Aimé Césaire', in *Tropiques*, 2 vols. (Paris: Jean-Michel Place, 1978), vol. i, pp. v–xxxv: viii. For a nuanced analysis of a Baudelairean intertext ('L'Albatros') in the context of the themes of self-alienation and assimilation in the *Cahier*, see Mireille Rosello, *Littérature et identité créole aux Antilles* (Paris: Karthala, 1992), 98–112.

have long wandered and I am returning to the deserted hideousness of your wounds.' (87)

Césaire's self-conscious effort to recover an original authenticity to be found in his Antillean and even more alienated African roots confronts the legacy of European exoticism that projected a distant elsewhere as a realm of return to primal rejuvenation and wholeness. For Césaire, the voyage is an actual one to be made, it is an actual return. The elsewhere to be rediscovered is his native land of Martinique and perhaps through it, Africa, from which he has been in physical, cultural, and psychological exile.

The poem must transform the poetic voyage, in which travel phenomenalizes a model for poetic transport, and in which the crossing is a poetic crossing. An exemplary intertext is found in Baudelaire's 'Parfum exotique', in which the exotic destination of the metaphorical journey is the realm of poetry. I quote the poem in its entirety:

> Quand, les deux yeux fermés, en un soir chaud d'automne,
> Je respire l'odeur de ton sein chaleureux,
> Je vois se dérouler des rivages heureux
> Qu'éblouissent les feux d'un soleil monotone;
>
> Une île paresseuse où la nature donne
> Des arbres singuliers et des fruits savoureux;
> Des hommes dont le corps est mince et vigoureux,
> Et des femmes dont l'œil par sa franchise étonne.
>
> Guidé par ton odeur vers de charmants climats,
> Je vois un port rempli de voiles et de mâts
> Encor tout fatigués par la vague marine,
>
> Pendant que le parfum des verts tamariniers,
> Qui circule dans l'air et m'enfle la narine,
> Se mêle dans mon âme au chant des mariniers.[31]

---

[31] Baudelaire, *Œuvres complètes*, 24. My attention was drawn to the aptness of this poem for my purposes by a quotation of 'Parfum exotique' in Césaire's play *Une tempête*, a rewriting of Shakespeare's *The Tempest*, in which the quoted lines bespeak the character's canonical literacy:

ANTONIO

Oui!
> Des hommes dont le corps est mince et vigoureux
> Et des femmes dont l'œil par sa franchise étonne...

GONZALO

Il y a de ça! Je vois que vous connaissez vos auteurs. Seulement, dans ce cas, attention. Cela nous imposerait, à nous, de nouveaux devoirs.

See Aimé Césaire, *Une tempête* (Paris: Seuil, 1969), 40–1. Although the constraint of space

> These warm fall nights I breathe, eyes closed, the scent
> of your welcoming breasts, and thereupon appears
> the coast of maybe Malabar—some paradise
> besotted by the sun's monotonous fire;
>
> an idle isle where Nature grants to men
> with bodies slim and strong, to women who
> meet your eye with amazing willingness,
> the rarest trees, the ripest fruit; and then,
>
> guided by your fragrance to enchanted ground,
> I glimpse a harbor filled with masts and sails
> still troubled by the slow-receding tide,
>
> while the aroma of green tamarinds
> dilates my nostrils as it drifts to sea
> and mingles in my soul with the sailors' song.[32]

The first line abdicates the power of the poetic voice to effect the journey on its own. The vision of the destination depends on alterity, the fragrance of the woman's breast, which serves as the bridge in the imagination to transport the speaker from his current locale to the wished-for land. The poem posits a naturalized confluence between the woman's fragrance and the 'charmants climats', between means and destination. The sails and masts are synechdochal reminders of the distance that must be covered to reach this destination, the figural work that must be done.

Ultimately, on this 'île paresseuse', the olfactory ('parfum'), the visual ('je vois un port'), and the aural ('chant des mariniers') blend together into a sensory unity ('se mèle dans mon âme'). This synaesthesia suggests the confluence of the synecdochal breast and the exotic destination as a parallel blending. Not only is poetry posited as a realm where differences amalgamate into a unity, but this erasure of difference functions as homologous to a blending of the metaphorical bridge with the metaphorical destination. The erasure of the distance between here and elsewhere is in effect the erasure of mediation.

A poem often compared to 'Parfum exotique' is Mallarmé's 'Brise marine'. However, in the latter poem, the unity desired and effected

---

prevents me from elaborating at length here, the close association of shipwreck, which is central to *The Tempest*, and intertextuality in this rewriting lends additional nuance to the reading that I am about to present.

[32] Charles Baudelaire, *Les Fleurs du Mal*, trans. Richard Howard (Boston: David Godine, 1982), 29–30.

in the former is reread as an oppressive weight to be escaped. I quote the poem in its entirety:

> La chair est triste, hélas! et j'ai lu tous les livres.
> Fuir! là-bas fuir! Je sens que des oiseaux sont ivres
> D'être parmi l'écume inconnue et les cieux!
> Rien, ni les vieux jardins reflétés par les yeux
> Ne retiendra ce cœur que dans la mer se trempe,
> Ô nuits! ni la clarté déserte de ma lampe
> Sur le vide papier que la blancheur défend
> Et ni la jeune femme allaitant son enfant.
> Je partirai! Steamer balancant ta mâture,
> Lève l'ancre pour une exotique nature!
>
> Un Ennui, désolé par les cruels espoirs,
> Croit encore à l'adieu suprême des mouchoirs!
> Et, peut-être, les mâts, invitant les orages
> Sont-ils de ceux qu'un vent penche sur les naufrages
> Perdus, sans mâts, sans mâts, ni fertiles îlots...
> Mais, ô mon cœur, entends le chant des matelots![33]
>
> The flesh is sad, alas, and there's nothing but words!
> To take flight, far off! I sense that somewhere the birds
> Are drunk to be amid strange spray and skies.
> Nothing, not the old gardens reflected in the eyes,
> Can now restrain this sea-drenched heart, O night,
> Nor the lone splendor of my lamp on the white
> Paper which the void leaves undefiled,
> Nor the young mother suckling her child.
> Steamer with gently swaying masts, depart!
> Weigh anchor for a landscape of the heart!
>
> Boredom made desolate by hope's cruel spells
> Retains its faith in ultimate farewells!
> And maybe the masts are such as are inclined
> To shipwreck driven by tempestuous wind.
> No fertile isle, no spar on which to cling...
> But oh, my heart, listen to the sailors sing![34]

In this poem, the voyage to a *là-bas* is driven by an effort to flee a tired literary legacy and to grope for a radically new poetic idiom: 'j'ai lu tous les livres. | Fuir! là-bas fuir!'. The sudden spasmodic

---

[33] Stéphane Mallarmé, *Œuvres complètes*, ed. Henri Mondor and G. Jean-Aubry (Bibliothèque de la Pléiade, 65; Paris: Gallimard, 1945), 38.

[34] Id., *Collected Poems*, trans. Henry Weinfield (Berkeley and Los Angeles: University of California Press, 1994), 21.

pronouncements of independence, 'Ô nuits!', 'Je partirai!', are made in vain against a backdrop of constraint, in which the very means of declaring defiance ('Rien, ni . . . ni . . . ni') confines the utterance to a monotonous enumeration. As in 'Parfum exotique' the poetic escape is the exotic destination: 'Lève l'ancre pour une exotique nature!'. But tellingly, the first stanza breaks off here, to be followed by 'Un ennui, désolé par les cruels espoirs'.

In the second and final stanza, the hope of reaching this new destination is destroyed. Ultimately, there is recognition that there is no travel to an entirely new place; the effort results in a shipwreck. There are no masts, no fertile isles, no new poetic realms to be discovered that are completely free of the old poetic language. The final image of hope, 'Mais ô mon cœur, entends le chant des matelots!' is a metonymic echo of Baudelaire's poem which ends with 'chants des mariniers'. In contrast to the wholeness and unity of the successful transport of 'Parfum exotique', this stanza recounts a failure of travel signalled by the disparate and incomplete fragments—masts, islands, songs—lost at sea in the wreckage. The 'chant des matelots', a twist on the sirens' song conventionally associated with shipwrecks, is the disembodied voices of poetic predecessors, voyagers all. If the metaphorical blending of 'Parfum exotique' is a successful transport, the metonymic disparateness of 'Brise marine' is a shipwreck.

'Brise marine' adds a new level to the exotic voyage of 'Parfum exotique': the difficulty of seeking a new poetic idiom that is free from the legacy of precursors. The exotic would-be destination at the end of the first stanza, initially presented as an escape, is retrospectively revealed to be illusory. Exoticism itself becomes, rather, a trope for the old poetic language. At the cost both of not reaching its destination and of becoming a non-destination of poetic incompleteness and disunity, the poem refuses the known comfort of exoticism.

In Mallarmé's 'Brise marine' one already sees a reorientation of the exotic voyage that is about poetics or textuality to refer additionally to the problem of literary inheritance.[35] Bloom's notion of the Oedipal rivalry between a text and its precursor is given a twist in the relationship of the *Cahier* to its precursors. If exoticism itself becomes

---

[35] For an excellent analysis of Mallarméan intertextuality, see Johnson, 'Les Fleurs du Mal Armé: Some Reflections on Intertextuality', in ead., *World of Difference*, 116–36. For an examination of textual relations between Mallarmé and Césaire, see Annie Pibarot, 'Césaire lecteur de Mallarmé', in Janos Reisz (ed.) *Frankophone Literaturen Ausserhalb Europas*, (Frankfurt on Main: Peter Lang, 1987), 17–27.

CROSSINGS, RETURNS 35

a trope for the French literary legacy, how much the more so for Antillean poetry, in which the black poet engages a tradition of which he is the exotic object. In the *Cahier* we find explicit refusals of exoticism: 'je lis bien à mon pouls que l'exotisme n'est pas provende pour moi' (100; 'I clearly read in my pulse that exoticism is no provender for me', 101). The poem is replete with stark and startlingly repellent descriptions of the poverty, illness, and alienation of the Antilles:

Au bout du petit matin bourgeonnant d'anses frêles les Antilles qui ont faim, les Antilles grêlées de petite vérole, les Antilles dynamitée d'alcool, échouées dans la boue de cette baie, dans la poussière de cette ville sinistrement échouées. (72)

At the brink of dawn budding with frail creeks, the hungry West Indies, the West Indies pockpitted with smallpox, the West Indies blown up by alchohol, stranded in the mud of this bay, in the dust of this town sordidly stranded. (73)

In contrast to the 'mince et vigoureux' bodies of the natives in Baudelaire's 'Parfum exotique', Césaire's islands are bodies racked by pain, starvation, and disease. Images that disgust make up the descriptions of the embodied land: pustules, smallpox, leprosy, bulimia, malarial blood. These pointedly unparadisiacal and indeed infernal descriptions are associated with being 'échoué', washed up: the result of a failed voyage.

Just as the land is 'en rupture de faune et de flore' (72; 'alienated from its own flora and fauna', 73), the Antillean crowd is alienated from its collective identity:

Et dans cette ville inerte, cette foule criarde si étonnamment passée à côté de son cri comme cette ville à côté de son mouvement, de son sens, sans inquiétude, à côté de son vrai cri, le seul qu'on eût voulu l'entendre crier parce qu'on le sent sien lui seul; parce qu'on le sent habiter en elle dans quelque refuge profond d'ombre et d'orgueil, dans cette ville inerte, cette foule à côté de son cri de faim, de misère, de révolte, de haine, cette foule si étrangement bavarde et muette. (74)

And in this inert town, this squabbling crowd so strangely swayed from its own cry as the town is swayed from its own movement and meaning, without concern, swayed from its only true cry, the only cry one would have liked to hear because one senses that this cry alone is its own; because one senses that it is alive in some deep shelter of darkness and pride, in this inert town, this town swayed from its cry of hunger, of poverty, of rebellion, of hate, in this crowd so strangely chattering and dumb. (75)

The crowd, 'cette foule qui ne sait pas faire foule' (74; 'this crowd which doesn't know how to be a crowd', 75), is described as unable to formulate its own purpose. The missing collective 'vrai cri' is figured as being perhaps alive in the shadowy depths of racial pride: 'dans quelque refuge profond d'ombre et d'orgueil'. The rediscovery and recuperation of this deeply buried meaning, which would mend the splitting of the 'foule' from peoplehood, is the poem's project.

In the above discussion of the exotic voyage as a textual voyage and as a voyage that reorients the poetic legacy, I have pointed to the ways in which the voyage becomes a useful rhetorical manoeuvre that draws attention to a set of discontinuities, differences in level, and heterogeneities that engender poetry, be it linguistic utopia or dysfunction. It is in this vein that I read the voyage of the *Cahier*. If, as others have argued, this poem represents a sudden break with poetic predecessors,[36] I would suggest that this is the case precisely to the extent that it successfully engages the trope of travel and its potential to draw attention to breaks. I suggested that Baudelaire's exotic, nostalgic, poetic destination itself is reused as a trope for an inherited poetic language that leads to shipwreck in Mallarmé. I similarly suggest that Césaire continues this process of troping, both responding to and writing himself into the tradition, by adding new levels to the chain of reference that the crossing already carries. The voyage of the *Cahier* aims to produce a political engagement, a reclamation of cultural and racial identity, a reunion with a collectivity, and a restitution of a bond with Africa, in addition to a return to the homeland. But rather than constituting a break with the past, the crossing of the *Cahier*, precisely in drawing attention to discontinuity, is also in rich re-encounter with the problematic exoticism, textuality, and the 'anxiety of influence' that the voyage has previously produced. The poem's anxiety about its familiarity with and retracing of routes already travelled coincides with its anxiety about its ability to negotiate the gaps between the levels of reference that the voyage of the *Cahier* must both create and bridge.

---

[36] Abiola Irele, introd. to Aimé Césaire, *Cahier*, p. xvii: 'Not the least importance of Césaire's Cahier was the decisive way it put an end to French West Indian poetry of exotic orientation.'

POINTS OF DEPARTURE

Against the backdrop of Paris, Baudelaire's poems gesture across the ocean toward afar. In 'Mœsta et errabunda', the speaker wants his lover to carry him away from the city 'Vers un autre océan où la splendeur éclate | Bleu, clair, profond, ainsi que la virginité?'.[37] Exclaiming 'Comme vous êtes loin, paradis parfumé', the speaker dreams of a place of perfect love, delight, youth, innocence: a lost past, a lost origin. In the final strophe, 'Est-il déjà plus loin que l'Inde et que la Chine?', we see a questioning of the poem's own geographical projection of this anteriority onto these faraway places. The alterity of India and China might be sites where perfection could be found. But here, the speaker doubts whether this otherness is enough to recall this splendid past. The final lines, 'Peut-on le rappeler avec des cris plaintifs | Et l'animer encor d'une voix argentine, | L'innocent paradis plein de plaisirs furtifs?' suggest that poetic potency is what is at stake, that the poem must rely on its own voice to recall and reanimate the lost object. The poem ends with a question, an uncertainty, with the distinct possibility of the failure of the poetic voyage.

This distance is reminiscent of the *négresse* of 'Le Cygne', Baudelaire's exemplary exile, 'Piétinant dans la boue, et cherchant, l'œil hagard, | Les cocotiers absents de la superbe Afrique'.[38] As Christopher Miller observes, the *négresse* is an exemplar of all those who have lost something that will never be regained.[39] The *négresse*'s distance from her native Africa forms an image evoking all the nostalgia, all the exile in the world. Not only is black alterity a stand-in for the lost object to which exoticism tends, but the black person becomes an archetypal representative of the state of exile itself. The *Cahier* is aware of the status of blackness in the European imagination, as both lost object *and* exemplary exile. The voyage of the *Cahier* undertakes a self-conscious recovery of the lost object and the undoing of exile, on the levels of reclamation of a land, a people, an identity, *négritude*. The poem's stakes in evoking something lost are raised by the actual voyage to be made. If Baudelaire figures paradise as distant and irretrievably lost to the *négresse*, Césaire's poem uses that distance to project blackness itself as a birthright to be reclaimed.

[37] *Œuvres complètes*, 60–1.
[38] Ibid. 81–3.
[39] See Miller's insightful reading of the poem in *Blank Darkness*, 125–30.

The first passage of the *Cahier* reads:

Au bout du petit matin . . .
Va-t-en, lui disais-je, gueule de flic, gueule de vache, va-t-en je déteste les larbins de l'ordre et les hannetons de l'espérance. Va-t-en mauvais gris-gris, punaise de moinillon. Puis je me tournais vers des paradis pour lui et les siens perdus, plus calme que la face d'une femme qui ment, et là, bercé par les effluves d'une pensée jamais lasse je nourrissais le vent, je délaçais les monstres et j'entendais monter de l'autre côté du désastre, un fleuve de tourterelles et de trèfles de la savane que je porte toujours dans mes profondeurs à hauteur inverse du vingtième étage des maisons les plus insolents et par précaution contre la force putréfiante des ambiances crépusculaires, arpentée nuit et jour d'un sacré soleil vénérien. (72)

At the brink of dawn . . .
Get lost I said you cop face, you pig face, get lost, I hate the flunkies of order and the cockchafers of hope. Go away bad grigri bedbug of monklet. Then I turned toward paradises lost to him and his kin, calmer than the face of a woman who lies, and there, lulled by the flow of never-tiring thought, I nurtured the wind, I unlaced monsters and I heard, rising on the far side of a disaster, a river of turtledoves and savannah clover which I always carry inside me as deep down as the twentieth story of the most arrogant houses is high to protect me against the putrefying strength of twilight atmospheres surveyed day in day out by a blessed venereal sun (73).

This poem begins with an injunction, 'Va-t-en', an act of decisive displacement and distancing directed at the policeman ('flic') and the priest ('moinillon'), who represent the order, repression, and constraint authorized by Europe. This defiant act of distancing then leads immediately to a turning toward a desirable alternative: 'Puis je me tournais vers des paradis pour lui et les siens perdu'. The poem defines the paradise initially by its status of being lost to Europe: 'pour lui et les siens perdu'. The displacement establishes a division between two realms: 'Va-t-en' opens up the gulf between the two sides of the divide, a discontinuity out of which this poem is produced; there is now a distance to be crossed. The paradise is on 'l'autre côté du désastre'. The disaster, recalling the middle passage of the slave ship, which figures prominently later in the poem, is the 'in-between' space in which the poem is inaugurated.

The enactment of distance that produces the disastrous space of poetry and crossing also corresponds to a simultaneous displacement at the level of subjectivity. What lies on the other side of the disaster, 'un fleuve de tourterelles et de trèfles de la savane' of an African past, is then relocated inside the speaking subject: 'que je porte toujours dans mes profondeurs'. Horizontal is transposed to vertical, and simultaneously, the two sides of the disaster are transposed to an oppositional relation between inside and outside. The paradise that is lost to Europe is to be found inside the speaking subject, 'dans mes profondeurs'. This first strophe appropriates the familiar move of projecting a paradise onto the exotic other, and locates this lost paradise deep inside the black subject. Thus the crossing of the gulf that the first lines establish is posited as the recovery of this 'refuge profond d'ombre et d'orgueil'.

In the gulf, we discover the ambivalence the journey has in store. The speaker is 'plus calme que la face d'une femme qui ment'. Like the female addressee's 'traîtres yeux' of Baudelaire's 'L'Invitation au voyage' and the 'femmes dont l'œil par sa franchise étonne' of 'Parfum exotique', the speaker's 'face d'une femme qui ment' is a feminine disruption of paradise. This line is also an echo of 'la face qui ment' in Baudelaire's 'Le Masque', a poem that figures the deceptive doubleness of art as a statue with two heads, one true and one a mask.[40] The attribution of mendacity to the speaker's face is an early sign of the dangerous allegorical character of the *Cahier*. It is a reminder that the crossing to paradise involves the negotiation of the divisions between the different levels of reference that the voyage produces. The wholeness of paradise is threatened by the very breaks and distances that the crossing presupposes, and that are embodied here by the lying feminine face of the speaker.

Elsewhere, when the woman appears in the landscape, she provides an image of inscrutability: she is 'la femme qui avait mille noms', 'le regard du désordre'. The woman appears as the multiple, disorderly, perhaps threatening component of paradise. The people of the island are compared to 'une femme, toute on eût cru à sa cadence lyrique, interpelle brusquement une pluie hypothétique et lui intime l'ordre de ne pas tomber'. The woman is the disruption to the fulfilment of the collective identity of the crowd. The woman becomes the potential principle of dissolution, disunity, miscarriage of the return to unity with the collectivity. The anxiety about failure is expressed by the woman's 'two-faced' presence as an anxiety about the poem's ability to achieve unity through the operation of metaphor. This anxiety can be seen in the peculiar lines

pourquoi une femme semble faire la planche à la rivière Capot (son corps

---

[40] Baudelaire, *Œuvres complètes*, 22–3.

lumineusement obscur s'organise docilement au commandement du nombril) mais elle n'est qu'un paquet d'eau sonore. (76)

why a woman seems to be floating in the Capot river (her luminously dark body obediently organises itself at her navel's command) but she is only a bundle of resounding water. (76)

Paradoxically, the temptation to impose the organizing shape of the drowned woman's body to read the landscape is abruptly refused by the very same utterance that renders her body one with that landscape. The movement from 'semble' to 'n'est que' exemplifies the tension between metaphor and being. The 'n'est que' refuses the body's likeness to the shape of the river at the same time that it posits the body *as* 'un paquet d'eau sonore', as nothing outside its identity with the landscape. The difference of the woman's body from the landscape is erased by a gesture that simultaneously refuses the metaphorical construction ('semble') and in doing so retains it ('elle n'est qu'un paquet d'eau sonore'). On the literal level, this phrase shows the metaphor of the woman's body for the landscape to have been a lie or a misreading: it is just 'un paquet d'eau' after all. On my reading, however, this exposure of the metaphor as a lie is the expression of an anxiety about the doubleness and difference of metaphor, an anxiety that accompanies the simultaneous reliance on and refusal of metaphor.

In spite of the fixing of the opposition between the realms of inside and outside, the two worlds are contaminated by each other's properties. For example, consider the lines 'que je porte toujours dans mes profondeurs . . . par précaution contre la force putréfiante des ambiances crépusculaires, arpentée nuit et jour d'un sacré soleil vénérien'. The 'ambiances crépusculaires', it seems, are posed in opposition to the anaphoric 'petit matin'. Both are liminal points in the day, moments of hovering between day and night, yet one is putrefying and to be protected against, while the other is the object of an affectionate mantra. If anything, the *crépuscule* would also be a space of escape from the surveillance by the 'soleil vénérien', precisely because of the in-betweenness of it. What is desired is a respite from this constant surveillance, a respite that the 'petit matin' carves out. However, in turning toward the desired paradise, we encounter 'là, bercé par les effluves d'une pensée jamais lasse'. In the context of the opposition between the two realms, the 'pensée jamais lasse' is the

[40] Baudelaire, *Œuvres complètes*, 22–3.

contamination of paradise by the constant surveillance without break, not unlike 'arpentée nuit et jour'. Although an opposition is being posited, desired and undesired properties are present in both sides of the divide. From the first strophe, the poem exhibits ambivalence about the opposition between two realms, between the colonizing European force and the African essence, between outside and inside. That both the reviled 'ambiances crépusculaires' and the affectionate 'petit matin' are themselves, in a sense, in-between spaces is indicative of this ambivalence.

What is the destination of the crossing, what lies on the other side of the disaster? Along with Césaire's descriptions of the reality of the island as repulsive, diseased, and famished, gestures toward paradise are present, even as they are ironized. Calling the island 'une vieille vie, menteusement souriant', the poem ironizes the anterior life that the paradise is supposed to conjure, but which is undercut by the stark reality of the island's poverty and misery. The poem recognizes that its voyage is inevitably bound up with the quest for origins, even while it acknowledges its futility and impossibility: 'Et nos gestes imbéciles et fous pour faire revivre l'éclaboussement d'or des instants favorisés, le cordon ombilical restitué à sa splendeur fragile.' Even while positing the voyage as a means to an originary state, the poem also sees this mythic origin as a means to the present reality of the *pays natal:* 'Et cette joie ancienne m'apportant la connaissance de ma présente misère.' Although the 'joie ancienne' orients us toward a glorious African past, the past returns us to the present, so that African anteriority is not merely an implied destination but also a means to an Antillean contemporaneity.

The anxiety about the (in)compatibility of the metaphoricity of the means of transport and the wholeness that is an essential component of the desired destination becomes the major preoccupation of the poem's narration of its departures, arrivals, shipwrecks, and all that happens in between. It is in these in-between spaces that the poem must negotiate between its different levels of reference. The first instance of departure in the *Cahier* is fraught with anxieties of betrayed loyalty, as the speaker prepares to leave Martinique for Europe: 'Au bout du petit matin, le vent de jadis qui s'élève, des fidélités trahies, du devoir incertain qui se dérobe et cet autre petit matin d'Europe' (84; 'At the brink of dawn, rising is the wind of yore, of betrayed loyalties, of an unclear duty shying away and this other little European dawn', 85). Between the two *petit matins* in this stanza, the possibility of leaving and returning opens up. It is precisely the space between departure and return that is of particular interest.

> Partir.
> Comme il y a des hommes-hyènes et des hommes-panthères, je serais un homme-juif
> un homme-cafre
> un homme-hindou-de Calcutta
> un homme-de-Harlem-qui-ne-vote-pas (84)
> To leave.
> As there are hyena-men and panther-men, I shall be a Jew-man
> a kaffir-man
> a Hindu-from-Calcutta-man
> a man-from-Harlem-who-does-not-vote (85)

Je retrouverais le secret des grandes communications et des grandes combustions. Je dirais orage. Je dirais fleuve. Je dirais tornade. Je dirais feuille. Je dirais arbre. Je serais mouillé de toutes les pluies, humecté de toutes les rosées. Je roulerais comme du sang frénétique sur le courant lent de l'œil des mots en chevaux fous en enfants frais en caillots en couvre-feu en vestiges de temple en pierres précieuses assez loin pour décourager les mineurs. Qui ne me comprendrait pas ne comprendrait pas davantage le rugissement du tigre. (86)

I would rediscover the secret of great communications and of great combustions. I would say storm. I would say river. I would say tornado. I would say leaf, I would say tree. I would be soaked by all the rains, moistened by all the dews. Like frantic blood over the slow stream of the eye, I would roll words as crazy horses as fresh children as bloodclots as curfew as vestiges of temples as gems deep enough to discourage miners. Whoever would not understand me would not understand the roaring of the tiger either. (87)

What follows the infinitive 'Partir' in this first instance of departure is the wish for identification with and connection to all oppressed people, the rediscovery of 'le secret des grandes communications' (with its echoes of the Baudelairean *correspondances*), and a primal union with nature. This rediscovery is the poetic project at hand: to the poetic word is attributed the power to achieve this union, as 'je dirais' leads into 'je serais', 'je roulerais'. As in the first lines of the poem, in which a displacement leads to a turning toward a desired alternative, the displacement of 'Partir' enables the possibility of the connection with other groups and with the land, and unleashes the capacity of the poetic utterance to effect wholeness. Only in declaring a leave-taking is the possibility for identification and connection produced.

Having staged the departure from the native land, the poem immediately wants to return to it in familiar terms:

il me suffirait d'une gorgée de ton lait jiculi pour qu'en toi je découvre toujours à même distance de mirage—mille fois plus natale et dorée d'un soleil que n'entame nul prisme—la terre où tout est libre et fraternel, ma terre (86)

I would only need one mouthful of your jiculi milk to discover in you always as distant as a mirage a land—a thousand times more native and turned to a golden tan by a sun that no prism divides—a land where everything is free and fraternal, my land (87)

This is a vision of wholeness attributed to the native land, similar in rhetoric to Baudelaire's elsewhere. We recall the fragrance of the addressee's breast in 'Parfum exotique' that is sufficient to bring about the travel to the primal place, and the fragrance of the addressee's hair in Baudelaire's 'La Chevelure': 'Fortes tresses, soyez la houle qui m'enlève!'.[41] In the *Cahier*, it is the taste of the 'lait jiculi', the milk of a native plant, that enables the journey to the native land. The speaker of 'La Chevelure' posits his addressee's head of hair as repository of the otherness that creates the possibility of transport to another locale: 'Je plongerai ma tête amoureuse d'ivresse | Dans ce noir océan où l'autre est enfermée.' In the *Cahier* passage I have quoted, the 'lait jiculi' becomes a similarly exotic repository. The speaker's departure from Martinique in effect creates a distance through the 'Partir' that renders the native land other to him, and this otherness is called upon in his wish for transport to a primacy, as signalled by the milk's recalling of the lost object of the mother's body. The relationship between distance ('toujours à même distance') and wholeness ('soleil que n'entame nul prisme') also emerges here.[42] The hope for discovery of the intensity of the primal land ('mille fois plus natale') is made possible by distance. The last line of the passage, 'la terre où tout est libre et fraternel, ma terre', recalls the familial wholeness of the destination of 'L'Invitation au voyage'. It is only in leaving the island home that a union with it can be craved and conceived. The possibility of a return to an original unity of experience is opened up in the wake of a departure.

[41] *Œuvres complètes*, 25–7.
[42] Compare to the 'soleil monotone' of 'Parfum exotique'.

SHIPWRECKS

The second instance of 'Partir' which follows shortly refers to the departure from Europe for Martinique:

Partir. Mon cœur bruissait de générosités emphatiques. Partir . . . j'arriverais lisse et jeune dans ce pays mien et je dirais à ce pays dont le limon entre dans la composition de ma chair: 'j'ai longtemps erré et je reviens vers la hideur désertée de vos plaies'.
Je viendrais à ce pays mien et je lui dirais: 'Embrassez-moi sans crainte . . . Et si je ne sais que parler, c'est pour vous que je parlerai'.

Et je lui dirais encore:
'Ma bouche sera la bouche des malheurs qui n'ont point de bouche, ma voix, la liberté de celles qui s'affaissent au cachot du désespoir'.

Et venant je me dirais à moi-même:
'Et surtout mon corps aussi bien que mon âme, gardez-vous de vous croiser les bras en l'attitude stérile du spectateur, car la vie n'est pas un spectacle, car une mer de douleurs n'est pas un proscenium, car un homme qui crie n'est pas un ours qui danse . . .'
Et voici que je suis venu! (86–8)

To leave. My heart was rustling with empathic generosities. To leave . . . I would arrive smooth and youthful in this land of mine and I would say to this land whose clay has been incorporated into my flesh: 'I have long wandered and I am returning to the deserted hideousness of your wounds.'
I would come to this land of mine and I would say: 'Kiss me without fear . . . And if I can only speak, it is for you that I shall speak.'

And I would also say:
'My mouth will be the mouth of those griefs which have no mouth, my voice, the freedom of those that collapse in the dungeon of despair.'
And on my way I would say to myself:
'And above all beware, my body and my soul too, beware of crossing your arms in the sterile attitude of the spectator, because life is not a spectacle, because a sea of sorrows is not a proscenium, because a man who screams is not a dancing bear.'
And so I have come back. (87–9)

There is a development from the infinitive 'Partir' to the conditional 'j'arriverais', 'je viendrais', 'je lui dirais', and then abruptly to the declaration of the arrival as having taken place: 'Et voici que je suis venu!'. What happens in the space between the 'partir', the potential return, and the assertion that the destination has been reached? How is this arrival accomplished?

The speaker's desire to return to the Antilles coincides with his desire to speak for his collectivity: 'ma bouche sera la bouche des malheurs qui n'ont point de bouche, ma voix, la liberté de celles qui s'affaissent au cachot du désespoir'. The voyage is figured as a process of becoming *representative* of the people. In the gap between the departure from Europe and the asserted arrival in the Antilles, however, there is a warning, a reminder that the real suffering of people is at stake: 'gardez-vous de vous croiser les bras en l'attitude stérile du spectateur, car la vie n'est pas un spectacle, car une mer de douleurs n'est pas un proscenium'. This warning urges the distinction between real suffering and performance, between 'un homme qui crie' and 'un ours qui danse'. The distant stance of the 'spectateur', the speaker, from the collectivity, poses the danger of performativity for the voyage's attainment of representativeness. This is precisely because the return is a *staging* of a return. It is in the very performativity of the 'partir' and the 'voici que je suis venu!' that the poetic voyage is completed: the poetic voice asserts the arrival and in doing so makes it happen. The hope of becoming representative is endangered by the very performative means necessary for its execution. While the poem posits the voyage's process of becoming representative as an undoing of the distance between the speaker and the collectivity, that distance is the very distance that being representative, 'standing for' and 'speaking for', entails.

Several lines hence, the danger turns into a failure, symbolized by a shipwreck:

tragiques futilités éclairées de cette seule noctiluque et moi seul, brusque scène de petit matin où fait le beau l'apocalypse des monstres puis, chavirée, se tait (88)

tragic futilities lit by this unique noctiluca and I alone, sudden stage of this dawn when the apocalypse of monsters shows off only to capsize and fall silent (89)

The 'brusque scène de petit matin' reveals the space in which the poem takes place to have been an explicitly performative space. The image of a boat capsizing is directly tied to the performativity of poetry. The aspiration to be unified with the collectivity is disappointed ('moi seul') and has a silencing effect precisely because the crossing is enacted by the poetic word. The claim 'voici que je suis venu!' signals the success of the poetic voyage, while the shipwreck signals a failure on other levels; it implies that the poetic voyage may be in tension with the motivated and repoliticized goals of the return.

Hence a few lines later comes an admission of the persistence of distance still: 'me voici divisé des oasis fraîches de la fraternité . . . cet horizon trop sûr tressaille comme un geôlier' (88; 'I am divided from the fresh oases of brotherhood. . . . this overconfident horizon shudders like a gaoler', 89). Ironically, it is the confidence of the poetic voice to manoeuvre the voyage ('fait le beau', 'horizon trop sûr'), its comfort and familiarity with the tropes of past poetic voyages, that is the principle of failure.

André Breton's 1947 preface to the *Cahier*, 'Un grand poète noir', picks up the shipwreck theme. Breton appropriates the poem's dynamics of exile and return to describe the French surrealist's own relationship to Martinique and Césaire's blackness. Breton had been one of the European writers named as sources of inspiration (along with Marx, Hegel, Lautréamont, Rimbaud) by the Martinican student signatories of the manifesto *Légitime défense* in 1932. The narrative of Breton's preface, which first appeared in Aimé and Suzanne Césaire's journal *Tropiques* in 1944 as 'Martinique, charmeuse de serpents: un grand poète noir',[43] takes place during World War II. Breton was briefly interned in Vichy-controlled Martinique on his way to voluntary exile in New York. Breton tells of his confinement in a concentration camp in Fort-de-France, his subsequent release, and his accidental discovery of Césaire's poetry.

He begins the preface with a shipwreck:

Avril 1941. Bloquant la vue une carcasse de navire, scellée de madrépores au sol de la plage et visitée par les vagues . . . par sa fixité même ne laissait aucun répit à l'exaspération de ne pouvoir se déplacer qu'à pas comptés, dans l'intervalle de deux baïonnettes: le camp de concentration du Lazaret, en rade de Fort-de-France.

April 1941. The view was blocked, blocked by the carcass of a ship riveted to the beach by coral and visited by the waves . . . The very fixedness of the ship made it all the more exasperating not to be able to move more than a few inches away, between two bayonets: we were in the Lazaret concentration camp in the harbour of Fort de France.[44]

[43] André Breton, 'Martinique, charmeuse de serpents: Un grand poète noir', *Tropiques*, 11 (May 1944), 119–26. Breton also wrote a book with this title: *Martinique charmeuse de serpents* (Paris: Sagittaire, 1948). For a creative account of the encounter of Breton and the Césaires, see Ronnie Scharfman, 'De grands poètes noirs: Breton rencontre les Césaire', in D. Lefort, P. Rivas, and J. Chénieux-Gendron (eds.), *Nouveau monde, autres mondes: Surréalisme & Amériques* (Collection Pleine Marge, 5; Paris: Lachenal & Ritter, 1995).

[44] Breton, 'Un grand poète noir', preface to Aimé Césaire, *Cahier d'un retour au pays natal*, bilingual edn., trans. Émile Snyder (Paris: Présence africaine, 1971), 8–27: 8–9. All further references are given in the text.

Breton finds himself trapped on the island and yet unable to see it because of a physical obstruction in the form of a shipwreck. This shipwreck, blocking the view of the landscape, becomes a metaphor for Breton's own confinement in the concentration camp and for his frustrated gaze.

When finally released from captivity, Breton goes eagerly in search of a landscape moulded by the exotic travels of the European literary imagination:

> Libéré au bout de quelques jours, avec quelle avidité ne m'étais-je pas jeté dans les rues, en quête de tout ce qu'elles pouvaient m'offrir de jamais perçu, l'éblouissement des marchés, les colibris dans les voix, les femmes que Paul Éluard, au retour d'un voyage autour du monde, m'avait dites plus belles que partout ailleurs. (9)

> I was released after a few days and I thrust myself with devouring curiosity into the streets, seeking their never perceived riches: the dazzling splendor of markets, the voices that sounded like colibris, the women whom Paul Eluard back from a trip around the world had described to me as more beautiful than anywhere else. (8)

However, he is soon disappointed:

> Bientôt pourtant une épave se précisait, menaçait d'occuper à nouveau tout le champ: cette ville elle-même ne tenait à rien, elle semblait privée de ses organes essentiels. Le commerce, tout en vitrines, y prenait un caractère théorique, inquiétant. (9)

> And yet I soon felt that another shipwreck was looming, threatening to block the view once again: this town in fact had no roots, no vital organs of its own. The shops, mere shop windows, took on a theoretical, disquieting turn. (8)

When the blockage of the shipwreck is removed, the exotic expectation is not fulfilled. Instead, Breton finds to his chagrin the grim reality of the island in its poverty and inertia. This harsh contrast between the island's depressing reality and the exotic images usually associated with it is, of course, precisely the shock-producing strategy with which Césaire so effectively begins his poem, whose voyage is in part a conscious disavowal of exoticism. Here we see Breton deploying a similar strategy of contrast between the desired exotic island of the European literary imagination and the actual landscape that he confronts.

Breton also echoes Césaire's evocation of the shipwreck, but puts it to different use. If Césaire's shipwreck signals, among other things, the dangers and traps of the familiar tropes of exoticism, Breton's shipwreck poses a bothersome obstacle to exoticism. The first shipwreck (of Breton's confinement) is removed only to reveal another one. In the landscape of his preface, the shipwreck, which in the first instance posed a blockage to his view, now returns ('une épave se précisait, menaçait d'occuper à nouveau tout le champ') as a blockage to exoticism. This second, and this time figurative, shipwreck is the reality of the actual island, which inconveniently frustrates his exotic desire.

Why might Breton be invested in constructing this situation as a shipwreck, a remaining trace of an historical accident that is, more likely than not, unexplained and unreadable? All this serves as a prelude to his accidental discovery of Césaire. It is out of the historical contingency of Breton's imprisonment in Martinique that he comes to know Césaire. According to the narrative, Breton comes upon Césaire's poems while glancing through an issue of *Tropiques* in a shop. If Breton's access to this island is obstructed by a shipwreck, it is Césaire who will restore his access, and make readable the 'bruit trop clair comme à travers les choses échouées' (9; 'noises too limpid as if coming through a wilderness of wrecks', 8). Describing his reaction upon reading Césaire's poems for the first time, Breton exclaims, 'Toutes ces ombres grimaçantes ce déchiraient, se dispersaient . . . ainsi la voix de l'homme n'était en rien brisée, couverte, elle se redressait ici comme l'épi même de la lumière' (11; 'All those grimacing shadows (I had sensed) were at last torn asunder and scattered away . . . man's voice had evidently not been stifled and subdued—here it rang, upright like spikes of light', 10). A play of dark and light renders Césaire's voice the luminous remedy to the darkness that afflicts the island. What the shipwreck hides, Césaire reveals. Furthermore, once brought to light, the island can be claimed as Breton's own: 'Cette terre qu'il montrait . . ., mais oui, c'était aussi ma terre, c'était *notre* terre que j'avais pu craindre à tort de voir s'obscurcir' (11; 'The land he revealed . . . was also my land— yes, it was *our* land which I had wrongly assumed to be one day overcome by darkness', 10). Césaire's salvation of the island from falling into darkness makes it possible for Breton to claim the land as 'ma terre'. All along, the shipwreck has cast a shadow, an obstacle standing in the way of Breton's ownership, now implemented by the mediation of Césaire's illuminating presence.

The play of dark and light, of hiding and revealing, also colours

Breton's first meeting with Césaire: 'Je retrouve ma première réaction tout élémentaire à le découvrir d'un noir si pur, d'autant plus masqué à première vue qu'il sourit' (13; 'I recapture my first immediate reaction at finding him so purely black—a blackness that his smile kept away from you at first sight', 12). Césaire's pure blackness is masked by his (white) smile, in Breton's blatantly stereotypical characterization. Like the shipwreck that blocks the landscape, the smile here is posed as a mask obscuring blackness. It is ultimately Césaire's blackness that Breton does discover, and of which he becomes inordinately enamoured. Breton's frustrated desire for the exotic is seamlessly replaced with a desire for blackness, embodied by Césaire himself:[45]

Et c'est un Noir celui qui nous guide aujourd'hui dans l'inexploré. . . . Et c'est un Noir qui est non seulement un Noir mais tout l'homme, qui en exprime toutes les interrogations, toutes les angoisses, tous les espoirs et toutes les extases et qui s'imposera de plus en plus à moi comme le prototype de la dignité. (15)

A black man it is who guides us today through unexplored lands. . . . A black man it is who embodies not simply the black race but all mankind, its queries and anxieties, its hopes and ecstasies and who will remain for me the symbol of dignity. (14)

Breton's narrative seeks to pose the black man as the explorer, not the explored; yet Breton's evident excitement at his 'découverte' of Césaire, blackness, and Martinique, gives the lie to this putatively empowering presentation.

The shipwreck that threatens to obscure the island now transmutes into a metaphor for the moribund state of European arts and letters: 'une époque . . . où l'art même menace de figer dans d'anciennes données, le premier souffle nouveau, revivifiant, apte à redonner toute confiance est l'apport d'un Noir' (13–15; 'an age. . . . when art itself is on the verge of being stultified in obsolete forms and values, the first new breath of life that can give us back our trust and

---

[45] The extent to which Breton's appropriation of Césaire contributed to a continuing exoticism is demonstrated in a telling contemporary example. The epigraph to the *Ulysses Travel Guide to Martinique*, ed. Claude Morneau, 2nd edn. (Ulysses Travel Publications, 1996) quotes Breton on the *Cahier*: 'En effet, ce poème, il écrit à Paris, alors qu'il vient de quitter l'Ecole normale supérieure et qu'il s'apprête à revenir à la Martinique. Le pays natal, oui comment en particulier résister à l'appel de cette île, comment ne pas succomber à ses ciels, à son ondoiement de sirène, à son parler tout de cajolerie?' —André Breton (1886–1966) speaking about Aimé Césaire and his *Cahier d'un retour au pays natal* found in *Martinique Charmeuse de Serpents*.'

vigour comes from a black poet', 12–14). In a familiar turn toward the other as the ultimate source of rejuvenation, Césaire becomes the great black hope for a tired European imagination.[46] The shape and structure of 'Un grand poète noir', which is in direct interaction and juxtaposition with the dynamics of exile and return in the *Cahier*, traces a trajectory from shipwreck and obscurity to happy discovery, arrival, and renewal. In this process, Césaire becomes representative not only of his people, but of all humanity.

This conjunction of the two contemporaries reveals that Césaire's literary encounter with exoticism is not limited to past literary texts that must be confronted and rewritten. It reveals that Césaire's own tropes at the moment of their textualization, and indeed his person, are immediately appropriated to contribute to a continuing exoticism—another version, another iteration—that desires blackness as a means to European access, ownership, and recovery.[47] The slippage between exoticism and *négritude* alerts us to the extent that even the repoliticized aspect of the voyage of recuperation in the *Cahier* may continue, as much as it breaks with exoticism. The ease with which Césaire's text could plausibly be integrated into Breton's exoticism calls into question any simplified notion that Césaire, by writing back to the tradition, had transcended it or brought about its demise.

ARRIVALS

Three major passages narrate arrival in the *Cahier*. I have discussed the first, in which a shipwreck undercuts the capability of the poetic word to bring about a successful arrival. In the second, the crossing is effected by the poet's 'prière virile':

> et voici au bout de ce petit matin ma prière virile que je n'entende ni les rires ni les cris, les yeux fixés sur cette ville que je prophétise, belle,
> donnez-moi la foi sauvage du sorcier

[46] Sartre's 'Orphée noir' displays a similar desire for blackness as an essential source of a much-needed political engagement in French literature.

[47] The encounter of Breton and Césaire is, of course, an important instance of the wider convergence of European avant-garde movements and black anticolonialism. See James Clifford's insightful account of the role of European ethnography in the convergence that he calls 'ethnographic surrealism', in *The Predicament of Culture: Twentieth-Century Ethnography, Literature, and Art* (Cambridge, Mass.: Harvard University Press, 1988), 117–51. An excellent discussion of primitivism in European art can be found in Hal Foster, 'The "Primitive" Unconscious of Modern Art, or White Skins Black Masks', in id., *Recordings: Art, Spectacle, Cultural Politics* (Seattle: Bay Press, 1985), 181–208.

donnez à mes mains puissance de modeler
donnez à mon âme la trempe de l'épée
je ne me dérobe point. Faites de ma tête une tête de proue
et de moi-même, mon cœur, ne faites ni un père, ni un frère,
ni un fils, mais le père, mais le frère, mais le fils,
ni un mari, mais l'amant de cet unique peuple.
Faites-moi rebelle à toute vanité, mais docile à son génie
comme le poing à l'allongée du bras!
Faites-moi commissaire de son sang
faites-moi dépositaire de son ressentiment (116)

and at the brink of this dawn this is my virile prayer may I heed neither
laughs nor cries, eyes rivetted on this city which I prophesy,
beautiful,
give me the savage faith of the sorcerer
give my hands the power to mould
give my soul the temper of a sword
I do not dodge. Make of my head a prow-head
and of myself, my heart, do not make a father nor a brother
nor a son, but the father, but the brother, but the son
nor a husband, but the lover of this unique people.

Make me refractory to any vanity but docile to its genius
like the fist to the outstretching of the arm
Make me representative of its blood
Make of me trustee of its rancour (117)

Drawing on the tropes of masculine virility and insemination, the 'prière virile' asks specifically that the poet be able to accomplish the oceanic crossing as a metaphoric crossing, the 'crossing' of metaphor. The line 'Faites de ma tête une tête de proue' entreats that the speaker be transformed into a metaphor. This process is figured in navigational terms, as a process of crossing the ocean. The prayer implores that the speaker be uniquely representative of his people ('ni un père, ni un frère ... mais le père, mais le frère ... de cet unique peuple'). The transformative power of metaphor is called upon to enable the speaker to stand for, represent, and transform the plight of his people. The prayer concerns the ability of the poet to avert the rhetorical manoeuvres of the voyage so that the textual arrival and representation coincides with the political. There is an abrupt shift from the poet's pleas to a description of the movements of a small lone canoe making its way to shore:

> La voici avancer par escalades et retombées sur le flot pulverisé
> la voici danser la danse sacrée devant la grisaille du bourg

la voici barir d'un lambi vertigineux
voici galoper le lambi jusqu'a l'indécision des mornes
et voici par vingt fois d'un labour vigoureux la pagaie forcer l'eau la
pirogue se cabre sous l'assaut de la lame, dévie un instant,
tente de fuir, mais la caresse rude de la pagaie la vire, alors elle fonce, un
frémissement parcourt l'échine de la vague,
la mer bave et gronde
la pirogue comme un traîneau file sur le sable. (118)

Here it is advancing, climbing up and falling down into the pulverised waves,
here it is dancing the sacred dance in front of the dull grey town
here it is trumpeting out of a vertiginous lambi
here is the lambi galloping all the way to the indecisiveness of the mornes
and here, twenty times over, the vigorous ploughing of the paddle forces the water
the pirogue rears under the assault of the swell, swerves for a moment, tries to flee, but the rough caress of the paddle turns it around, then it surges forward, a shiver runs along the spine of the wave
the sea slobbers and growls
the pirogue like a sleigh beaches on the sand. (119)

What can we make of the relationship between the 'prière virile', the speaker's entreaty for the arrival, and the description of the advancing of the boat? There are several levels of metaphoricity at stake in the prayer for the arrival: among them the voyage as a textual crossing, the poet as a representative for the collectivity, and the textual voyage as a metaphor for political representation. We have seen that anxieties about the distance between the levels of the poetic voyage constitute the potential for shipwreck. The pirogue reaching shore is not only an allegory of the success of the poet's voyage, but an allegory of the bridging of the gap between the different levels of the voyage. The abrupt turn to the allegorical story of the pirogue is an allegory of the ability of allegory to forge connections between levels of reference. The prayer beseeches:

> donnez-moi sur cet océan divers
> l'obstination de la fière pirogue
> et sa vigueur marine. (118)

> give me on this diverse ocean
> the obstinacy of the proud pirogue
> and its marine vigour. (119)

It begs, 'donnez-moi les muscles de cette pirogue sur la mer démontée' (118; 'give me the muscles of that pirogue on the raging sea', 119). The prayer appeals for the pirogue's steadfast 'obstination' in the face of the heterogeneity and disorder produced in the oceanic space. The boat's moment of arrival on the beach is invested with the union of heterogeneous levels of meaning, even as the allegorical boat adds another level of heterogeneity to the crossing. In effect, the 'prière virile' is a paradoxical prayer for allegory.

This prayer is answered by the final successful voyage. A far cry from the various shipwreck images appearing throughout the text, this final triumphant crossing is made, ironically, by the slave ship, an image that is central to the *Cahier*. This passage narrates slaves taking over a ship in revolt, storming each part of the ship, one by one:

le négrier craque de toute part . . . Son ventre se convulse et résonne . . . L'affreux ténia de sa cargaison ronge les boyaux fétides de l'étrange nourrisson des mers! (128)

the slave-ship cracks everywhere . . . Its belly convulses and resonates . . . The atrocious tapeworm of its cargo gnaws at the foetid bowels of the strange suckling of the sea! (129)

> La négraille aux senteurs d'oignon frit retrouve dans son sang répandu le goût amer de la liberté
>
> Et elle est debout la négraille
>
> la négraille assise
> inattendument debout
> debout dans la cale
> debout dans les cabines
> debout sur le pont
> debout dans le vent
> debout sous le soleil
> debout dans le sang
>   debout
>   et
>   libre (130)

Negridom with its smell of fried onion rediscovers the sour taste of freedom in its spilt blood

Negridom is standing
sitting-down negridom
unforeseenly standing

>   standing in the hold
>   standing in the cabins
>   standing on the deck
>   standing in the wind
>   standing under the sun
>   standing in the blood
>   standing
>   and
>   free (131)

That this time it is a 'navire lustral' (130; lustral ship, 131), not a lone 'pirogue', signals the arrival of a collective consciousness. The takeover of the slave ship assumes another level of meaning in this context. The figurative arrival of the slave ship that is taken over by slaves on the high seas becomes an image of a reversal of the voyages of the triangular trade that brought blacks from Africa to the West Indies.

In earlier parts of the *Cahier*, we have seen ambivalence about the ability of poetry to bring about a successful voyage. The shipwreck of the first arrival signals the internal contradictions between performative textuality and the poem's project of bringing about a unity between the poet and the collectivity. The second arrival's 'prière virile' concerns the power of allegory to effect a connection between levels, textual and extra-textual. By contrast, the final allegorical crossing of the *Cahier* involves a transformation of the historical terms of the arrival. The slaves take over the ship, owning each part. What is invested in this successful takeover of the slave ship is the reclamation of a collective history—another, metaphorical, form of arrival. This brings out an important aspect of the return, across to 'l'autre côté du désastre' (72; 'the far side of disaster', 73), by which the voyage of the *Cahier* attempts to set itself apart from previous literary voyages. It is ultimately this level, of historical transformation by the allegorical slave ship, that is presented as constituting the success of the voyage of the *Cahier*, a voyage whose potential for failure has been at hand throughout the poem.

The arrival of a slave ship as a success is, of course, redolent with irony on which the text capitalizes to underline the paradox of its crossing. The relationship between success and failure of crossing is the crux of the paradoxical dynamic that has been the focus of this chapter. That which threatens to make the crossing a failure is also the condition for its success. This is so when the voyage attempts to produce authenticity and originality in the face of the exotic influence of precursors. It is equally so when the voyage becomes an allegory of allegory that simultaneously achieves and undercuts unity. The distance and difference that the crossing aims to erase is also the very distance and difference that makes crossing possible. Whether deployed by French or Antillean poet, the alterity invoked by travel to an ailleurs can serve as a means to a nostalgic experience of wholeness, with alterity enabling a literary experience of authenticity. Thus, the crossing takes place in a space of paradox, of difference that brings about unity, of figures that reveal through hiding, of the simultaneous success and failure of structures of reference.

As we have seen, the crossing in the *Cahier* bears the weight of antecedent crossings, which inform its concerns about poetic autonomy and the effectiveness of poetic language. This weight is especially borne by the poem's presentation of the crossing as a process of the poet's reunion with his collectivity, a return that is bound up with a recuperation of collective history. The crossing, the wrestling and wresting of poetic autonomy, the regaining of wholeness, the effectiveness of the poetic word, are all challenges of the process of coming to represent.[48] The final triumph of arrival in the *Cahier* is in tension with the continual ambivalences and doubts that obtain in the poem's encounter with its textual status. Historical rewriting is presented as that which is finally capable of bridging the distances that the voyage confronts in its encounter with problems of representation. In what follows, I shall discuss the interaction between historical rewriting and the inherent discontinuities of allegorical representation. The *Cahier*, then, is the touchstone for this study not only because of its foundational position in Antillean literature, but because of its profound engagement with this problematic.

[48] Of course Césaire did in fact come to represent in his well-known political career as mayor of Fort-de-France and *député* in the Assemblée nationale constituante (1945–93). Most famously in this capacity, Césaire oversaw the 1946 departmentalization of Martinique, Guadeloupe, Guyane and Réunion. His political ambivalence about this 'solution' arguably parallels the poetic ambivalence that I have been discussing. Confiant has attacked Césaire for his 'paradoxe assimilationiste' in *Aimé Césaire*, 86–93, 125–9. For an informative and more fair view of Césaire's political ambivalences, see Auguste Armet, 'Aimé Césaire, homme politique', *Études littéraires*, 6/1 (1973), 81–96.

3
GLISSANT, *DÉTOUR*, AND HISTORY

I have chosen in the previous two chapters to focus on two themes, crossing and allegory. I have suggested that both function as figural models for a certain paradox. Each chapter points to the expression of a desire for unity that depends on a principle of heterogeneity; the drive to regain a prior authenticity and an awareness of a break with the past; nostalgia and the renunciation of nostalgia. Whether in Césaire's poetic journey to his native land, in Jameson's theory of Third World literature, or in the orientation of allegory toward a pure anteriority, the precondition of the intense longing for a return to origins is the consciousness of the rupture with origins.

Paul Gilroy chooses the ship in motion as an organizing symbol for the project of writing a history of the black Atlantic because 'ships immediately focus attention on the middle passage, on the various projects for redemptive return to an African homeland, on the circulation of ideas and activists as well as the movement of key cultural and political artefacts'.[1] In the context of the history of the African diaspora, the ship not only becomes a rich and useful metaphor for the return to origins across space and time, but also a repetition of the memory of the 'originary' moment of discontinuity, the middle passage, that transported Africans to slavery. The return to the first place and concept of discontinuity may be envisioned as constituting the organizing principle of the historical project. One can, with Gilroy, usefully imagine the historical project as a ship travelling in between destinations, one that makes connections possible, and repeats the first crossing that brought about the need for precisely those connections.

The previous chapters have sketched two major examples of paradoxical return. Both the metaphor of travel and the rhetorical device of allegory, with their self-conscious attention to breaks and discontinuities, forge connections. Travel allegorizes and allegory travels in the gap left by a discontinuity that preoccupies postcolonial literature: the problem of history. The twin themes of severance from one's own past and of the pressing need to reinstate historical continuity recur in efforts to articulate personal and collective identity.

[1] *The Black Atlantic: Modernity and Double Consciousness* (London: Verso, 1993), 4.

I explore in this chapter the possibility of a postcolonial project that is directed not toward recovering a lost authentic anteriority, but toward the discontinuity itself and what is produced in the gap.[2] I shall argue that the space of discontinuity can be seen not as negating, but as engendering, history. My argument is divided into three parts. First, I shall show how Édouard Glissant in *Le Discours antillais* (1981) suggests an epistemological model for the Antilles that is structured around missing origins, indirect approaches, and repeated departures. Next, I shall elaborate on Glissant's *antillanité* as an in-between space usefully compared to a version of textuality in which the absence of a structural centre engenders the play of signification. Finally, I shall apply these discussions to the problem of the absence of history in the Antilles, and propose an approach to reinterpreting the discontinuity at the centre of Antillean experience. More generally, this chapter probes the intriguing background of the political and intellectual stakes of the idea of history for postcolonial discourses. It questions what it means to be in possession of a history that is 'one's own', and what implications this has for thinking about tradition and diaspora.

RETOUR AND *DÉTOUR*: MISSING ORIGINS

Novelist, poet, playwright, philosopher, and the most influential theorist of Caribbean identity, Édouard Glissant departs in his theoretical work from *négritude*'s essentialism and notions of absolute racial and cultural difference.[3] *Antillanité*, a term Glissant coined in *Discours*, denotes a process of relativity, contact, interdependence, and hybridity that the Antilles exemplify. The Creole language becomes the linguistic paradigm of this cultural phenomenon. Glissant subsequently became the inspiration for the *créolité* movement, launched by a younger generation of Martinicans, Jean

---

[2] One way to think of this shift in focus is expressed by Gilroy's homonym 'routes' rather than 'roots': 'marked by its European origins, modern black political culture has always been more interested in the relationship of identity to roots and rootedness than in seeing identity as a process of movement and mediation that is more appropriately approached via the homonym routes' (ibid 19). James Clifford also explores this idea in his work on travelling cultures in *Routes: Travel and Translation in the Late Twentieth Century* (Cambridge, Mass.: Harvard University Press, 1997).

[3] Glissant's biography can be found in J. Michael Dash, *Édouard Glissant* (Cambridge: Cambridge University Press, 1995), 6–25. See also Danel Radford, *Édouard Glissant* (Poètes d'aujourd'hui, 244; Paris: Seghers, 1982), 13–27.

Bernabé, Patrick Chamoiseau, and Raphaël Confiant, with the publication of their manifesto, *Éloge de la créolité* (1989).[4] *Créolité* emphasizes the creation of a distinctive Caribbean culture out of a multiplicity of sources, and endorses the use of the Creole language in literary forms. Rejecting both the universalism of the West and the oppositional thinking of black singularity, Glissant's *Discours* refuses, in a nuanced way, the temptations of purity and authenticity. Despite *créolité*'s indebtedness to Glissant, it has had the tendency to reinscribe essentialism in its insistence that Creole be understood as the authentic voice of the Antillean people.[5] *Discours* already contains a warning against this possibility.[6]

In the Afro-Caribbean context, geographical exile is a common starting point for writers due to the ancestral displacement caused by slavery. In texts that posit Africa as the place of origin, or that attempt to recuperate an estranged Caribbean identity, the endeavour inevitably grapples with distance—physical, cultural, spiritual, historical. In *Discours*, Glissant presents a theory of Antillean history that is a thoroughgoing alternative to the teleology of return. He begins by distinguishing the situation of Caribbean people as different in kind from that of populations who are simply transplanted from one land to another and continue to survive as the same people in the newer place of exile. In contrast to a people 'qui maintient l'Être' ('that maintains its original nature'),[7] Glissant sees the Caribbean population, most of whose ancestors were transferred by the slave trade, as having changed and constantly changing into another people. It is from this first premise that he advances his theory of *Relation*: he abandons the notion of the uncontaminated, unchanging *Être* as the principle of peoplehood in favour of 'histoires entrecroisées . . . qui

---

[4] Patrick Chamoiseau speaks affectionately of his own and his generation's debt to Glissant, 'père d'une littérature future', in 'En témoignage d'une volupté', *Carbet*, 10 (1990), 143–52: 143.

[5] For a useful discussion of Glissant's refusal of the essentialist regressions of the *créolité* movement that he inspired, see Chris Bongie, 'Resisting Memories: The Creole Identities of Lafcadio Hearn and Edouard Glissant', *SubStance*, 84 (1997), 153–78.

[6] In *Conquérants de la nuit nue: Édouard Glissant et l'H(h)istoire antillaise* (Tübingen: Gunter Narr Verlag, 1988), Bernadette Cailler warns of the risk in *antillanité* of the return to *négritude*'s privileging of the male conqueror. This is due to the emphasis on *marronnage*, the optic through which, for example, Suzanne Crosta reads the project of transforming history in Glissant's oeuvre, in *Le Marronage créateur: Dynamique textuelle chez Édouard Glissant* (Québec: GRELCA, 1991).

[7] Édouard Glissant, *Le Discours antillais* (Paris: Seuil, 1981), 29; *Caribbean Discourse*, trans. J. Michael Dash (Charlottesville, Va.: University Press of Virginia, 1989), 15. All further references are given in main text.

produisent de l'étant' (28; 'mingling of experiences . . . producing the process of being', 14). A population that enters into *Relation*, a constant process of creolization, does so because

cette population-ci n'a pas emporté avec elle ni continué collectivement les techniques d'existence ou de survie matérielles et spirituelles qu'elle avait pratiquées avant son transbord. Ces techniques ne subsistent qu'en traces, ou sous forme de pulsions ou d'élans. (29)

the latter has not brought with it, not collectively continued, the methods of existence and survival, both material and spiritual, which it practiced before being uprooted. These methods leave only dim traces or survive in the form of spontaneous impulses. (15)

According to Glissant, this is what differentiates, for example, 'la Traite des Nègres' from the Jewish diaspora, whose traditional texts and practices have been maintained and passed on in a deliberate and conscious manner against a history of persecution.[8]

In the absence of the systematic preservation of transported collective practices after geographical displacement, a population can be said to have entered the process of *Relation*. The old practices of the group are 'preserved' only in traces that are by and large unconscious, uncontrolled, and not organized by collective will. Rather than maintaining the original and continuous character of its peoplehood, the group becomes transformed into something different. For many, this might occasion the mourning of a loss. For Glissant, however, this recognition of loss is the starting point for *Relation*, which can only be enacted when a people abandons the purity of origins and becomes open to the possibilities of cultural contact and synthesis.

---

[8] While Glissant mentions the Jewish diaspora here to point out an important difference, themes common to both the Jewish and African diasporas—the notion of a return to a point of origin, exile from the homeland, a history of suffering, survival, and resistance in the face of oppression—provide a rich store of correspondences between the two groups. Several Caribbean writers have explored these suggestive commonalities. Some examples include Edward Brathwaite in his important poem *Rights of Passage* (London: OUP, 1967), Caryl Phillips in *The Nature of Blood* (London: Faber and Faber, 1997), Césaire in *Soleil cou coupé* (Paris: Éditions K, 1948), and Condé in *Moi, Tituba, soriere . . . Noire de Salem* (Paris: Mercure de France, 1986). Gilroy writes: 'In the preparation of [*Black Atlantic*] I have been repeatedly drawn to the work of Jewish thinkers in order to find both inspiration and resources with which to map the ambivalent experiences of blacks inside and outside modernity', *Black Atlantic*, 205–6. See his discussion (ibid. 205–17) of ways in which Jewish diaspora concepts and modern Zionism may have provided philosophical models for Pan-Africanism and black nationalism. See also Clifford's discussion of connections between the black Atlantic and anti-Zionist Jewish diasporism in 'Diasporas', in id., *Routes*, 244–77.

Of course the risk of this openness to change is that, in response to domination, a colonized people may come to mimic the colonizer. Glissant specifies that, in his vision of *Relation*, a group's transformation into another people occurs 'sans pourtant qu'elle succombe aux réductions de l'Autre' (29; 'without, however, succumbing to the reductive pressures of the Other', 15): he argues for the possibility and necessity of entanglement without co-optation. Nonetheless, the line to be drawn between assimilation and *Relation* is clearly tricky, since both involve leaving behind the notion of pure origins and undergoing transformative change. I shall return to this point later in the chapter.

I would like to explore the notion of group *absence* to the meaning of its 'techniques d'existence', which survive only in sparse, spasmodic vestigial impulses and drives. The relationship between *Relation*, a people's loss of its orientation toward origins, and unconsciousness, lies at the very heart of Glissant's characterization of the Antillean experience. For example, consider Glissant's comparison of Caribbean history to a group experience of a psychic trauma:

> Serait-il dérisoire ou odieux de considérer notre histoire subie comme cheminement d'une névrose? La Traite comme choc traumatique, l'installation (dans le nouveau pays) comme phase de refoulement, la période servile comme latence, la 'libération' de 1848 comme réactivation, les délires coutumiers comme symptômes et jusqu'à la répugnance à 'revenir sur ces choses du passé' qui serait une manifestation du retour du refoulé? . . . L'histoire a son inexplorable, au bord duquel nous errons éveillés. (133–4)
>
> Would it be ridiculous to consider our lived history as a steadily advancing neurosis? To see the Slave Trade as a traumatic shock, our relocation (in the new land) as a repressive phase, slavery as the period of latency, 'emancipation' in 1848 as a reactivation, our everyday fantasies as symptoms, and even our horror of 'returning to those things of the past' as a possible manifestation of the neurotic's fear of his past? . . . History has its dimension of the unexplorable, at the edge of which we wander, our eyes wide open. (66)

Glissant suggests a correspondence between the chronology of Antillean history and the experience of trauma.[9] This mapping of key events in the history of the people of the Antilles onto a psychoanalytic model of neurosis goes some way toward explaining the

---

[9] Compare Stuart Hall's characterization of 'the ruptures and discontinuities that constitute, precisely, the Caribbean's uniqueness' in 'Cultural Identity and Diaspora', in Jonathan Rutherford (ed.), *Identity: Community, Culture, Difference* (London: Lawrence and Wishart, 1990), 225–37: 225.

uncontrolled 'pulsions' or 'élans' that survive as the displaced symptoms of a repression.[10] Trauma may be defined most generally as 'an overwhelming experience of sudden or catastrophic events in which the response to the event occurs in the often delayed, uncontrolled repetitive appearance of hallucinations and other intrusive phenomena'.[11] On this interpretation, the spontaneous impulses that survive are delayed symptoms of the rupture: the middle passage. The unconscious nature of the later survival of vestigial impulses, then, is produced by the initial overwhelming catastrophic event. This unconsciousness comes to be because the event was not assimilated into the understanding at the time of its occurrence.

If Glissant's 'traces' are really to be understood as symptoms of 'le refoulé historique' (134; 'what is repressed in our history', 66), then it is unsurprising to notice in Antillean literature a repeated focus on the narrative of return as well as on different kinds of involuntary returns. However, it is not in the simple drive towards return that Glissant finds an answer for Antillean discourse. On the contrary, it is the impossibility of return that inaugurates the theory of *Relation*. Glissant sees the impulse to return, however powerful in a displaced people, as misguided:

> La première pulsion d'une population transplantée, qui n'est pas sûre de maintenir au lieu de son transbord l'ancien ordre de ses valeurs, est le Retour. Le Retour est l'obsession de l'Un: il ne faut pas changer l'être. Revenir, c'est consacrer la permanence, la non-relation. Le Retour sera prôné par les sectateurs de l'Un ... Dans les conditions actuelles, une population qui mettrait en acte la pulsion de Retour, et cela sans qu'elle se fût constituée en peuple, serait vouée aux amers ressouvenirs d'un *possible* ... à jamais perdu. (30)

> The first impulse of a transplanted population which is not sure of maintaining the old order of values in the transplanted locale is that of reversion. Reversion is the obsession with a single origin: one must not alter the absolute state of being. To revert is to consecrate permanence, to negate contact. Reversion will be recommended by those who favor single origins. ... In the contemporary situation a population that would activate the impulse towards return without having become a people would be destined to face bitter memories of *possibilities* forever lost. (16–17)

---

[10] Few critics of Glissant have focused as explicitly and as heavily on psychoanalytic models as I do in this chapter. Jacques André performs Freudian readings of Glissant in *Caraïbales* (Paris: Éditions caribéennes, 1981).

[11] Cathy Caruth, *Unclaimed Experience: Trauma, Narrative, and History* (Baltimore: Johns Hopkins University Press, 1996), 11.

This impulse to return is not merely a yearning for a return to one's homeland, but implies an ideological commitment to and belief in the notion of an authentic, unchanging, original state ('l'obsession de l'Un').

Must people transplanted by the slave trade abandon *Retour* simply because return is impossible; because it is too late when a tremendous set of transformations has already occurred; because the population has become too estranged from its roots to recuperate them wholesale? While this impossibility is a real factor, Glissant's focus away from the return to roots is less a pragmatic strategy for dealing with an unfortunate reality than a reflection on the new set of possibilities that are available once *Retour* ceases to be an available or desirable option.

The desire for return to the homeland can gradually disappear as a population comes to terms with the new land. Glissant locates this possibility in the maintenance and renewal of 'la mesure technique' (31; 'technical know-how', 18). The maintenance and renewing of technical prowess for dealing with the new place is vital to collective survival. This is so whether in immigration, where after several generations the population comes to accept the new land as home, or in diaspora where, even in the absence of the immediate need for return, the orientation toward the ancestral homeland continues to be an organizing principle of peoplehood.[12] A people that does not collectively come to terms with the new land, does not accept it as home nor use collective techniques for the construction of a sense of peoplehood within it, can neither deactivate the impulse toward nor effect *Retour*:

En Martinique, où la population transbordée s'est constituée en peuple, sans que pourtant la prise en compte de la terre nouvelle ait pu être effective, la communauté a tenté d'exorciser le Retour impossible par ce que j'appelle une pratique du Détour. (31–2)

In Martinique, where the relocated population has evolved into a people, without, however, coming effectively to terms with the new land, the com-

---

[12] William Safran's definition of diaspora exemplifies this orientation toward a root. He defines diasporas as communities that (1) are dispersed from an original centre, (2) retain a collective 'memory, vision, or myth about their original homeland', (3) believe they are not or cannot be accepted by their host society, (4) see the homeland as a place of eventual return, (5) are committed to the maintenance of the homeland, and (6) define ethnocommunal consciousness by relation to the homeland. See 'Diasporas in Modern Societies: Myths of Homeland and Return', *Diaspora*, 1 (1991), 83–99: 83–4.

munity has tried to exorcise the impossibility of return by what I call the practice of diversion. (18)

In the Antilles, the desire for *Retour* has not gradually disappeared, but remains in its impossibility, and is expressed indirectly through the practice of *Détour*. Again, Glissant characterizes this Antillean practice as unsystematic, involuntary habit, 'negative' in the sense of not being undertaken from a collective consciousness and will. A group resorts to *Détour* when it finds itself in a situation of oppression and misery in which there is no clear enemy nor a tangible system of domination against which a people would otherwise organize, mobilize, and struggle collectively. In contemporary departmental Martinique, blame for economic exploitation, underdevelopment, and nonentity cannot be so directly assigned. *Détour* is the response to this situation: 'il faut aller chercher *ailleurs* le principe de domination, qui n'est pas évident dans le pays même: parce que le mode de domination (l'assimilation) est le meilleur des camouflages' (32; 'it then must search elsewhere for the principle of domination, which is not evident in the country itself: because the system of domination . . . is not directly tangible', 20).

If the mode of domination is indirect and camouflaged, *Détour* is an indirect and camouflaged response, which also functions at first *as* camouflage. Glissant's primary example of *Détour* in the Antilles is the Creole language, which began and is marked still by a strategy of trickery: 'La langue créole s'est constituée autour une telle ruse' (33; 'The Creole language was constituted around this strategy of trickery', 21). This trickery, he claims, came about as a response to the imposition of the French language on slaves, and functioned as an appropriation of French. Creole speakers used French in a deriding and deforming way, to wreak violence on the language itself. This strategy, in its derision of and attack on French, nonetheless remains dependent upon contact and interaction with it: 'Je vois surtout dans la poétique du créole un exercice permanent de détournement de la transcendance qui y est impliquée: celle de la source française' (32; 'For me what is most apparent in the dynamics of Creole is the continuous process of undermining its innate capacity for transcending its French origins', 20). Creole continually works *not* to transcend the French language, but as a diversion, a turning away, from the language's own impulse to transcend the French language. 'Transcendence' would entail the definition of a Creole authenticity as separate from a 'contaminating' French; French would be transcended and ultimately left behind in favour of a distinct Creole.[13] Glissant acknowledges that this desire is inherent to Creole itself. However, the *détournement* is a diversion of the impulse to refuse the French source. It is the active continuation of the entangled presence of French, even in struggle, derision, mockery, and discomfort. Whereas Creole may now have the capacity to think its identity as separate from French, it continues to create new ways of being constituted by contact with French. This *détournement* can be seen as a form of the search *ailleurs* in response to the dominance of assimilation. The answer lies not in the avoidance of contact with an oppressive French language by focusing on an oppositional Creole authenticity, but in an indirect resistance to assimilation precisely by making Creole embody contact without assimilation.

This *détournement* refuses the binarity that presupposes a commitment either to assimilation or to authenticity. Refusing this linguistic resistance draws attention to the mechanism of political resistance: Glissant's approach appears open to the charge of political quietism, because it turns away from active opposition. Another example of *Détour* is the experience of Antillean immigrants to France, who, according to Glissant, only in France first become aware of themselves as Other: 'Voici bien une illustration de l'occultation, en Martinique même, de l'aliénation: il faut aller la chercher *ailleurs* pour en prendre conscience' (34; 'Here is a fine example of the concealment, in Martinique itself, of alienation: one must look for it *elsewhere* in order to be aware of it, 23). Arrival in France produces consciousness of a self-alienation of which Antilleans were previously unaware. It is in France that consciousness of an Antillean identity is suddenly experienced with an unexpected force. In the logic of Glissant's *Détour*, the success of the French policy of assimilation is such that one's alienation from one's Antillean identity in Martinique is concealed, and Antillean consciousness must be approached indirectly through the *ailleurs* of France.[14]

Maryse Condé writes about her state of mind on leaving Guadeloupe to study in Paris: ' Si on m'avait demandé à ce moment-

---

[13] The ambiguity of this sentence makes it equally plausible to read the transcendence alternatively as a property of the French language, so that Creole's 'détournement de la transcendance' would be a practice that diverts and subverts the claim of the French language to transcendent properties. This reading is compatible with my view that this subversion comes about through continual renewal of contact with French rather than getting beyond and away from it.

[14] Compare to my related discussion in Ch. 2, above of the need for an *ailleurs* in poetry.

là "Qu'est-ce que ton pays natal?" Je n'aurais rien eu à dire; j'aurais dit que c'était peut-être deux ou trois palmiers à coté de la mer qui encadraient le vide le néant.'[15] In Paris, 'La première découverte que je fais, c'est que je ne suis pas française.'[16] It is in Paris that Condé first comes to reflect on her identity. She discovers for the first time the writing of Aimé Césaire and the existence of an Antillean literary heritage. Condé's experience, as an example of Glissant's *Détour*, can be seen as an approach to identity forced by consciousness of difference. This does not, however, merely lead to the comfort of a simple discovery of identity. Rather this *Détour* leads to a new consciousness of alienation, of identity as alienation, a discovery of home as a place of exile.[17]

While being not-at-home in a different land might make one aware of the comfort of home, realizing that one is not French in France makes the Antillean aware of being not-at-home in the Antilles:

> conscience d'autant plus dramatique et insupportable que l'individu ainsi enhavi par le sentiment de son identité ne pourra quand même pas réussir la réinsertion dans son milieu d'origine (il trouvera la situation intolérable, ses compatriotes irresponsables; on le trouvera assimilé, devenu blanc de manières, etc.) et qu'il repartira. Extraordinaire vécu du Détour. (34)

> an awareness that is all the more disturbing and unliveable, since the individual so possessed by the feeling of identity cannot, however, manage to return to his origins (there he will find that the situation is intolerable, his colleagues irresponsible; they will find him too assimilé, too European in his ways, etc.), and he will have to migrate again. (23)

This new consciousness does not result then in a happy arrival, but in *another departure*, in the face of another alienation, another exile. It is this constant and repeating process of departures between places, without real arrivals, that makes up the logic of *Détour*. It may be necessary to depart in order to know what it means to arrive, but it is not long before it becomes necessary to depart again.

Toward what, then, is *Détour* ultimately directed? Glissant claims 'Le Détour *mène donc quelque part*, quand l'impossible qu'il contourne tend à se résoudre en "positivités" concrètes' (33; 'The strategy of

---
[15] 'Notes sur un retour au pays natal', *Conjonction: Revue franco-haïtienne*, 176, suppl. (1987), 6–23: 10.
[16] Ibid.
[17] In the face of the impossible homeland of Africa, the Antilles themselves can be seen as a place of *Détour*. In Condé's case, this also led eventually to repeated departures and an oeuvre focused on the issues of home and diaspora.

diversion can therefore lead somewhere when the obstacle for which the detour was made tends to develop into concrete "possibilities"' 22); 'Le Détour *ne mène nulle part*, quand sa ruse originelle ne rencontre pas les conditions concrètes d'un dépassement' (34; 'Diversion leads nowhere when the original trickster strategy does not encounter any real potential for development', 23). *Détour* leads somewhere only when it finally becomes an expression of a collective will, when the population's unconsciousness of the 'occultation' is transformed into a collective consciousness. But where is it supposed to lead? Directed not toward arriving, but rather toward the various routes that are traced in the in-between spaces of repeated departures, Glissant's *Détour* provides the insight that becoming a collectivity is tied to a process of continual departures. It is by departing that collective consciousness is made possible, for it is only in the continuous movement in the in-between space that collectivity is to be found. 'Leading somewhere' is the transformation of the obstacle, which is a state of non-collectivity. It designates the travel itself rather than the destination, and travel constitutes collective becoming. The need for repeated departures is poignantly captured by Césaire's lines towards the end of the *Cahier:* 'Il y a encore une mer à traverser | oh encore une mer à traverser' (132; 'There is one more sea to cross | oh, one more sea to cross', 133).[18] The collective project and the notion of elsewhere come together in the notion of an 'Ailleurs partagé' (36; 'shared elsewhere', 26), which is ultimately where *Détour* should lead: an elsewhere in which becoming a collectivity is possible.

Détour, it turns out, is actually an indirect return:

Il faut revenir au lieu. Le Détour n'est ruse profitable que si le Retour le féconde: non pas retour au rêve d'origine, à l'Un immobile de l'Être, mais retour au point d'intrication, dont on s'était détourné par force; c'est là qu'il faut à la fin mettre en œuvre les composantes de la Relation, ou périr. (36)

We must return to the point from which we started. Diversion is not a useful ploy unless it is nourished by reversion: not a return to the longing for origins, to some immutable state of Being, but a return to the point of

---

[18] According to Glissant, Césaire's *négritude* is a *Détour* that leads somewhere. Césaire's *négritude* displays the properties of *Détour* in several ways. First, it played a much greater role in the political struggles of African nations than it has yet to play in Césaire's native Martinique. Second, the 'retour au pays natal' is a *substitute* for the return to Africa. The effects of contact and cross-fertilization with other parts of the black world, as well as of displacement and substitution (in both directions), are characteristics of *Détour* that Césaire's poetry possesses.

entanglement, from which we were forcefully turned away; that is where we must ultimately put to work the forces of creolization, or perish. (26)

Détour does not desire or effect a return to origins but to the 'point d'intrication', the point of contact and creolization of different entities, precisely the point at which the notion of a unique origin must be abandoned to the forces of *Relation*.[19] It is at this point that collective consciousness can be articulated.

DÉTOUR AND THE MOVEMENT OF SUPPLEMENTARITY

What, then, is the nature of the 'point d'intrication', the locus of *Relation*, to which *Détour* is ultimately directed, and which comes to replace the unique origin of *Retour*? Glissant's rejection of the return to origins can usefully be compared to the renunciation of logocentrism. In Derridean terms, the fixed origin constitutes the structural centre to which the system ultimately refers; it is the terminal point that grounds the play of the system, a centre that underwrites the meaning of the system but is itself beyond its play. Glissant abandons the fixed origin for the 'point d'intrication', authenticity for creolization. Glissant's focus on the 'point d'intrication' of *Détour* over 'l'Être' of *Retour* is a move that re-evaluates the presence of the centre to be a 'non-lieu dans lequel se jouaient à l'infini des substitutions de signes'.[20] The origin becomes a non-locus in the Antilles: group unconsciousness to the meaning of original practices of which only involuntary traces remain, as well as the obscured nature of the source of oppression and misery, underscore the notion of central origin as absence. In Derrida's terms, 'ce mouvement du jeu, permis par le manque, l'absence de centre ou d'origine, est le mouvement de la *supplémentarité*'.[21] In the absence of the grounding centre, *Détour* is a play of substitutions, as a movement that supplements the impossibility of *Retour*.[22] Absence is supplemented by repeated departures for *ailleurs*, a play inaugurated by the missing point of origin:

[19] Although Césaire's poem of return may be seen as a displacement or substitution of the return to Africa, this *Détour* does not in fact lead to Africa as origin, but to a space of contact and shared collective identification.
[20] Jacques Derrida, *L'Écriture et la différence* (Paris: Seuil, 1967), 411.
[21] Ibid. 423.
[22] Homi Bhabha relies on the notion of supplementarity to argue that diasporic postcolonial temporality is characterized by the experience of being belated and extra. See 'DissemiNation: Time, narrative, and the margins of the modern nation', in Id. *Location of Culture*, 139–170.

Le signe représente le présent en son absence. Il en tient lieu. Quand nous ne pouvons prendre ou montrer la chose, disons le présent, l'étant-présent, quand le présent ne se présente pas, nous signifions, nous passons par le détour du signe.

The sign represents the present in its absence. It takes the place of the present. When we cannot grasp or show the thing, state the present, the being-present, when the present cannot be presented, we signify, we go through the detour of the sign.[23]

The traumatic shock of the slave trade, and the destructiveness of assimilation, are in effect unpresentable origins. *Détour* refers indirectly and represents what cannot be shown. In the Antilles, the absence of a central presence makes this signification both possible and necessary.

The meaning of Antillean identity is always deferred to *ailleurs*. The destination of *Détour* is always deferred to yet another departure for yet another elsewhere: 'il *repartira*' (34). *Détour* is deferred *Retour*, the return to the origin deferred repeatedly through stand-ins: Césaire's return to *négritude* deferred through the triangulated substitution of France, Martinique, and Africa; the West Indian revolutionary potential of Fanon deferred through his political struggle in Algeria. Does *Détour* then have an arrival? If *Détour* can be seen as a process of signification, supplementarity, and deferral, is the 'point d'intrication' just another way of thinking of and naming a non-locus of endless substitution? The 'point d'intrication' is a point of absence; the Antillean people were 'détourné par force'. *Détour*, as a means of getting back to that point, can be seen as a play of substitutions that supplement that lack. But rather than being endless, it seems that the 'point d'intrication' is designated in Glissant as an arrival, a stop, a return. Is it a place at which the substitutive *Détour* is ultimately grounded? Does the *Détour* that 'mène *quelque part*' stop needing to depart when it gets there?

Glissant claims that it is at this arrival point that *Relation*, the process of creolization, can be put to work. The 'point d'intrication' is the place of the contact and mixture of ancestry, languages, cultures. *Relation* can be understood as a play of combination and contiguity. *Détour* is the process by which substitutive play ultimately leads to the contiguous combination of *Relation*. Translating this into an idiom that Jakobson has made familiar, we might see the transfor-

---

[23] Derrida, *Marges de la philosophie* (Paris: Minuit, 1972), 9; *Margins of Philosophy*, trans. Alan Bass (Chicago: University of Chicago Press, 1982), 9, emphases added.

mation of the absent locus of substitution into the 'point d'intrication'—the locus of contiguity—as a 'poetic function'.[24] While *Détour* is primarily a metaphorical operation based on vertical substitution, *Relation* is a metonymic one based on horizontal combination. On this view, Glissant's *Antillanité* projects the vertical into the horizontal. Through the process of substitution one engenders a relationship of equivalence between contiguous elements.[25] The horizontal force of *Relation* and the vertical tendency of *Détour*, activated by absence, at once feed into and undercut each other, and Glissant's *Antillanité* becomes a way out of a limiting binarity.

It is in the place of the projection of the vertical into the horizontal axis, then, that Glissant finds the possibility for collective consciousness. We see that 'ailleurs partagé' denotes two categories: first, the distance, difference, and indirectness of metaphor that is needed to set off the approach of a shared Antillean identity; second, the space where *Antillanité* is constituted by another sense of sharing—that of contact, mixture, coexistence with others. In this latter context, the relationship of identity and difference itself is destabilized. This place where the vertical yields to the horizontal coincides with the engendering of a collectivity. It is the point at which absence or unconsciousness becomes consciousness of absence, which has the capacity to set off a sense of collective will that can engage in the process of *Relation*.

Relation evades direct approach and so substitution is necessary. The return to the 'point d'intrication' through *Détour* enables collective control over the changes, mixtures, contact that constitute *Antillanité*, in contrast to the passive experience of uncontrolled 'pulsions' and 'élans' that prevent a crowd from becoming a people.

Pour nous Martiniquais, ce lieu est déjà les Antilles: mais nous ne le savons pas. Du moins, de manière collective. Le pratique du Détour est la mesure de cette existence-sans-savoir . . . La tangence du Détour devient, au stade

---

[24] Recall Roman Jakobson's notions of selection and combination: 'The selection is produced on the base of equivalence, similarity, dissimilarity, synonymity and antonymity, while the combination, the build up of the sequence, is based on contiguity. *The poetic function projects the principle of equivalence from the axis of selection into the axis of combination*' ('Closing Statement: Linguistics and Poetics', in Thomas A. Sebeok (ed.) *Style in Language* (Cambridge, Mass.: MIT Press, 1960), 350–77: 358).
[25] For example, through a process of substitution, France, Africa, and the Antilles enter into a relationship of lateral combination. Also consider the relationship of Creole and French, which at once brings out the possibility of substitutive translation and combination through contact.

de l'expression, conquête sur le non-dit ou sur l'édit (c'est-à-dire sure les deux modes principaux de la répression). (36 n. 7)

For us Martinicans, this place already is the Caribbean: but we do not know it. At least, in a collective way. The practice of diversion can be measured in terms of this existence-without knowing.... The tangential movement from Diversion becomes, at the level of self-expression, the conquest of the unspoken or the unspeakable (that is of the two main forms of repression). (26)

Antillean collective identity consists of the consciousness of the Antilles as the in-between space toward which *Détour* is undertaken.

UNSPEAKING THE UNSPEAKABLE RUPTURES OF HISTORY[26]

For Glissant, the most serious manifestation of this missing centre in the Caribbean is the problem of history.[27] History in the Caribbean is experienced as

le combat sans témoins, l'impossibilité de la datation même inconsciente, conséquence du raturage de la mémoire en tous. Car l'histoire n'est pas seulement pour nous une absence, c'est un vertige. Ce temps que nous n'avons jamais eu, il nous faut le reconquérir. (278)

our struggle without witnesses, the inability to create even an unconscious chronology, a result of the erasing of memory in all of us. For history is not only absence for us, it is vertigo. This time that was never ours, we must now possess. (161)

The problem is a perceived absence of collective memory. Glissant's description of this vertigo is the starting point for a reflection on the specific character of history and its possibility in the Antilles. History in the Antilles is experienced as an absence, in the sense not only of an erasure of memory, but of the danger of falling into an abyss. This abyss is tied to a lack of ownership of history ('ce temps que nous

[26] I borrow this heading from the title of Toni Morrison's 'Unspeakable Things Unspoken: The Afro-American Presence in American Literature', *Michigan Quarterly Review*, 28/1 (1989), 1–34, in which she argues that in 19th-cent. American literature, slavery is a repressed absence which is never spoken directly, but can be discerned as a presence. The unspeakability of race is spoken through allegory, hence unspoken.

[27] In his fiction Glissant has sought to reconstruct an absent, opaque Martinican history. His novels, *La Lézarde* (Paris: Seuil, 1958), *Le Quatrième Siècle* (Paris: Seuil, 1964), *Malemort* (Paris: Seuil, 1975), *La Case du commandeur* (Paris: Seuil, 1981), and *Mahagony* (Paris: Seuil, 1987), are interlaced, cross-referenced narratives of slaves, maroons, and their descendants. Patterns of recurrence and correspondence throughout the oeuvre underscore the structure of repetition and missed opportunities underlying Glissant's conception of Antillean history.

n'avons jamais eu'). My argument concerns the gap at the heart of Antillean historical consciousness, and how this gap relates to a Derridean account of the absent centre that both makes signification necessary and permits it.

It is not surprising that, whether through the rewriting of historical events in fictional forms, figuring the writer as historian, allegorizing collective history in a character's story, or positing history as literary activity, the theme of history is persistently present in postcolonial literatures. The need for literary rewritings of history has been articulated by many postcolonial critics and writers, who equate the search for a lost history with the quest for a collective identity. Paradigmatically, the contemporary postcolonial writer speaks for a hitherto silenced collectivity. Angela Davis writes of Condé's *Moi, Tituba*:

> Tituba's revenge consists in having persuaded one of her descendants to rewrite her moment in history in her own African oral tradition. And when Tituba takes her place in the history of the Salem witch trials, the recorded history of that era—and indeed the entire history of the colonization process—is revealed to be seriously flawed.[28]

Davis comments that the most general problem with history in postcolonial contexts is that what is known as history is a received account given by the colonizer. The chronologies produced depend upon narratives of the dominant power, narratives that are likely to be 'seriously flawed' when seen from the perspective of the colonized. There appears to exist a need to articulate one's own place in a history that has been previously subsumed by hegemonic 'white mythologies'.[29] The remainder of this chapter questions what it would mean to be in possession of a history that is one's own in a context in which history is apparently absent, incomplete, suppressed, or too overwhelming to understand. This may illuminate the question of what is to be gained by fictionality, and why postcolonial literature functions as an arena for historical revision.

One of the problems addressed by Glissant is the periodization of Antillean history in terms of the continuous narrative of the colonizer's history, upon which an account of Antillean history seems to depend. Edward Said has described this historical narrative

---

[28] Foreword to Maryse Condé, *I, Tituba, Black Witch of Salem*, trans. Richard Philcox (Charlottesville, Va.: University of Virgina Press, 1992), pp. xi–xiii: xii.

[29] Robert Young, *White Mythologies: Writing History and the West* (London: Routledge, 1990).

as the 'homogenizing and incorporating world-historical scheme that assimilated non-synchronous developments, histories, cultures, and peoples, to it'.[30] The divisions and organization into periods appear inevitably determined by the French colonial historical narrative. A basic experience of discontinuity results from this overlay of French history upon the lived experience of Antilleans: 'Il y a ainsi un discontinu réel sous le continu apparent de notre histoire' (157; 'There is therefore a real discontinuity beneath the apparent continuity of our history', 91). The underlying discontinuity comes from the fact that despite an apparently continuous series of periodizations—beginning in the mid-1600s with the slave trade, the plantation system, the appearance of the bourgeois elite, the collapse of the cane sugar economy, departmentalization, and the policy of assimilation—these key periods were not brought about by the repeated rebellions of slaves (which were unsuccessful), but 'en fonction d'une autre histoire' (157; 'in relation to another history', 91).[31] Because the historical narrative is organized into periods that themselves result from external impositions, there is an underlying lack of correspondence between history and lived experience.[32] History in the Antilles is an account of events that happened to the population rather than of events that the people made happen. 'Pour nous, reconquérir le sens de notre histoire, c'est connaître le discontinu réel pour ne plus le subir passivement' (157; 'For us, the repossession of the meaning of our history begins with the awareness of the real discontinuity that we no longer passively live through', 92). Glissant attributes the discontinuity underlying the apparent continuity of history to its not

[30] *Orientalism*, (London: Routledge, 1978), 8.
[31] The time directly leading up to the last of these, departmentalization, has been the subject of several literary revisions in Glissant's *La Lézarde*, Raphaël Confiant's *Le Nègre et l'amiral* (Paris: Grasset, 1992), and Patrick Chamoiseau's *Chronique des sept misères* (Paris: Gallimard, 1986). The short period of blockade by the Allied Fleet during German occupation of France saw Martinique's relative autonomy and Césaire's rise to power. Departmentalization in 1946, however, put an end to the island's self-sufficiency. This historical juncture, which Glissant sees as one of a series of 'occasions ratées' that make up Antillean history, could be understood as a traumatic rupture and hence the occasion of historical rewriting.
[32] One striking response to this felt imposition of periodization may be found in Patrick Chamoiseau's Prix Goncourt-winning novel *Texaco* (Paris: Gallimard, 1992), which is divided into four periods, each corresponding to a phase of Martinican history. Chamoiseau characterizes these periods by the names of the building materials used by Martinicans themselves to construct their dwellings: 'temps de paille' (1823?-1902), 'temps de bois-caisse' (1903–1945), 'temps de fibrociment' (1946–1960), 'temps béton' (1961–1980). His project, after all, is about the literal and figurative construction of Martinican space, hence the use of building materials to articulate periodization.

being possessed.[33] There is a need to reconquer history precisely by coming to terms with a constitutive discontinuity. This discontinuity is also manifested in the lack of connection between the imposed continuum of historical time and Antillean reality:

> Dans un tel contexte, l'histoire en tant qu'elle est discipline et qu'elle prétend éclairer la réalité que vit ce peuple souffrira d'une carence épistémologique grave: elle ne saura pas par quel bout s'attraper. (130)

> In such a context, history as far as it is a discipline and claims to clarify the reality lived by this people, will suffer from a serious epistemological deficiency: it will not know how to make the link. (61).

The imposition of a historical narrative based on French colonial periodization is interpreted as the constraint of a monolithic temporality. Glissant sees the Antillean tendency to think chronology primarily in terms of natural disasters as resistance to French historical time.

> [L]'histoire obscurcie s'est souvent réduite pour nous au calendrier des événements naturels, avec leurs seules significations affectives 'éclatées'. Nous disions: 'l'année du grand tremblement', ou 'l'année du cyclone qui a tombé la maison de monsieur Céleste', ou 'l'année de l'incendie dans la Grande Rue'. Et c'est bien là le recours de toute communauté désamorcée d'un acte collectif et engoncée loin de la conscience de soi. (131–2)

> [O]bscured history was often reduced for us to a chronology of natural events, retaining only their 'explosive' emotional meanings. We would say: 'the year of the great earthquake,' or 'the year of the hurricane that flattened M. Celeste's house,' or: 'the year of the fire on Main Street.' And that is precisely the recourse open to any community without a collective consciousness and detached from an awareness of itself. (63)

For Glissant this tendency to mark the passage of time mainly by reference to natural disasters is antithetical to a historical consciousness. He sees implicit in this practice, however, a resistance to historical temporality. It is a practice that implies that colonization is also the colonization of temporality: 'L'une des conséquences les plus terrifiantes de la colonisation sera bien cette conception univoque de l'Histoire, et donc du pouvoir, qui l'Occident a imposée aux peuples' (159; 'One of the most disturbing consequences of colonization could well be this notion of a single History, and therefore of power, which

---

[33] The importance of the possession of history is also expressed by Frantz Fanon in *Les Damnés de la terre* (Paris: François Maspéro, 1961).

has been imposed on others by the West', 93). History itself then, and historical method, is seen as an imposition of the colonial power. Yet it is precisely the urgent need for history in the Antilles with which Glissant is concerned. Consider the explosive character of the calamities that Glissant gives as examples that structure a sense of temporality: an earthquake, a hurricane, a fire. Tellingly, all are catastrophic events. Consider the idea that a community's past could be envisioned and retold in terms of these violent, life-threatening, overwhelming occurrences that are completely beyond one's control. It is in a sense of time marked by catastrophe and rupture that an alternative historical temporality can be found and articulated:

> Les Antilles sont le lieu d'une histoire faite de ruptures et dont le commencement est un arrachement brutal, la Traite. Notre conscience historique ne pouvait pas 'sédimenter, ... mais s'agrégeait sous les auspices du choc, de la contraction, de la négation douloureuse et de l'explosion. Ce discontinu dans le continu, et l'impossibilité pour la conscience collective d'en faire le tour, caractérisent ce que j'appelle une non-histoire. (130–1)

> The French Caribbean is the site of a history characterized by ruptures and that began with a brutal dislocation, the slave trade. Our historical consciousness could not be deposited gradually and continuously like sediment, ... but came together in the context of shock, contradiction, painful negation, and explosive forces. This dislocation of the continuum, and the inability of the collective consciousness to absorb it all, characterize what I call nonhistory. (61–2)

The beginning of Antillean history is constituted by the displacement from Africa and the relocation into slavery. Glissant locates in this beginning the inability of Antillean people to have a sense of history as a continuous narrative that proceeds gradually, subsuming and explaining all. The initial displacement persists in preventing such a continualist, linear historical consciousness from developing. The shock, contraction, negation, explosion, and lack of assimilation into the consciousness is fundamentally a problem of unrepresentability that results in a situation of historylessness. It might thus appear to follow that the solution would entail domesticating and inserting the experience of slavery into linear memory; but this is emphatically not Glissant's implication.

Glissant's catastrophic characterization of the Antillean historical (or non-historical) consciousness is traumatic. In *Unclaimed Experience*, Cathy Caruth calls on the phenomenon of trauma to rethink history away from a model of straightforward reference: 'permitting *history* to arise where *immediate understanding* may not'.[34] Trauma seems at first to offer a paradoxical model in which a powerfully unusual event is at once inaccesible to the person who 'experienced' it, and yet all too available in nightmare, hallucination, and unwanted repetition.[35] Glissant writes: 'Le passé, notre passé subie, qui n'est pas encore histoire pour nous, est pourtant là (ici) qui nous lancine' (132; 'The past, to which we were subjected, which has not yet emerged as history for us, is, however, obsessively present', 63). The event evades direct reference and knowledge, and yet provides constant torment.

Caruth finds in the phenomenon of trauma as presented in Freud's *Moses and Monotheism* a way of making compatible the epistemological problems raised by poststructuralism and the possibility of history.[36] The traumatic event in Freud's text is the murder of Moses by the Jews, whom he liberated from slavery and led out of Egypt. Freud diverges from the biblical story in which Moses was one of the Hebrews in captivity, became their leader, and delivered them from Egypt to the border of Canaan. He claims that Moses was an Egyptian who led the Hebrews out of Egypt in order to preserve his own sun-centred monotheism, and that this act transformed the Hebrews into the Jews.[37] Moses gave them his monotheistic religion and liberated them, after which they murdered him and repressed the crime. After several generations, however, Moses was not completely erased from the Jewish historical memory: eventually the acts of Moses (the Egyptian) came to be attributed to a later priest called Moses; and his sun-god came to be merged with another god named Yahweh. Thus according to Freud, a key moment of Jewish history is constituted by murder, its repression and return.

Caruth notes that the Jewish exodus, often understood as a return to a freedom once enjoyed in the Jews' past, becomes in Freud, not really a return but a departure into a new peoplehood organized

---

[34] *Unclaimed Experience*, 11.

[35] I have quoted Caruth's definition of trauma earlier in this chapter.

[36] As I have mentioned earlier, Jewish history, tradition, and culture potentially provide a rich resource of inspiration, correspondence, and point of comparison and mutual reference for black discourse and imagination, as Gilroy and others have begun to show. My argument here, however, does not undertake comparisons between entire cultural traditions, but between certain specific mythical structures. I refer to Freud's text in my argument because of the potency of the model of trauma presented in it for the postcolonial, particularly Caribbean, situation.

[37] Condé's *La Colonie du nouveau monde* (Paris: Robert Laffont, 1993) may represent an allusion to this story: the forcibly exiled Guadeloupean protagonists attempt to establish a religion centred around an Egyptian sun-god in Latin America.

around the newly given monotheistic religion: 'In this rethinking of Jewish beginnings, then, the future is no longer continuous with the past but is united with it through a profound discontinuity. The exodus from Egypt, which shapes the meaning of the Jewish past, is a departure that is both a radical break and the establishment of a history.'[38] The notion of the past and the future being linked through a profound discontinuity (departure) that establishes a history seems paradoxical. For Glissant, however, this 'discontinu dans le continu' impedes Antilleans' historical consciousness. How is it possible to see the moment of discontinuity itself as constituting a link that actually enables history rather than making it impossible?

The answer lies in the structure of repression and return that constitutes this moment of discontinuity. The memory of Moses is repressed after his murder, but it returns powerfully after the second Moses receives credit for the liberating acts of the first Moses. At that point, 'the shadow of the god whose place he had taken became stronger than himself; at the end of the historical development there arose beyond his being that of the forgotten Mosaic god'.[39] The Mosaic monotheistic religion returns powerfully after a period of latency, 'after the breaking away of the Moses religion, during which no trace is to be found of the monotheistic idea', to become the fundamental surviving mark of Jewish peoplehood.[40] Caruth argues that the meaning of a founding historical moment, the departure from Egypt, is only available to the Jews through the distortion of traumatic repression and return. The experience of trauma constitutes the link between the past of the Hebrews who were slaves in Egypt and the historical Jewish people.

Glissant describes a period of 'blocus idéologique' (131; 'ideological blockade', 62) during which Antilleans forgot the heroic revolt of Colonel Delgrès and his men who blew themselves up at Fort Matouba, Guadeloupe, rather than surrender to French troops.[41] Now, however, the situation has changed:

le bruit de cette explosion ne retentit pas immédiatement dans la conscience des Martiniquais et des Guadeloupéens. C'est que Delgrès fut vaincu une seconde fois par la ruse feutrée de l'idéologie dominante, qui parvint pour

[38] *Unclaimed Experience*, 14.
[39] Sigmund Freud, *Moses and Monotheism*, trans. Katherine Jones (New York: Vintage Books, 1939), 62.
[40] Ibid. 84.
[41] Slavery was abolished in 1794, but Napoleon reimposed slavery in 1802. It was against this reimposition that Delgrès fought.

un temps à dénaturer le sens de son acte héroïque et à l'effacer de la mémoire populaire. . . . Aujourd'hui, pourtant, nous entendons le fracas de Matouba. (131)

the noise of this explosion did not resound immediately in the consciousness of Martinicans and Guadeloupeans. It happened that Delgrès was defeated all over again by the sly trickery of the dominant ideology, which succeeded for a while in twisting the meaning of his heroic act and removing it from popular memory. . . . Today, however, we are hearing the blast from Matouba. (62)

The literal repression by the French troops of the revolt is repeated in the dominant ideology's repression of the meaning of the heroic act, and then again in the repression in the memory of Antilleans themselves. Here as with the acts of Moses, the repressed event returns, so that after a period of erasure and forgetting, the meaning of Delgrès's heroic act is only now being felt.[42] If Antilleans are at last hearing the explosion at Matouba today, it is because the meaning of Delgrès's act is only available through this repression and return.

In both Freud's account of Jewish history and Glissant's account of Antillean history, the traumatic event is not experienced as it occurs, and a period of latency interposes between event and experience. It is worth noting that in the histories of both the Jews of *Moses and Monotheism* and the Antilleans of *Discours*, the beginning is a literal act of leaving one place for another, the former from bondage to freedom, the latter from freedom to bondage. For both groups the departure marks the discontinuity between a past and a future. Caruth argues: 'Centering his story in the nature of the leaving, and returning, constituted by trauma, Freud resituates the very possibility of history in the nature of a traumatic departure'.[43] In the relationship between trauma and the act of leaving, the discontinuity that is inherent to departing demonstrates this period of latency in which a traumatic event is repressed and forgotten. The middle passage that constitutes the first break in Antillean history is a departure that is itself a traumatic beginning.

Typically, historical memory is understood to entail the existence of an archive in the memory in which a certain set of events are recorded. In *Mal d'archive*, Derrida describes a notion of archival recording that is not historical in the ordinary sense.[44] He responds

---

[42] Delgrès's heroic act is one of the stages of struggle for Guadeloupean independence that are revisited in Daniel Maximin's novel, *L'Isolé Soleil* (Paris: Seuil, 1981).

[43] *Unclaimed Experience*, 15.

[44] *Mal d'archive: Une impression freudienne* (Paris, Galilée, 1995).

to historian Yosef Hayim Yerushalmi,[45] who, pointing to the absence of any recording of murder in Jewish biblical or rabbinic sources, appears to argue against Freud that Moses was in fact not murdered:

Or Yerushalmi sait très bien que le propos de Freud, c'est d'analyser, à travers l'apparente absence de mémoire et d'archives, toutes sortes de symptômes, signes, figures, métaphores et métonymies qui attestent, au moins virtuellement, une documentation archivale là où l'"historien ordinaire" n'en identifie aucune. Qu'on le suive ou non dans sa démonstration, Freud a prétendu que le meurtre de Moïse a effectivement laissé des archives, des documents, des symptômes dans la mémoire juive et même dans la mémoire de l'humanité. Simplement les textes de cette archive ne sont pas lisibles selon les voies de l'"histoire ordinaire".[46]

Now Yerushalmi knows very well that Freud's intention is to analyse, across the apparent absence of memory and of archive, all kinds of symptoms, signs, figures, metaphors, and metonymies that attest, at least virtually, an archival documentation where the 'ordinary historian' identifies none. Whether one goes along with him or not in his demonstration, Freud claimed that the murder of Moses effectively left archives, documents, symptoms in the Jewish memory and even in the memory of humanity. Only the texts of this archive are not readable according to the paths of 'ordinary history' and this is the very relevance of psychoanalysis if it has one.[47]

Where ordinary historical enquiry would come up against an absence of archive, an alternative historical archive exists in the symptoms of a repression. Reading these symptoms lets speak a truth that historical memory misses and cannot archive.

Il y a une vérité du délire, une vérité de la folie ou de la hantise. Analogue à cette 'vérité historique' que Freud distingue . . . de la 'vérité matérielle', cette vérité est refoulée ou réprimée. Mais elle résiste et revient, à ce titre, comme vérité spectrale du délire ou de la hantise. Elle revient à la vérité spectrale . . . La vérité est spectrale, voilà sa part de vérité irréductible à l'explication.[48]

There is a truth of delusion, a truth of insanity or of hauntedness. Analogous to that 'historical truth' which Freud distinguishes. . . . from the 'material truth,' this truth is repressed or suppressed. But it resists and returns, as such as the spectral truth of delusion or of hauntedness. It returns, it belongs, it

---

[45] Yosef Hayim Yerushalmi, *Freud's Moses: Judaism Terminable and Interminable* (New Haven: Yale University Press, 1991).
[46] Derrida, *Mal d'archive*, 103–4.
[47] Id., *Archive Fever: A Freudian Impression*, trans. Eric Prenowitz (Chicago: University of Chicago Press, 1996).
[48] Id., *Mal d'archive*, 136.

comes down to spectral truth. . . . The truth is spectral, and this is its part of truth which is irreducible by explanation.[49]

This suggests that historical truth of a sort can be found in ways of knowing and remembering that are peculiar to disorder. As Caruth similarly has it, 'historical memory, or Jewish historical memory at least, is always a matter of distortion, a filtering of the original event through the fictions of traumatic repression, which makes the event available at best indirectly'.[50] One might say that because traumatic experience makes the event too overwhelming to be known in an 'ordinary' fashion, it is not possible to refer directly to it, and so it becomes a gap in the historical understanding. It becomes knowable through the indirect reference of repression and return. Thus, what begins as a gap in historical understanding ultimately engenders a history that becomes available through a form of disorder.

Similarly in the postcolonial context, the notion of historical memory may have to be revised to account for events that do not bear the direct reference to which historical method lays claim:

'Là où se joignent les histoires des peuples, hier réputés sans histoires, finit l'Histoire'. (Avec un grand H.). . . . C'est ce procès de hiérarchisation que nous nions dans la conscience commençante de notre histoire, dans ses ruptures, sa soudaineté à investir, sa résistance à l'investigation (Glissant, *Discours*, 132–3).

'History [with a capital H] ends where the histories of those peoples once reputed to be without history come together'. . . . It is this hierarchical process that we deny in our own emergent historical consciousness, in its ruptures, its sudden emergence, its resistance to exploration. (Glissant, *Carribbean Discourse*, 64)

The resistance to investigation that characterizes Antillean history for Glissant corresponds closely to Derrida's account of the unreadability of repressed events to methods of ordinary history. In the Antillean context particularly, the depriveleging of *Histoire* also entails a complicated notion of reference. In order to elucidate this notion, I turn again to Freud.

The structure of delay, metaphoric substitution, and indirect reference at the heart of Freud's text lies in the account of the two Moseses. Their identities are discontinuous, yet they become one Moses in the historical memory, the second Moses substituting for

---
[49] Id., *Archive Fever*, 87.
[50] Caruth, *Unclaimed Experience*, 15–16.

and referring to the first. The violent murder of the first Moses, the repression of his memory, and the rise to power of the second Moses's new religion outline a model of substitutive reference. The traumatic discontinuity of the two Moseses is a delayed and metaphorical act of substitution. However, the monotheism of the first Moses returns through the *Détour* of the second. In the story of Moses and his double we can see that substitutive reference displays a traumatic structure of repression and return.

Caruth claims that 'the traumatic nature of history means that events are only historical to the extent that they implicate others'.[51] If history can be seen as indirectly referential, then it is through the *Détour* of other groups' histories that one can refer to one's own history. Glissant articulates the need for the history of Martinique and Guadeloupe to discover its connections to the histories of other islands in the Caribbean, with whom links might currently be tenuous or non-existent:

Aujourd'hui nous entendons le fracas de Matouba, mais aussi la fusillade de Moncada. Notre histoire nous frappe avec une soudaineté qui étourdit. L'émergence de cette unité diffractée (de cette conjonction inaperçue d'histoires) qui constitue les Antilles en ce moment nous surprend, avant même que nous ayons médité cette conjonction. (132)[52]

Today we hear the blast from Matouba, but also the volley of shots fired at Moncada. Our history comes to life with a stunning unexpectedness. The emergence of this common experience broken in time (of this concealed parallel in histories) that shapes the Caribbean at this time surprises us before we have even thought about this parallel. (62)

The delayed blast of Matouba is interpreted as referring to and as referred to by another blast separated in time and space. While Matouba's blast ended a failed revolution, Moncada was the failed first attack of an ultimately successful revolution. Indeed, Moncada itself is an example of latency and return: although Castro's attack was violently suppressed and Castro was tried for organizing it, the effect of Moncada was ultimately to play an important symbolic role in the Cuban consciousness and revolutionary struggle.

By drawing on the meaning of the history of another island, Glissant implies that latency may also prove effective in the Antillean context. Out of the discontinuity between two histories, two islands,

---

[51] *Unclaimed Experience*, 18.
[52] The Moncada Barracks Attack, led by Fidel Castro in 1953, launched the Cuban revolution.

comes a relationship of mutual reference and merging. The discontinuity between histories is manifest in a period of traumatic latency in which they are mutually unaware of each other. History is envisioned not only as the delayed and indirect reference to unassimilated events in one's own past, but also as a forging of referential relationships between one's own and others' histories.[53] The idea of 'transversality', of lateral connections between histories, functions in Glissant as a multiplicitous and diverse alternative to a linear, unique *Histoire*:

L'irruption à elle-même de l'histoire antillaise (des histoires de nos peuples, convergentes) nous débarasse de la vision linéaire et hiérarchisée d'une Histoire qui courrait son seul fil. Ce n'est pas cette Histoire qui a ronflé sur les bords de la Caraïbe mais bel et bien des conjonctions de nos histoires qui s'y font souterrainement. La profondeur n'était pas le seul abysse d'une névrose mais avant tout le lieu de cheminements multipliés. (134)

The implosion of Caribbean history (of the converging histories of our peoples) relieves us of the linear, hierarchical vision of a single History that would run its unique course. It is not this History that has roared around the edge of the Caribbean, but actually a question of the subterranean convergence of our histories. The depths are not only the abyss of neurosis but primarily the site of multiple converging paths. (66)

Pointing to the link between trauma and substitutive reference, I have argued that in Freud's text, we see a traumatic structure in the metaphorical substitution of the two Moseses (who become connected through discontinuity and delay). In Glissant's account of history in the Antilles, however, it is within the space of latency inherent to trauma, in the period of delay necessary to substitutive reference, that a certain transformation occurs. This transformation can be understood, as I noted above, as a shift from the vertical metaphoric to the horizontal metonymic pole. The discontinuity of parallel histories and their dynamic of repetition are transformed into contiguity and contact. Finally Glissant articulates a version of the notion of history that aims to go beyond the traumatic model of repression

---

[53] Celia Britton formulates the relationship between the absence of history, *Relation*, and otherness thus: 'The absence of historical origin, then, leads to a conception of existence as a plurality of relations with otherness ... "Relation" is above all an attitude to cultural difference. Thus a particular attitude to history, an attempt to wrest something positive from the trauma and lack underlying Caribbean history, ends up as an ethical framework for conceptualizing cultural difference'. See 'Opacity and Transparency: Conceptions of History and Cultural Difference in the Work of Michel Butor and Édouard Glissant', *French Studies*, 49 (1995), 308–20: 315.

and return, of substitution, delay, and repetition: 'Se battre contre l'un de l'Histoire pour la Relation des histoires' (159; 'The struggle against a single History for the cross-fertilization of histories', 93). From the very limits and parameters of trauma, history emerges in relation to other histories, as the referential relationship of multiple merging and crossing histories.

I close this chapter with a reflection on one of the most unsettling features of Glissant's thought. Glissant not only analyses the particular 'disorders' of the Antillean situation; I would argue that he takes them to constitute *antillanité* itself. One must ask whether his emphasis on the productive use-value of disorder comes dangerously close to being an unintentional apology for the slave trade. Glissant walks a difficult tightrope: his bold, nuanced position is not as politically straightforward as the oppositional language of anticolonial resistance associated with *négritude*, Afrocentrism, and nationalism. The danger is that the acceptance, even privileging, of traumatic modes of experience, thinking, and narration that arise out of a history of slavery and colonialism, may bear a disturbing resemblance to a quietism that may blunt the militancy of Glissant's intended political edge.[54] There is also the possibility that glossing the unlimited multiplicity, openness, and indeterminacy of *antillanité* as a version of literariness, as I have done, could have the effect of neutralizing and harnessing political passions.

In the process of acknowledging pain and turning an unspeakable situation into a privileged site, there is reason to feel unease at seeing a positive side to tragedy. These concerns are also present in other counter-discourses that locate within a disadvantaged position a subjective vantage point in order to enable critique of the epistemological hierarchy entailed by domination. The undoing of Western History's power to define the narratives and lives of the colonized, however, requires an articulation of the ways in which the epistemologically oppressed speak from their peculiar positions and histories. Glissant's critique brings out the inadequacy of *Histoire*, which misses the truth of disorder.

The 'abysse d'une névrose' is the gaping absence of history at whose edge Glissant's Antilleans vertiginously stand. In arguing that this abyss is the period of latency inherent to trauma, I have sug-

[54] It is worth noting, however, that the privileging of alternative modes of representing history is grounded in 'the urgent political need to recover the capacity for action', as argued by Celia Britton in '*Discours* and *histoire*, Magical and Political Discourse in Édouard Glissant's *Le Quatrième Siècle*', *French Cultural Studies*, 5 (1994), 151–62: 161.

gested that it is the very site of substitutive reference. The situation of a lack of ownership, of a vertiginous break in continuity in one's history is symptomatic of a vertical epistemological model. In the transformation of this traumatic gap into a site that engenders history, the gap becomes the occasion of the relation and contact of histories, of the merging of the exclusive binaries of the vertical and the horizontal. When the need for possession of a history that is continuously 'one's own' is understood to depend on this limiting binarity, the 'abysse d'une névrose' becomes an abyss of infinite potential.

In the face of rupture, Antillean literary discourse recapitulates structures of continual yearning: the longing to erase the distance at the heart of exile; the search for lost origins as a means to reimagining and revaluing identity; the desire and burden to undo the distance between the writer and the collectivity; the desire for history in the aftermath of colonialism; and the desire of allegory for wholeness and readability. Paradoxically, the attempt to recuperate or get beyond what has been lost repeats the very fracture at the source that occasioned the search. Whether the Antillean 'pays natal' or an anterior African origin is the object of longing, the distance of the sea that must be (re)crossed is both the literal and allegorical in-between space that constitutes the originary break in Antillean literary imagination. In the (middle) passage of time at the heart of allegory and trauma, the notion of crossing takes on multiple meanings, including the merging of histories. Antillean writers, from Aimé Césaire to Maryse Condé, have allegorized this crossing. In examining in relation the paradoxes of allegory and the problem of history and historylessness in the Antilles, this book probes the possibilities of representation that exist when the relationship of centre to periphery is destabilized, when the centre drops out to leave the relation between peripheries. It asks what acts of representation and making readable have to do with the crossing of in-between spaces: between self and other, between individual and collective histories. In the chapters that follow, I set out to read one Antillean writer's productive response to these paradoxes of postcoloniality.

4
ARCHETYPAL RETURNS: *HÉRÉMAKHONON* AND *UNE SAISON À RIHATA*

Maryse Condé's oft-cited biography compares suggestively with the intellectual and ideological development of Antillean postcoloniality.[1] Indeed, Condé's biography is a story of migration, and her oeuvre the product of the migrant's 'oblique gaze'.[2] Born in Guadeloupe in 1937, she left at the age of 16 for Paris. She later spent a decade in West Africa before being exiled to London, teaching in Paris and the USA, and returning to Guadeloupe. When her first novels, *Hérémakhonon* (1976) and *Une saison à Rihata* (1981), set in Africa, were published, critics immediately read them as autobiography, a tendency that Condé has explicitly rejected. In this chapter, I shall suggest conceptual interferences, similarities, and conflicts between the author's relationship to fictional identity and the Antillean intellectual's relationship to Africa, through a reading of Condé's first two novels.

Born Maryse Boucolon, Condé was the youngest child of a prominent black bourgeois family. Her mother was a schoolteacher and her father the founder of a bank. At 16, she received a scholarship and left Guadeloupe to study in Paris. After being expelled after two years at the Lycée Fénélon for disciplinary problems, she continued her studies at the Sorbonne in French, Classics, and English. In Paris in the 1950s, through her contact with West Indian and African students, she became politically aware and engaged with the struggles of anticolonialism and decolonization facing the black world. She met and married an African actor, Mamadou Condé, in 1959.

---

[1] The biographical information that follows is gathered from a number of published interviews: Françoise Pfaff, *Conversations with Maryse Condé* (Lincoln, Nebr.: University of Nebraska Press, 1996); ead., *Entretiens avec Maryse Condé* (Paris: Karthala, 1993); Vèvè A. Clark, '"Je me suis réconciliée avec mon île": Une interview de Maryse Condé', *Callaloo*, 12/1 (1989), 86–132; Mohamed B. Taleb-Khyar, 'An Interview with Maryse Condé and Rita Dove', *Callaloo*, 14/2 (1991), 347–66. See Pfaff, *Conversations*, 139–65 for a bibliography of works published by and about Condé (in francophone countries and in the USA).

[2] Iain Chambers, *Migrancy, Culture, Identity* (London: Routledge, 1993), 14.

In 1960, she went to the Ivory Coast as a schoolteacher for the French Ministry of Cooperation, and a year later went to Guinea to live with her husband. In post-independence Guinea, Condé befriended Marxist militants and became a Marxist. She was quickly disabused of her admiration of Guinean President Sékou Touré and his regime, especially after witnessing the teachers' strikes of 1962 and the government's brutal repression, arrests, and tortures, which are the bases for the events depicted in her first novel, *Hérémakhonon*.

With her marriage now failed, Condé went to Ghana in 1964 as a French teacher for Kwame Nkrumah's Institute for Ideological Training, placing her hopes anew in the socialism of Nkrumah. When Nkrumah lost power in 1966 and fled to Guinea, Condé was accused of being a spy for Sékou Touré, arrested, imprisoned, and then deported. She went to London to work at the BBC. Soon afterwards, she returned to Africa and worked as a translator and a teacher in Senegal. There she met Richard Philcox, who later became her husband and the English translator of several of her novels.

In 1970 she went to Paris and worked at *Présence africaine*. She resumed her studies and received a doctorate in Caribbean literature from the Sorbonne in 1975. She began teaching African and Caribbean literature at the University of Paris IV and wrote *Hérémakhonon* (1976). She had already published two plays: *Dieu nous l'a donné* (1972) and *Mort d'Oluwémi d'Ajumako* (1973). During this period, she published several works of literary criticism: *La Poésie antillaise* (1977), *Le Roman antillais* (1977), *Cahier d'un retour au pays natal: Césaire* (1978), and *La Civilisation du Bossale* (1978). During this time Condé also worked at Radio France internationale, reviewing and discussing books and interviewing francophone authors.

Condé was invited to the USA in 1978 to teach at the University of California, Santa Barbara, and has since taught at various American universities including Occidental College, University of California, Berkeley, University of Virginia, University of Maryland, Harvard, and Columbia, establishing residence in the USA. She published a book of criticism on Antillean women's writing, *La Parole des femmes* (1979), and two more novels set in Africa, *Une saison à Rihata* (1981) and the best-selling epic *Ségou* novels (1984 and 1985). Then came her first novels to take place, at least in large part, in the Caribbean, *Moi, Tituba, sorcière . . . Noire de Salem* (1986), for which she received the

Grand Prix littéraire de la femme, and *La Vie scélérate* (1987), which won the Prix de l'Académie française 1988 (bronze medal), and a collection of stories, *Pays-mêlé* (1985). In 1986, Condé decided to go back to Guadeloupe to live, after thirty-three years of wandering. There she wrote *Traversée de la Mangrove* (1989). In the 1980s she also published two plays: *Pension Les Alizés* (1988), *An Tan Revolisyon: Elle court, elle court la liberté* (1989).

Condé now divides her time between Guadeloupe and the USA, where she currently teaches at Columbia University. Her most recent novels continue her characteristic *errance*, taking her characters to North and South Americas, Cuba, Dominica, and France: *Les Derniers Rois mages* (1992), *La Colonie du nouveau monde* (1993), *La Migration des cœurs* (1995), and *Désirada* (1997). Condé's growing published oeuvre now comprises eleven novels, four plays, a collection of short stories, three books for children, a memoir (*Le Cœur à rire et à pleurer*, 1999), and several works of literary criticism and textbooks. She is one of the most popular (both academically and generally), prolific, versatile, and outspoken writers of the French Antilles, in a variety of genres. Known for her engagement of the 'frictions and harmonies of multicultural junctures', Condé herself has undertaken extensive travel along a route that is strikingly mapped in her novelistic itinerary.[3]

One result of the apparent correspondence between Condé's oeuvre and her biography has been a marked critical temptation to confound the author with her heroines. This was especially true of her early 'African' novels, which I shall analyse in this chapter. Both of Condé's first novels, *Hérémakhonon* and *Une saison à Rihata*, are stories of Guadeloupean women protagonists living in West African countries in the aftermath of independence. As if to confirm Glissant's view that 'La première pulsion d'une population transplantée, qui n'est pas sûre de maintenir au lieu de son transbord l'ancien ordre de ses valeurs, est le Retour' (30), the Antillean women in Condé's first works of fiction direct their 'identity quests' to Africa as the 'arrière-pays culturel'.[4] The return to Africa in these novels is often written of

---

[3] Leah Hewitt, *Autobiographical Tightropes* (Lincoln, Nebr.: University of Nebraska Press, 1990), 167.

[4] The return to Africa has been a powerful theme for some of the major writers of the African diaspora. e.g Alex Haley, *Roots* (London: Hutchinson, 1977); Myriam Warner-Vieyra, *Juletane* (Paris: Présence africaine, 1982); and Simone Schwarz-Bart, *Ti-Jean l'Horizon* (Paris: Seuil, 1979).

as an initial 'return to Africa' phase of her oeuvre.[5] Of all of her works, *Hérémakhonon* and *Saison* have also been the most susceptible to biographical interpretation because the author, like each of her women protagonists, went to live in West Africa in the 1960s after completing her university education in Paris. A major tendency has been to take the Guadeloupean women characters' experiences in Africa as an indication of the author's own attitudes and feelings toward the continent.[6]

Condé's protagonists, Véronica and Marie-Hélène, become disillusioned with the notion of the central importance of Africa to Antillean identity. Condé has stated: 'La quête d'identité d'un Antillais peut très bien se résoudre sans passer, surtout physiquement, par l'Afrique, ou si l'on veut, le passage en Afrique prouve simplement qu'elle n'est pas essentielle dans l'identité antillaise.'[7] Condé's statements on the subject of Africa are devoid of idealism about origins: 'je n'ai jamais commis l'erreur de penser que l'Afrique était ma terre natale. J'aurais aimé que l'Afrique devienne une mère adoptive, mais elle ne peut être une mère naturelle.'[8] She has described the return to Africa largely as a failure for diaspora blacks:

Les partisans de la Négritude ont fait une grave erreur et ont causé beaucoup de torts aux Antillais aussi bien qu'aux Américains noirs. Nous avons été amenés à croire que l'Afrique était la source. C'est la source mais nous avons cru que nous trouverions une patrie alors que ce n'est pas une patrie. Sans la négritude, nous n'aurions pas subi un tel degré de désillusion.[9]

It is nevertheless the case that Véronica in *Hérémakhonon* and Marie-

---

[5] Condé's first four novels are set in Africa, including the two-vol. historical saga *Ségou: Les Murailles de terre* (Paris: Robert Laffont, 1984) and *Ségou: La Terre en miettes* (Paris: Robert Laffont, 1985). Her second published play, *Mort d'Oluwémi d'Ajumako* (Paris: Pierre-Jean Oswald, 1973), takes place in Africa during the same era as *Hérémakhonon* and *Saison*.

[6] For example, Jonathan Ngaté reads Condé's protagonists' disparagement and distancing of Africa as evidence of her tortured ambivalence toward Africa, as a recalcitrant daughter's feelings toward her mother, in 'Maryse Condé and Africa: The Making of a Recalcitrant Daughter?', *Current Bibliography on African Affairs*, 19/1 (1986–7), 5–20. Pius Ngkandu Nkashama sees Condé as an ethnocentric missionary, in 'L'Afrique en pointillé dans *Une saison à Rihata* de Maryse Condé', *Notre librairie*, 74 (1984), 31–7.

[7] Marie-Clotilde Jacquey and Monique Hugon, 'L'Afrique, un continent difficile: Entretien avec Maryse Condé', *Notre librairie*, 74 (1984), 21–5: 22.

[8] Ibid. 23.

[9] Clark, '"Je me suis réconciliée avec mon île"', 116. Condé's polemical early views on *négritude* are expressed in 'Pourquoi la Négritude? Négritude ou Révolution?', in Jeanne-Lydie Gore (ed.), *Négritude africaine, Négritude caraïbe*, (Paris: La Francité, 1973), 150–4.

Hélène in *Saison* do go to Africa (through the mediation of Paris), and that as a writer, Condé chooses to devote these first two novels to the story of an Antillean woman's return to Africa. In light of Condé's statements, it is possible to read her first novels, as others have done, as parables of identity quests that fail, of an Africa that ultimately cannot be mother to the diaspora, of the return to Africa as a misdirected search for a home.[10] Recently, in the wake of Glissant's picture of *Retour* and *Détour* and his emphasis on *antillanité*, critics of Condé have tended to consider the return to Africa as a misguided stage in an identity quest that ultimately finds its truest, happiest place in the Caribbean.[11]

While not underestimating the importance of these themes, in this chapter I adopt a different focus, and concentrate instead on the question of the relationship between self, fictionalized self, and stereotype/archetype that is raised by the confluence of autobiographical concern and paradigmatic return. Rather than ask why Africa cannot be a satisfactory place of return for the Antillean person in search of identity, I focus on why Africa does serve as the setting and occasion for the writing of self-fictionalized return in these novels. I ask, what is the relationship between the much-vaunted identity quest in Africa and the difficulty and necessity of self-distancing? What role does the fictionalization of the self play in this negotiation? I enquire how post-independence Africa becomes an arena for the enactment of return on a variety of axes. I draw on the significance in these novels of the particular historical moment following African independence to suggest further implications for the concept of postcoloniality.

AN AUTHORIAL ARCHETYPE

In Condé's first novel, *Hérémakhonon*, the Guadeloupean protagonist Véronica recalls how her love affair with a light-skinned mulatto

---

[10] See e.g. Adele King, 'Two Caribbean Women go to Africa', *College Literature*, 18/3 (1991), 98–105.

[11] See Françoise Lionnet, 'Happiness Deferred: Maryse Condé's *Hérémakhonon* and the Failure of Enunciation', in ead., *Autobiographical Voices: Race, Gender, Self-Portraiture* (Ithaca, NY: Cornell University Press, 1989); Arlette Smith, 'Maryse Condé's *Hérémakhonon*: A Triangular Structure of Alienation', *CLA Journal*, 32/1 (1988), 45–54; Wangari wa Nyatetu-Waigwa, 'From Liminality to a Home of her Own?: The Quest Motif in Maryse Condé's Fiction', *Callaloo*, 18/3 (1995), 551–64.

man scandalized her family's black bourgeois community.[12] Within the ideological mores of the island's rigidly colour-conscious 'négro-bourgeoisie', Véronica's romantic choice is interpreted as the product of a black woman's self-hating desire to whiten the race. In the midst of her vociferous denial of this distasteful motivation, she claims: 'Je ne suis pas une Mayotte Capécia' (55; 'I'm no Mayotte Capécia', 30). In his analysis of the complexes and obsessions plaguing the Antillean psyche in *Peau noire, masques blancs* (1952), Fanon reads Capécia's novel *Je suis martiniquaise* as a transparent window into the black woman's soul, as her internalization of the colonizer's myth of black racial inferiority and her resulting desire for a white man.[13] Without need of elaboration, Véronica's distancing of herself from Mayotte Capécia functions as a response to Frantz Fanon's famous condemnation of the black woman's presumed wish for 'lactification', her desire to become white.[14]

Véronica's allusion to Fanon's dreaded lactification complex is more than a demonstration of 'diaspora literacy'.[15] The stakes of Véronica's distancing of Mayotte Capécia are no less than those of being apprehended as a race traitor.[16] Véronica claims that she is not 'une Mayotte Capécia'; we recall Fanon's generalizing vilification of the 'Mayotte Capécias de tous les pays' ('the Mayotte Capécias of all nations').[17] As Condé herself has pointed out elsewhere, in singling Capécia out as exemplar of the black woman's self-abnegating long-

[12] All references are to the most recent edition, *En attendant le bonheur (Hérémakhonon)* (Paris: Robert Laffont, 1997), and will be given in the text. This book was originally published as *Hérémakhonon* (Paris: Union générale, 1976) and repr. as *En attendant le bonheur (Hérémakhonon)* (Paris: Robert Seghers, 1988; repr Robert Laffont, 1997). All translations are from *Heremakhonon*, trans. Richard Philcox (Washington: Three Continents Press, 1982) and references to it will be given in the text.

[13] Mayotte Capécia's *Je suis martiniquaise* (Paris: Corréa, 1948) chronicles a black woman narrator's feelings of inferiority in the context of her relationship with a white man.

[14] Frantz Fanon, *Peau noire, masques blancs* (Paris: Seuil, 1995), 38.

[15] Vèvè Clark's 'diaspora literacy' is the possession of a set of cultural reference points that enable the reader to comprehend literatures of the diaspora from an informed perspective. See 'Developing Diaspora Literacy: Allusion in Maryse Condé's *Hérémakhonon*', in Carole Boyce Davies and Elaine Savory Fido (eds.), *Out of the Kumbla: Womanist Perspectives on Caribbean Literature* (Trenton: Africa World Press, 1989), 315–31, and 'Diaspora Literacy and *Marasa* Consciousness', in Hortense Spillers (ed.), *Comparative American Identities: Race, Sex, and Nationality in the Modern Text* (New York: Routledge, 1991), 40–61.

[16] Susan Z. Andrade reads *Hérémakhonon* as a mirroring political response to Fanon's text that reflects his anxieties about betrayal and female sexuality. See 'The Nigger of the Narcissist: History, Sexuality and Intertextuality in Maryse Condé's *Hérémakhonon*', *Callaloo*, 16/1 (1993), 213–26.

[17] Fanon, *Peau noire*, 36; *Black Skin, White Masks* (New York: Grove Weidenfeld, 1967), 44.

ing to whiten the race through a relationship with a white man, Fanon deliberately elides the distance between the author and the subject of her fiction.[18] Fanon's erasure of distance between self and fictionalized self in effect enables him to reproach the author for her character's thoughts and actions. He in turn directs his animadversion toward her act of writing: 'Un jour, une femme du nom de Mayotte Capécia, obeissant à un motif dont nous apercevons mal les tenants, a écrit deux cent deux pages—sa vie—où se multipliaient à loisir les propositions les plus absurdes' ('One day a woman named Mayotte Capécia, obeying a motivation whose elements are difficult to detect, sat down to write 202 pages—her life—in which the most ridiculous ideas proliferated at random').[19] He attributes to the mere fact of her writing the detestable motives of her character. Fanon reads the novel *Je suis martiniquaise*, ('sa vie') as autobiography. However, one might note that the acknowledged unintelligibility of Capécia's random motivations may undermine Fanon's ability to read the narrative as a transparent authorial confession. Nevertheless Fanon relies on this erasure of distance between author and character to hold the author out as a cautionary tale. The representative, 'martiniquaise' status of the first-person subject in Capécia's title becomes fodder for Fanon's desire to make an example of her and multiply her representativeness as he warns the Mayotte Capécias of all nations.

We might thus read Véronica's distancing of Capécia in view of the distance between authorial and fictionalized selves that Fanon so readily erases. On one level, Véronica's 'Je ne suis pas une Mayotte Capécia' seems quite simply to be her rejection of an exemplary woman race-traitor. However, on closer reflection, her refusal to be read as 'une Mayotte Capécia' is the refusal of a label, a stereotype, the expected story: what Anthony Appiah calls a 'scripted identity'.[20] Furthermore, if Fanon's very rendering of Mayotte Capécia into an

[18] Condé, 'Order, Disorder, Freedom, and the West Indian Writer', *Yale French Studies*, 83/2 (1993), 121–35: 131.
[19] Fanon, *Peau noire*, 34; *Black Skin*, 42.
[20] 'Identity, Authenticity, Survival: Multicultural Societies and Social Reproduction', in Charles Taylor (ed.), *Multiculturalism: Examining the Politics of Recognition*, expanded edn. ed. Amy Gutmann (Princeton: Princeton University Press, 1994), 160n. See also Appiah and Amy Gutmann, *Color Conscious: The Political Morality of Race* (Princeton: Princeton University Press, 1996), where Appiah observes that collective identities come with the notion of 'loose norms or models' of behaviour and 'provide what we might call scripts' (97); 'An African-American after the Black Power movement takes the old script of self-hatred, the script in which he or she is a nigger, and works, in community with others, to construct a series of positive black life scripts' (98).

archetypal female race traitor depends so heavily on his erasure of the writer's estrangement from her fictionalized selves, the very exemplarity of Capécia's feminized betrayal of her race is born of that effacing. Thus, Véronica's allusive disavowal of the stereotype may intimate the demarcation of the distance between self and fictionalized selves that, as I shall argue, is pivotal to her own internal ironic self-distance and her vision of herself as divided.

Issues of self-distancing and self-fictionalizing become especially prominent in relation to the question of autobiography and Africa in Condé's work. When first published, some critics read *Hérémakhonon* as Condé's rejection of Africa, prompting her to clarify repeatedly in interviews that the book is not an autobiographical novel and that 'Véronica n'est pas moi'.[21] It is as if Véronica's 'Je ne suis pas une Mayotte Capécia' in *Hérémakhonon* prefigures the distance between authorial and fictionalized selves on which Condé herself would later have to insist. Indeed, the novel brought Condé accusations of being a Mayotte Capécia with regard to an alleged betrayal of Africa. In Condé's anecdotal account of the reception of *Hérémakhonon*, 'the word-of-mouth system worked, and I was labeled as a person who detests and says bad things about Africa.... An article in *Le Naif*... called me "a voyeur and a whore," added that "an odor of sperm could be smelled" in the book, and ended up comparing me to Mayotte Capécia'.[22] Remarkably enough, the critical censure of Condé's representation of Africa took the sexualized form and rhetoric identical to and convergent with the censure of Véronica's romantic choice within the fiction; the two women are both whores, or rather, there is only one woman, who is at once writer, prostitute, and race-traitor. Véronica's 'Je ne suis pas une Mayotte Capécia' is a pre-echo of Condé's 'Véronica n'est pas moi', and prescient of the interpretive overdetermination to which Condé herself was subjected.

FICTION AND CLICHÉ

Guadeloupean Véronica has recently finished her university studies in Paris and travels to a recently independent 1960s West African

---

[21] Pfaff, *Entretiens*, 63–4.
[22] Ead., *Conversations*, 46. See also Vèvè Clark, '"Je me suis réconciliée avec mon île"', 120–3.

country to teach Western philosophy as a French *coopérante*.[23] Intelligent and well educated, Véronica seeks her identity through a quest for her ancestral past. She has come to Africa 'pour essayer de voir ce qu'il y avait avant' (31; 'to try and find out what was before', 12). Véronica's first words in this first-person narrative are a self-conscious acknowledgement that her trip to Africa can be read as a cliché: 'Franchement on pourrait croire que j'obéis à la mode' (19; 'Honestly! You'd think I'm going because it is the in thing to do', 3). She recognizes that in light of the current fashion for things African, along with the history of European exoticism, her own desire for Africa is a cliché. Having herself drawn attention to the plausibility of such an interpretation, she simply insists: 'Or c'est faux. Je n'obéis pas à la mode' (19; 'Well, I'm not!', 3). Her self-consciousness about the cliché is that of living and enacting a fiction, not only in the sense of a falsehood, but of a narrative that is 'too tightly scripted'.[24]

This early highlighted tension captures the central struggle of Véronica's identity quest: the attempt to wrest away freedom from the imprisonment of overdetermined cultural and political meanings. Véronica is plagued by an awareness of the presence of language and thought that is second-hand, that belongs to the colonizer: 'Ils ont une façon silencieuse de se déplacer. Attention aux clichés! Mais non. Ils *se déplacent ainsi*' (37; 'They have a silent way of moving. Beware of cliché! No, that's how they move', 16). Rather than avoid and renounce clichés when they recur throughout her thought-narrative, Véronica pointedly revisits and maintains them. Her repeated reaction to the danger of the clichés is to note their presence and to affirm defiantly the individualized meaning of her derivative utterance. She insists upon her originality at the very moment that her unoriginality becomes manifest. The act of reappropriation is a means of creating a liberatory albeit fictional discourse.

If Véronica gives self-discovery as the reason for the voyage, for this she looks to a severed past. On being welcomed by her boss Saliou—whom she repeatedly refers to as 'l'échalas' ('bean pole')—at the Institute where she is to teach, she muses,

Bon, il efface d'un coup trois siècles et demi.... On a rejeté les Blancs à la mer. Elle s'est rougie de leur sang. A Nantes et Liverpool, on met le feu aux négriers. (21)

[23] Though unnamed, this country is modelled on Sékou Touré's post-independence Guinea, and the story inspired by events of 1962. See Maryse Condé's account in 'Avant-propos', in *En attendant le bonheur (Hérémakhonon)*, 11–15: 11–12.
[24] Appiah, in Appiah and Gutmann, *Color Conscious*, 99.

With one word, he has wiped out three centuries and a half.... They are driving the whites back into the sea. It is glowing red with their blood. The slave ships in Nantes and Liverpool have been set afire. (4).[25]

She wants to feel a connection with a glorious African past that precedes the slave trade that displaced and deracinated her ancestors.

Je suis venue chercher une terre non plus peuplée de nègres . . . mais de Noirs. C'est-à-dire, en clair, que je suis à la recherche de ce qui peut rester du passé. Le présent ne m'intéresse pas. Par-delà lui, je vise le palais des Obas, les ciselures de leurs masques et les chants de leurs griots. (89)
I came to seek a land inhabited by Blacks, not Negroes.... In other words, I'm looking for what remains of the past. I'm not interested in the present. Beyond that, I am seeking the Oba's palace, the carving on their masks, and the songs of the griots. (56)[26]

Privileging the past over the present in her search for a land of authentic blackness, Véronica posits the African past as the needed refuge from the 'scripting' of her words and actions. However, as she recognizes in the novel's opening lines, the very act of seeking this freedom in Africa is itself also a cliché that she must deny and against which she must guard.

The struggle against the colonization of her individuality forms the core of Véronica's quest for personal identity. She has suffered this colonization most painfully from her family and the black bourgeois community in Guadeloupe to which they belong. We learn that she was sent to Paris for her studies in the wake of the scandal of her affair with Jean-Marie de Roseval, the son of a prominent Guadeloupean mulatto family. The shock and censure of the community, and of her father, whose reaction was to call her a whore, came from a context in which such a relationship can only be understood as black women's desire to whiten the race. Recalling and recounting the relationship to her newly befriended 'échalas', she says:

Non, je le jure. Ce n'était pas sa couleur comme ils l'ont dit, parce que bien sûr, ils ne pouvaient penser à rien d'autre. C'était sa liberté. L'échalas me sourit. Il a un beau sourire. Des dents arrondies et très blanches. Attention! Se méfier des clichés: le nègre aux dents blanches. Enfin tout de même, il a vraiment les dents blanches. (26)

[25] Nantes and Liverpool were two of the principal European ports in the slave trade, whose prosperity led to later capitalist development in these cities, as Eric Williams argues in *Capitalism and Slavery* (New York: Russell & Russell, 1961).

[26] Novelistically, Condé has tried to recreate a glorious African past with the historical epic *Ségou*, about the Bambara kingdom, which 'illustre la grandeur et la décadence d'un peuple africain symbolisée par une famille précise' (Pfaff, *Entretiens*, 73).

Wasn't his color, I swear. That's what they all said because naturally, they could not think of anything else. No, it was his freedom. The bean pole smiles. He has a lovely smile, rounded teeth, very white. Careful! Beware of clichés: the nigger with flashing teeth. All the same, his teeth are very white. (8)

In this passage, yet another instance of Véronica's insistence on her individuality in the face of the cliché of clichés ('le nègre aux dents blanches') is juxtaposed with her recollection of her affair with Jean-Marie. This juxtaposition and her emphasis on her attraction to her white lover's 'liberté' draws attention to how the stereotyping of her romantic choices is a sign of the overdetermination from which she seeks escape. Her family, who call her a 'Marilisse' (39), see only what the relationship between a black woman and a light-skinned man represents politically.[27] Véronica's appeal to the freedom simply to be in love in effect converges with the appeal to be free from a pre-existing fiction or script: 'Non, je ne me faisais pas Marilisse. J'aimais. C'est tout. (39; 'I was not doing a Marilisse. I was in love. That's all', 18). In Paris, she encounters the problem again when she becomes involved with a white Frenchman, Jean-Michel. At a Caribbean festival in Paris with her lover, she is confronted by a group of young militant Antilleans who show their contempt by repeating, 'Marilisse! Tu te fais Marilisse!' (41). She loves Jean-Marie and Jean-Michel because of their lack of self-alienation: 'Ils étaient libres. D'être eux-mêmes. Vraiment. Profondément. . . . Rien à prouver, encore moins. Ils étaient ma Liberté. Je veux dire, j'y accédais à mon tour par eux' (63; 'They were free. To be themselves. Genuinely; deep down. . . . They had nothing to prove. They were my freedom. I mean it was through them that I got there', 36). Paradoxically, the freedom embodied by Jean-Marie and Jean-Michel can only be enjoyed theoretically by Véronica, who becomes most aware of being read as a cliché, and hence rendered most unfree, because of her relationships with them. Parallel to her 'je ne suis pas une Mayotte Capécia', her 'je ne me faisais pas Marilisse' signals her struggle against being read and aware of herself as a cliché, repeatedly around her romantic persona. Véronica's denial of her continuity

---

[27] 'Étant en partance, le sieur Cazeau habitant au Cul-de-Sac a mis en vente une jeune négresse de belle figure prénommée Marilisse, bonne blanchisseuse. On la prendra à l'essai' (*Hérémakhonon*, 39). According to Condé, Marilisse was a 'personnage . . . que j'ai trouvé dans l'Histoire: une négresse esclave qui vivait avec un Blanc dont elle avait des enfants' (Pfaff, *Entretiens*, 65).

with Marilisse, a historically scripted character, draws attention to the notion of historical script as cliché, as a fiction to be rewritten.

FEAR OF TWONESS, FEAR OF WHOLENESS

Véronica projects this self-consciousness about herself as cliché onto her black suitors in Guadeloupe. As she puts it, 'S'ils me faisaient horreur, c'est qu'ils n'étaient pas libres. Parce qu'ils avaient terriblement peur d'être ce qu'on disait qu'ils étaient. Parce qu'en fait ils croyaient être ce qu'on disait' (63; 'I detested them because they weren't free. Because they were terribly afraid of being what it was said they were. Because, in fact, they thought they were just that', 36). Antillean blacks' lack of freedom, Véronica implies, is due to their self-consciousness about their racial and political identity. The awareness of being read along a script and the necessity of reacting to it prevents one from simply being oneself.[28] Véronica sees Guadeloupean blacks as suffering from a splitting of identity, which we can see as a kind of 'double consciousness'.[29] In *The Souls of Black Folk* (1903), W. E. B. DuBois famously writes:

It is a peculiar sensation, this double-consciousness, this sense of always looking at one's self through the eyes of others, of measuring one's soul by the tape of a world that looks on in amused contempt and pity. One ever feels his twoness. . . . two souls, two thoughts, two unreconciled strivings; two warring ideals in one dark body, whose dogged strength alone keeps it from being torn asunder.[30]

Véronica's horror of her family and 'ses discours glorificateurs de la Race et, au cœur, sa conviction terrifiée de son infériorité' (86; 'its talk of glorifying the Race and its terrified conviction of its inferiority', 52), can be discerned as a dread of 'twoness'. Véronica experiences the fear of being what one claims not to be as a double-conscious self-alienation. Africa, for its part, represents the possibility of recovery of the split, occasioning for Véronica an indulgence in nostalgia:

Qu'est-ce que je donnerais pour 'être née dans le Nord'! Mon père assis sur

---

[28] Despite Véronica's consternation at being stereotyped, and labelled, her own discourse is replete with scripts through which she reads the people that she encounters. Her father is the 'marabout mandingue', Saliou is 'l'echalas', Ibrahima Sory is her African 'nègre avec aïeux', her white lover is 'ma Libérté', and 'Il y avait ces jeunes Antillais coiffés du béret noir des Black Panthers' (*Hérémakhonon*, 41).

[29] For discussions of double consciousness, see Ashcroft et al., *The Empire Writes Back: Theory and Practice in Post-Colonial Literatures* (London: Routledge, 1989); Fanon, *Peau noire*; id., *Les Damnés de la terre* (Paris: François Maspéro, 1961); Paul Gilroy, *The Black Atlantic: Modernity and Double Consciousness* (London: Verso, 1993).   [30] (New York: Penguin, 1989), 5.

sa peau de mouton reçoit les hommages des vassaux. Il ne parle jamais de la Race. Car en est-il une autre que la nôtre? (73)
What wouldn't I give to be born in the North? My father sitting on his sheepskin receiving homage from his vassals. He never talks of Race. Can there be another one apart from ours? (43)

She conceptualizes Africa as a place where she can recover from the doubleness that the awareness of one's race and one's otherness entails. She sees herself as divided, and for reunification she looks to her sexual relationship with Ibrahima Sory, an aristocratic, high-ranking minister of the corrupt ruling government. He is her 'nègre avec aïeux' ('nigger with ancestors'), a metonym for Africa: 'Je me suis mis dans l'idée que cet homme-là me réconcilierait avec moi-même' (83; 'I got it into my head that this man would reconcile my two selves', 50).

Véronica imagines the process of recovery from past trauma as a wresting of the personal away from the political. Her avowed indifference to the political appears repeatedly in anti-political mantras throughout her stay. She repeats them each time she inevitably encounters the realities and struggles of post-independence Africa: 'Je n'ai pas traversé les mers pour me mêler de leurs querelles' (54; 'I haven't crossed the oceans to get mixed up in their quarrels', 29); 'Je ne suis pas venue pour me lancer dans des débats sur la voie africaine du socialisme' (55; 'I didn't come to get mixed up in a debate on African socialism', 30). Her aggressive attempt to distance herself from the political realities into which she has arrived informs her decision to become romantically involved with the aristocratic Ibrahima Sory, whom her friends call 'assassin-du-peuple' (55; 'the people's assassin', 30). Proclaiming 'J'en ai ma claque des étiquettes' (55; 'I'm sick of labels', 30), she subordinates any concern for the political to her personal identity quest:

> Mais avouons franchement que des crimes passés et présents de cette aristocratique famille, je n'ai cure! Parce qu'en fait, c'est cela que je suis venue voir. D'authentique aristocrates. Pas des singes. Des petit-fils d'esclaves dansant le menuet. . . . Ainsi donc, ce nègre a des aïeux! (47)

> Quite frankly, I don't care a damn for the past and present crimes of this aristocratic family. They are the ones I came to see. Genuine aristocrats. Grandsons of slaves dancing the minuet. . . . This nigger has ancestors! (24)

She is crudely fascinated by Ibrahima Sory because he was not branded by slavery, and represents an African authenticity that is lost to diaspora blacks.

In a fashion that almost parodies Jameson's distinction between the West and the Third World, Véronica's relationship with Ibrahima Sory reveals the distance between her Western psychologizing needs and an African reality that seems to have no vocabulary for inner life apart from the political. She conceives of her encounter with Ibrahima Sory on a model of therapeutic confession and recollection that will lead to a cure for her malaise: 'Je me suis venue pour me guérir d'un mal. . . . Nous échangerons nos enfances et nos passés. Par lui, j'accéderai enfin à la fierté d'être moi-même' (71; 'I came to find a cure . . . We'll exchange our childhoods and our past. Through him I shall at last be proud to be what I am', 42). The cure, it seems, is to be effected through an exchange, a substitution of her past for his.

Il faut qu'il m'aide à guérir. Ma haine des uns, mon mépris des autres. Il faut que mes explications soient sincères; pas comme celles de ces malades qui mentent sur le divan à leur psychanalyste. (85)

He must help me find a cure. My hatred, my contempt. My explanations must be sincere—not like those patients who continue to lie to their psychiatrist. (51).

However, her repeated appeals to Ibrahima are only met with amused mockery, and she becomes aware of the absurd cliché of her position as one of his 'névrosés de la diaspora' (86). In response to her psychologizing, Ibrahima Sory patronizes: 'Ici, il n'y a pas de place pour les petits problèmes personnels, la sentimentalité, les caprices. Nous sommes au lendemain d'une révolution' (119).

Meanwhile, as she insists on taking her distance from politics, her unwillingness to judge the events taking place around her becomes less and less tenable, as the regime becomes increasingly authoritarian and repressive. The violent suppression of the strikes at her school, along with the arrests of her student Birame III and her friend Saliou for opposing the regime, makes it impossible to continue to play the neutral observer, especially as her lover is directly responsible for the repression of dissidents. Véronica's stance evolves from distanced irony to narcissistic resentment about being dragged into involvement in concerns that she wants to see as separate from her own. She is forced into caring as she realizes that her friends may be in danger, and that she may be complicit.

Véronica finds her romantic life subject to political scrutiny. Her friend Saliou interprets her relationship with Ibrahima Sory as a political betrayal. Her militant students write on her blackboard at school, 'Nous détruirons les Ministres, Leurs Mercedes, Et leurs Putains' (106; 'We shall destroy the ministers, their Mercedes and their whores', 68). What is the most personal of choices is read as a political one: 'Si je comprends bien, dans ce pays, faire l'amour revient à faire un choix politique' (106; 'If I understand correctly making love in this country comes down to making a political choice', 69). Though this is precisely what she came to Africa to escape, Véronica finds herself in the familiar position of being subject to political judgement for her sexual choices. She is forced to recall a similar event from the past: in effect, she experiences the intrusion of the political into her love life in Africa as a traumatic repetition of the past.

Festival des Caraïbes. Château de Vincennes.
Qu'est-ce qui m'avait prise? Neuf ans, je vous dis. Alors un coup de cafard!
Ils étaient debout à l'entrée, le béret noir incliné sur l'oreille.
Manquaient les fusils à répétition. Le créole, si je ne l'ai jamais parlé je le comprends tout de même et leurs injures entre leurs dents serrés se vrillaient dans ma chair.
Alors, j'ai déguerpi! (107)
The Caribbean Festival. Chateau de Vincennes. Whatever came over me? Nine years, I'm telling you. Homesickness.
They were standing at the entrance, their black berets tilted to one side. All that was missing were the rifles. Jean-Michel doesn't understand creole. I do. I did learn it after all and haven't forgotten it. Their insults, half out loud, between their teeth, drilled into my flesh. Well, I decamped. (69)

In this recollection, Véronica's homesickness while in Paris draws her to a Caribbean festival, where she is verbally abused for being with her white lover. Similarly, her desired 'return' and escape to Africa is accompanied by the repetition of being rendered a whore by her sexual decisions. The close association of nostalgia for the past and traumatic repetition suggests the extent to which the positing of return as a recovery from trauma backfires. For Véronica, whose quest for identity is so deeply tied to the narrative of her romantic life, these alienating, repetitive intrusions of the political into the personal are precisely the symptoms of the malaise that she has come to Africa to cure.

In Guadeloupe, Paris, and Africa, Véronica's sexual choices are read as politically symbolic acts, and always the wrong ones at that. Véronica perceives this erosion of public and private spheres as not only a problem in her own identity quest, but representative of the quandary of black people: 'A mon avis les Nègres, il serait grand temps qu'on leur foute la paix, qu'on les laisse danser, se saouler et faire l'amour, ils l'ont bien mérité' (123; 'In my opinion, it's high time they left the niggers in peace, let them dance, get drunk and make love. They've deserved it', 82). Her move to assign representative status to her situation also erodes the public–private separation. Whether under the oppressive Western gaze or the gaze of Africans themselves, individual actions are always constrained by political meanings, even or especially in the most intimate matters. Véronica remembers falling ill as a child upon realizing that her father, whom she ironically calls the 'marabout mandingue', must have engaged in sexual intercourse; she is disappointed at his being content to imitate the Whites in this as in other things. It pains her to see prostitution in Africa because despite its ubiquity, 'c'est une invention, encore une, que l'Afrique n'avait pas faite. . . . Elles sont la preuve que l'Europe est passée par là' (146; 'it's just another invention that Africa didn't make. . . . They're proof that Europe has been through these parts', 100). The saturation of the commonplace with colonial meaning forms the prison of black identity, which is just as shot through in an independent Africa. Véronica's efforts to be neutral are always doomed: 'Les sujets neutres, indifférents n'existent pas dans ce pays. On est constamment agressé, violé, sommé de prendre part' (124; 'Neutral, indifferent subjects don't exist in this country. You are constantly attacked, raped, and forced to take part', 82). Her comparison of the intrusion of the political into her life to rape emphasizes the colonization of her romantic life and her position as a woman who finds that she does not have control over the way in which her sexual choices are read.

RETURN, DISTANCE, AND IRONY

For Véronica, Africa is supposed to be an alternative to black alienation because it represents continuity with an ancestral past. Thus Véronica conceives of her quest as a search for her past. Sexual relations are central to the question of origins. We learn that her own family's 'origin' begins with a grandmother who was the illegitimate daughter of a *béké*. Véronica's relationship with Ibrahima Sory is an attempt to reverse this 'original' break with the past. The sexual relations between white men and black women that make up her ancestry constitute for Véronica the traumatic break from an African authenticity. Her repeated attempts to make individual sexual choices are plagued by the repetition of a determinism that is a kind of haunting by her familial past.

While her efforts to affirm the individuality of her present are haunted by her past, Véronica finds her search for an African past frustrated by the reality of an overwhelming African present that is thrust upon her against her will. This paradoxical interaction between the past and the present, whose boundaries and distinctions resist her control, is also played out at the formal level of the narrative. Making use of free direct and indirect discourse, the narrative moves confusingly between the past and the present, within Véronica's interior monologue. Her thoughts comprise myriad different voices and points of view that speak from the present or the past without any textual demarcation. In addition, the text makes no physical or visual distinction between Véronica's inner thoughts and her quoted speech. This technique, which makes abundant use of unattributed voices and intertextual references, produces the impression of a polyglossia that recalls the Bakhtinian concept of 'internal dialogization'.[31] The reader experiences a process of constant and jarring shifts—of positions, voices, values, temporality—moment to moment, without warning, all within Véronica's evolving inner world. The narrative moves between the past and the present, so that the present can seamlessly trigger an event or a voice from the past. This functions as the formal counterpart of Véronica's inability to escape from the painful memories of her past, which continue to be recalled in her effort to recreate herself in Africa. Yet, despite her search for Africa's past and her avowed distance from its present, the

[31] See Mikhail Bakhtin, *The Dialogic Imagination*, ed. Michael Holquist, trans. by Caryl Emerson and Michael Holquist (Austin, Tex.: University of Texas Press, 1981). However, Condé's oeuvre as a whole displays relatively little interest in the 'carnavalesque' as cited, especially in discussions of *créolité*, to stand for the subversive dialogization and the polyphonic multiplicity of discourses that characterize the culture of the Caribbean. See e.g. Richard Burton, *Le Roman marron: Etudes sur la litterature martniquaise contemporaine* (Paris: L'Harmattan, 1997), 201–58; Ronnie Scharfman, '"Créolité" is/as Resistance: Raphaël Confiant's *Le Nègre et l'Amiral*', in Maryse Condé and Madeleine Cottenet-Hage (eds.), *Penser la créolité* (Paris: Karthala, 1995), 125–34. 131–3; Thomas Spear, 'Jouissances carnavalesques: Représentations de la sexualité', in Condé and Cottenet-Hage (eds.), *Penser la créolité*, 135–52.

political present imposes itself upon her. The intrusion of the political thus simultaneously frustrates her desires both for the present and for the past.

Véronica's ironic stance toward events around her gradually gives way to panic. This becomes most evident on one occasion where Véronica suddenly needs to establish distinctions between the past and the present. This takes place during Véronica's crossing toward an island off the African coast. As is typical of this narrative, the passage moves without warning between Véronica's present crossing to Jean Lefèvre and Adama's vacation home and her childhood memories of sailing to les Saintes off the coast of Guadeloupe. What can we make of the interjections 'Est-ce le présent ou le passé? Le présent, le présent' (180; 'Is it the present or the past? The present, the present', 127) and 'C'est le présent? Ou est-ce que c'est le passé? . . . C'est le passé. C'est le passé' (181; 'Is it the present? Or is it the past. . . . It's the past. The past', 127). Suddenly, Véronica is compelled to reassure herself that she can demarcate the distinction between the past and the present. This need comes at a moment when Véronica's ironic distance has given way to emotional involvement: with one horrifying event after another, she begins to confront the impossibility of keeping separate the personal and the political. Her escape from the town, in the form of a crossing, much like her previous escapes to Paris from Guadeloupe and to Africa from Paris, coincides with her effort to re-establish boundaries between the past and the present, the personal and the political. But even this momentary escape is thwarted, as the police find her on the beach without her identity papers and take her back to town.

Véronica realizes that if she is forced to confront the political it is only through the personal. It is not the revolutionary struggle that ultimately moves her, but her feelings for Saliou, who is repeatedly imprisoned, and eventually dies in confinement.

Peut-être que ce à quoi j'assiste . . . c'est le combat-d'un-peuple-pour-la-liberté-et-la-justice? Mais s'il m'émeut, c'est parce qu'un ami est en danger. Est-ce que je suis à plaindre parce que, c'est certain, j'ignore les grands sentiments? Je ne connais que les petits: l'amitié, l'amour. Mes aïeux, mes aïeux, par Ibrahima Sory interposé, me jouent un mauvais tour. Un très sale tour. Emprisonnant Saliou, ils veulent me forcer à les haïr. (224)

Perhaps what I'm witnessing . . . is the fight of a people for their liberty and justice. But I am moved because a friend is in danger. Am I to be pitied because I have no idea of the major sentiments? I only know the minor ones—friendship, love. My ancestors, my ancestors via Ibrahima Sory are playing a dirty trick on me. A very dirty trick. By imprisoning Saliou they are trying to force me to hate them. (160)

Véronica privileges the personal, intimate concerns of 'l'amitié, l'amour' over 'les grands sentiments' of the political; yet she experiences their convergence everywhere. This is the problem with Africa. This has a disillusioning effect on a quest that she has posed as a refuge from the meanings that burden personal identity.

One critic calls this novel an 'allegorical treatment of the problem of exiled Antilleans'.[32] On this reading, Africa would not turn out to be a resolution of exile, but would represent the misguided attempt at *Retour*, one stage in a nomadism that would typify Antillean identity progression. *Hérémakhonon* ends with Véronica's departure from Africa, with her disillusionment with her quest, and her conclusion that looking to Africa for her identity has been an

erreur, cette tragique erreur que je ne pouvais pas ne pas commettre, étant ce que je suis. Je me suis trompée, trompée d'aïeux, voilà tout. J'ai cherché mon salut là ou il ne le fallait pas. Parmi les assassins. (244)

mistake, this tragic mistake I couldn't help making, being what I am. My ancestors led me on. What more can I say? I looked for myself in the wrong place, in the arms of an assassin. (176)

As a diaspora neurotic, Véronica's attraction to Africa has been a quest for a wholeness and authenticity that would cure the divisions plaguing her identity. The problem, however, is that there is too much wholeness and not enough division between the political and personal, private and public.

If this novel is indeed an allegorical treatment of Antillean identity, it can be traced in the cyclical appearance, recession, and reappearance of Véronica's irony. The final lines mark the return of her irony with regard to her own words and feelings: 'Allons, pas de grands mots! Toujours ce goût de drame. Le printemps? Oui, c'est le printemps sur Paris' (244; 'Come now, don't use big words. Always dramatizing. Spring? Yes, it's Spring in Paris', 176). The cliché of 'Paris in the springtime' is embraced tongue-in-cheek. The ironic distance from her own motivations that characterized her discourse initially but eventually gave way to sincere emotional involvement, returns and accompanies Véronica's decision to leave Africa. The wholeness and authenticity that Véronica sought in Africa in order

[32] Lionnet, *Autobiographical Voices*, 168.

to reconcile her 'twoness' has been manifested in the suppression of her self-distancing. Africa, we realize, has in its own way, forced an erasure of distance between self and fictionalized selves that is the hallmark of Véronica's self-mocking discourse. In a sense, the identity quest has not failed, but rather has succeeded with a vengeance. The return of Véronica's irony and her departure to Paris are signs of a possible acceptance of the hybridity on which 'double consciousness' and self-fictionalization rest.

While *Hérémakhonon* ends with Véronica's departure from Africa, Condé's second novel, *Une saison à Rihata*, plays out the alternative: remaining in Africa.[33] Marie-Hélène, a Guadeloupean who has moved to Africa with her African husband Zek, has been languishing for many years in a small and undistinguished town in a newly independent African country. Marie-Hélène is drained by her lacklustre marriage, the mediocrity of her husband and surroundings, and her own wasted potential. Her bitter personal disappointments have as their backdrop and political counterpart her hopes for a free Africa, dashed by a regime whose political repression and corruption form the fabric of the characters' everyday lives.[34]

Marie-Hélène is haunted by the past, and unable to integrate herself into the reality of her African present. The novel's opening description of her family's dilapidated house, the only one of its kind in the town, signals her exile, alienation, and marginality to the community. A grand structure built by a colonial magistrate before independence and abandoned after the departure of the French, the house is shunned by everyone for being too reminiscent of the colonial past. However, Zek sees a resemblance between the unique place in the town occupied by the house, and his family (11–12). For Marie-Hélène's nephew and adopted son Christophe, the house is a 'symbole de leur condition de semi-étrangers, mal intégrés à une communauté qui ne perdait jamais de vue les siens' (12; 'symbol that they were partly foreigners, poorly integrated into a community that put its own people first', 2). Although Zek is the son of a well-established Ngurka family, they are outsiders. The source of this malaise is Marie-Hélène's foreignness. The townspeople call her

---

[33] *Une saison à Rihata* (Paris: Robert Laffont, 1981; repr. 1997); *A Season in Rihata*, trans. Richard Philcox (London: Heinemann, 1988). All references will appear in the main text.

[34] The title of this novel alludes to Césaire's play *Une saison au Congo* (Paris: Seuil, 1966), about the traumatic decolonization of the Belgian Congo, the martyrdom of Patrice Lumumba, and the evaporation of the dream of a unified, decolonized Africa. Césaire's title itself alludes to Rimbaud's *Une saison en enfer* (1873).

'"Semela"', mot ngurka qui signifie "Celle-qui-vient-d'ailleurs"' (12; '"Semela", Ngurka for "the woman from over there"', 2). She lives amidst the cold exclusivity of an African society that she once anticipated as her own: 'Exclue? Pourquoi? Savaient-elles comme elle avait rêvé de l'Afrique quand toute sa génération réclamait l'indépendance comme un merveilleux gâteau d'anniversaire?' (33; 'Why was she excluded? Little did they realise how she and her entire generation had dreamed of Africa, demanding independence like a magnificent birthday cake', 22). Their once-elegant house, anachronistic, out of place, and fallen into disrepair from neglect, is a metonym for Marie-Hélène's state of exile, her failed hopes, and the burden of her past.

With this beginning, the novel introduces us to stories that go back a long way. The time frame of the novel is delineated by the official visit to Rihata of Zek's younger and more successful brother Madou, a minister in the government. Madou's visit occasions the return of painful ghosts. It triggers memories of sins, wounds, and tragedies, which then unsettle the characters' already uneasy lives. What is under the surface is gradually brought to light as the unfolding of the plot reveals crucial secrets. The most proximate is the recent memory of Marie-Hélène's affair with her brother-in-law, which has caused a rift between the brothers Zek and Madou.

The notion of a past that haunts, of the tracing of originary explanations for present misery, structures the characters' preoccupations. For Zek, his wife's preference for his younger brother is a reminder of her preference for another man, Olnel, while they were students in Paris. Both memories are but painful, haunting repetitions of his now-deceased father Malan's clear favouritism of his younger son. For Marie-Hélène, Madou's visit reactivates memories of 'le drame qui avait failli la détruire' (32; 'the drama that had almost killed her', 21), her younger sister Delphine's suicide, which troubles Marie-Hélène with guilt and personal responsibility. The details of the murky and interconnected pasts that these characters share are only gradually revealed. We eventually learn that in Paris during their student days, Delphine, while pregnant with Christophe, had been abandoned by her child's father—her lover Olnel—who had himself fallen in love with her sister Marie-Hélène. When Delphine had discovered the betrayal, she killed herself, leaving behind her infant boy. Olnel fled home to Haiti, and Marie-Hélène soon afterwards married Zek and moved to Africa.

Adopted and raised by Zek as his own, the now adolescent Christophe is tortured by the need to know the real reason for his mother's suicide, which has been hidden from him. Delphine's suicide leaves Christophe with a deep sense of loss and uncertainty, and he believes that recuperation lies in finding out the truth about the circumstances of her death. The loss of the mother coincides with the time of birth, as elsewhere in Condé's oeuvre.[35] Here it is a metaphor for an absence of history that Christophe experiences as an infantilizing obstacle to the formation of his identity: 'Comment devenir un homme quand on ne connaît pas son passé? Quand on ne sait d'où l'on vient?' (38; 'But how can you become a man when you don't know your past? When you don't know where you came from?', 27). Another term in this signifying chain is Christophe's status as an exile, a foreigner in Africa, born of a Guadeloupean mother and a Haitian father; he dreams of travelling to Haiti to seek his roots. Christophe's situation seems to allegorize the predicament of diaspora blacks, while reversing the usual model of Africa as homeland and the Caribbean as place of exile. His quest for the concealed story of his mother's suicide also provides a parallel to the pursuit of the narrative's roots within the text's play of partial hiding and revealing of crucial pieces of the past that inform the characters' present situations.

The relationship of the past to the present is primarily manifested in the characters' feelings of guilt. Marie-Hélène, Zek, and Madou are all weighed down by guilt and knowledge of past wrongdoing. The young Christophe, however, innocent and ignorant of these crimes, seems all the more to carry the burden of these sins on his shoulders. His frustrated search for the cause of his mother's suicide hovers around self-blame. The inheritance of guilt and blame in this novel are important figures for history. Like Francis Sancher in *Traversée* (as we shall see in Chapter 6), Christophe is a Christ-figure in this novel, the sufferer for the adults' past sins which have determined his life and caused his exile.[36]

Alongside Christophe, other references to archetypes abound in the characters' names. Christophe's aunt, adoptive mother, named after the two most important women in Christian and Greek myth—

---

[35] In *La Migration des cœurs* (Paris: Robert Laffont, 1995), *La Vie scélérate* (Paris: Seghers, 1987), *Ségou*, and as I shall discuss in Ch. 5, *Moi, Tituba*.
[36] The character of Christophe also represents an allusion to Henri Christophe, Haitian military leader who established a monarchy in Saint-Domingue in 1807–20. Césaire's play *La Tragédie du roi Christophe* (Paris: Présence africaine, 1963) is based on this legendary figure.

Mary and Helen of Troy—embodies a dangerous combination of innocence and guilt that wreaks havoc in the lives of those around her. The 'immaculate conception' of adoptive motherhood, that renders Marie-Hélène the mother of Christophe, functions as ever-present witness to her role in his real mother's death. The archetypal mother–son pairing evokes an interdependent simultaneity of nurture and treachery, birth and death, sinlessness and guilt.

Like Helen, whose beauty and romantic wrongdoing become the reason for the Trojan War and set off a chain of familial tragedies, Marie-Hélène is guilty by virtue of the seductive power that she wields even when the consequences of romance would be destructive. Marie-Hélène's winning away of her sister's lover and her affair with her husband's brother attest to this. Disastrous seduction is a specifically feminine capability in this text: the topic of Zek's numerous mistresses is treated casually, and his affairs seemingly have no remarkably wounding effects on his family. Like Helen's beauty, Marie-Hélène's loveliness may almost put her beyond blame; Zek blames himself for her unfaithfulness and his love for her does not wane. His and Marie-Hélène's evasive and opaque responses to Christophe's search for answers about Delphine's death leave the boy engaged in a 'Delphic' quest, in which he must wonder how to interpret the vague and enigmatic statements that surely mask a story of crucial importance. With the dead mother Delphine, whose story is obscured yet central to Christophe's sense of his identity, the novel's reference to the Delphic Oracle suggests an overarching paradigm of the search for the mother cum identity quest, the implications of which will become clearer later in my argument.[37]

The presence of archetypes in this novel extends beyond nomenclature to structural aspects of the characters' relationships. We find various parallels to biblical and classical relationships: the sibling rivalry and inequality of Jacob and Esau is repeated in Malan's favouritism of the younger Madou over Zek; Jacob's preference for Rachel over Leah and his marriage to both sisters is repeated in Olnel's romances with the sisters Marie-Hélène and Delphine, and then again in Marie-Hélène's romances with the brothers Zek and

[37] The search for familial stories and their relationship to the identity quest is the central theme of Condé's *La Vie scélérate*, where Coco strives to bring back to memory her family's story over four generations, and *Désirada* (Paris: Robert Laffont, 1997), where Marie-Noëlle uncovers the secrets of her mother and grandmother. The reconstruction of family archive by a young woman in search of her identity is also the central undertaking in Daniel Maximin's *L'Isolé Soleil* (Paris: Seuil, 1981).

Madou. The pairs of siblings also recall the sisters Helen and Clytemnestra, who married the brothers Menelaus and Agamemnon, all members of a cursed family within which crime set off a chain of further crime.[38]

Why this over-abundance of archetypal models? In addition to the repetitions of prior events within the boundaries of the narrative, there is in this text, as I have shown, a whole set of references to events and characters that are not only intertextual, but notably, glaringly, anterior and archetypal in nature. Perhaps these references even go so far as to become self-conscious markers of archetypal reference itself. But why would a text by an Antillean writer about an unhappy family living in Africa abound with archetypal material in this manner? Christophe, the text's allegorical figure for the African diaspora, searches for the key to his identity. Meanwhile, the others also struggle to locate the origins of their present misery, alternating between blaming themselves and wondering to whom and how far back blame can be traced. Still haunted by his father's lack of love, Zek conjectures that he may be paying the price for something that had happened between his father and his mother Sokambi, who herself was the disfavoured of Malan's two wives.

In these repetitions of kinship structures, events, and archetypal models, the text engages in a series of tropological displacements that use the inheriting of guilt and blame to refer from one level of reference to another. Within the narrative frame, guilt is traced through the repetition of structures and events, which also refer outside the narrative to archetypes. The repetition of pre-formed archetypes, in a sense, becomes the fate of the 'guilty' characters. To be guilty is to repeat. The tracing of the origins of guilt is coterminous with the reference to other instances, other levels of duplication, of which the archetype can offer the tease of 'origin'. The search for guilt-roots becomes a process of reference across differences of level, in which the origin is repeatedly displaced and redoubled. The mirrored sibling pairs are themselves markers of this process of redoubling.

In Christophe's positing of Delphine's opaque and unknown story as somehow integral to his own, we can discern a commentary on the quest for origins and identity, which not only likens the quest to a return to archetypes, but in doing so refers to an archetypal site of

---

[38] Although I am not aware of any comments she has made on classical myths in *Saison*, one of the subjects that Condé studied at the Sorbonne was Classics. To my knowledge, critics have not discussed this intertextuality.

opacity, enigma, interpretation, and foretelling. The reference to the Delphic Oracle, however, has yet another working valence of return: that of revenge. We recall that it is in obedience to the Delphic Oracle that Orestes, nephew of Helen, comes out of exile in order to avenge his father Agamemnon's murder, in a family in which an initial curse has made each generation of the house of Atreus come to disaster. Familial crime leads to further crime through the generations until the curse on the house of Atreus is finally expunged with the purification of Orestes.

Saison ends with the revenge killing of Madou by an adolescent guerrilla resistance fighter who is in many ways Christophe's double. The young Victor seeks to avenge the regime's imprisonment, torture, and probable murder of Muti, a matriarchal figure whose name, 'mother', signals her allegorical significance in this political side-story. The two alternating strands of the narrative, the family drama and the political intrigue, finally culminate together in Madou's assassination. It is as if the family narrative of transgenerational haunting is expiated at the moment of revenge, a moment that brings together the personal and the political strands of the novel.

Let us remain for the moment with the familial story. The murder of Madou appears to function as an expiation of familial guilt that weighs on the household. Sokambi's bitter uneasiness toward Marie-Hélène is due to her foreignness and her power over Zek, but above all to her affair with Zek's brother Madou, son of her husband's favoured wife. Sokambi is disturbed and worried that this 'incestuous' crime has been left unpunished by the gods, with Madou instead being rewarded with public success for his transgression of Ngurka codes of conduct:

> Vraiment, les dieux et les ancêtres ne savent pas toujours ce qu'ils font! Madou qui aurait dû être puni de façon spectaculaire, s'était vu attribuer un haut poste ministériel et avait même épousé une des jeunes sœurs du président. (18–19)

> The gods and the ancestors really do make a mess of things! Madou, who should have been given an exemplary punishment, had been appointed to a high ministerial position and had even married one of the President's younger sisters. (8)

Sokambi associates this divine neglect and laxity with a new Africa emasculated by colonialism:

> Cela se serait passé des années plus tôt, avant les Blancs n'imposent leur

mollesse et ne transforment les hommes en femmes à pantalons, on aurait lapidé l'infidèle, exilé le jeune frère incestueux et brûlé la case qui les avait abrités. Au lieu de cela, Zek avait pardonné. (54)

If it had happened years earlier, before the white man had imposed his soft manners and changed the men into trousered women, they would have stoned the infidel, exiled the incestuous young brother and burnt the hut they had used. Instead of which Zek had given his pardon. (41)

There is a sense in which things seem to be the reverse of what they ought to be. Madou ought to be punished, but he is rewarded. The younger brother outshines the older. Marie-Hélène still receives the adoration of her sexually betrayed husband. This reversal—which is eventually *symbolically* set right with Madou's assassination, indeed 'de façon spectaculaire'—is associated with a break with the past, a break that constitutes African independence:

Ah, cette nouvelle société née de l'indépendance! Tout y était sens dessus dessous. Les fils commandaient aux pères, les cadets aux aînés. Même les femmes qui en bien des cas prenaient le pas sur les hommes. (43)

So much for this new society born out of independence! Sons rule their fathers, the younger brothers their older. In many cases even women were taking precedence over men. (31)

On the one hand, independence represents a break with colonialism, but on the other, it is felt by certain characters as an even more severe break with traditional ways of life.[39] Madou, a minister in the newly independent government, represents a new Africa in which the community allows a grave crime to go unchecked.

That crime, of course, is incest. The incest of Marie-Hélène and Madou stands metonymically for a host of related disruptions that Marie-Hélène herself introduces into the ideal of an African past. She is a reminder of the 'contamination' of African ancestry that is the effect of slavery and diaspora: her father-in-law refuses to acknowledge a difference between whites and West Indian blacks. Her foreignness, femaleness, and 'whiteness', then, figure the undermining of African tradition and masculinity. Her incestuous affair with her brother-in-law, which breaks a tribal taboo, is the reason for the family's exile in Rihata, and for the rift between the two brothers. Like Helen, she, a woman, becomes the pretext for a war between

---

[39] This notion is also explored in Condé's play set in the same period, *Mort d'Oluwémi d'Ajumako*, about a Nigerian chief who refuses to commit the ritual suicide expected of him, and is struck dead by a mysterious illness.

men. Incest serves as the symbolic occasion of the breakdown of tradition, a breakdown attested by Zek's forgiveness and abandonment of the tribal, customary practice for dealing with such a crime. As the agent of incest, Marie-Hélène thus becomes the connection between colonialism and the abandonment of tradition: a virtual scapegoat for the destruction of old ways of life. Marie-Hélène's love for the younger brother Madou is very much tied up with his success in the newly independent African political arena, even as she is repulsed by the corrupt dictatorship in which he enjoys success. The younger brother's success in political life is predicated on unpunished incest; the cuckolding of his older brother is the personal counterpart of his precedence over him in the public realm. By extension, the political mess of the new Africa in the wake of independence is born out of the violation of taboos and laws of traditional Africa, and this rupture is uneasily repressed.

Naturally this guilt must be expunged. The incestuous younger brother Madou must be killed 'de façon spectaculaire' in order to abreact the repressed material of the collective psyche. As a result the denouement has the feel and effect of ritual. Madou's thoughts as he is about to be shot signal the text's self-consciousness about this ritual aspect of his murder:

[Victor] en tira un revolver et Madou considéra avec stupeur l'arme bien entretenue, luisante, totalement déplacée dans cette main maigre, encore adolescente. C'était comme s'il se trouvait entraîné dans une pièce de théâtre stupide dont les personnages seraient aussi faux que les situations. (173)

[Victor] drew out a revolver and Madou stared in astonishment at this gleaming, well-oiled gun that seemed totally incongruous in his thin, still adolescent hand. It was as if he had been dragged to a stupid play whose characters were just as false as the situations in which they found themselves. (153)

This sudden focus on theatricality and the fakeness draws attention to the performative role that the murderous moment occupies in the text. Madou's murder functions not merely as a punishment that is finally exacted, but also as the expiation of the familial curse. Madou's punishment for his violation and break with an anterior African life coincides with the expunging of the familial guilt. Tradition, violated and denigrated, itself effects a return, through what one could read as a ritual killing. The various ritual greetings, congratulations, and blessings that are uttered by characters throughout the text are remainders from an African past that seem out of place, and they are disdained by Marie-Hélène:

A ses yeux, toutes les manifestations de la vie communautaire africaine étaient privées de sens, vestiges mécaniques d'un passé dont rien ne subsistait. Elle s'y ennuyait à périr. On y récitait à chaque fois les mêmes salutations. On y poussait les mêmes exclamations. On y répétait les mêmes plaisanteries. On y faisait les mêmes gestes. (192)

In her opinion, all the events of African community life were devoid of meaning and paid lip-service to a past of which nothing was left. She was bored to death. The same greetings were recited every time. The same exclamations were made. The same jokes repeated. The same gestures. (171)

In contrast to the slightly anachronistic, rote, empty quality that the ritual sayings take on as part of the novel's political backdrop, the ritual suddenly regains function in Madou's assassination. As the final expression of a previously denied tribal will, the murder of Madou represents a sudden return of an anterior life, whose rupture has been repressed.

This ritual purification coincides with the birth of a first male child to Marie-Hélène and Zek. Their houseful of daughters had, up to this point, been another one of Sokambi's grievances against Marie-Hélène. It is as if a son can only finally be born to Marie-Hélène when expiation for her crime has occurred. It is as if her previous inability to bear a son is a kind of infertility tied to her incestuous act. Indeed, there has even been some doubt as to the paternity of one of Marie-Hélène's daughters. The birth of the son represents the possibility of a new beginning that can only come with expiation and revenge.

Yet the expectation of a new beginning appears but an ephemeral, momentary tease. If anything, in reality Madou's death actually deflates the family's hopes for renewal, for it was Madou who was to help get Zek a new job so that they could move out of their backwater town. Zek's initial resolution at his son's birth to eschew his bad habits and mediocre ambitions, to start anew, turns into unsatisfied resignation about his never-changing life. Marie-Hélène in mourning can only think of 'toutes ces promesses qui ne seraient jamais tenues. Jamais. Jamais. Jamais' (209; 'All those promises that would never be kept. Never. Never. Never', 186). Sia realizes with a heavy sense of lost potential that her mother, whom she has resented and would earlier have liked to see undermined, 'disait irrévocablement adieu à sa jeunesse, à la possibilité d'être séduite et de commettre des fautes, voire des crimes, de blesser les autres et soi-même' (209; 'was irrevocably saying farewell to her youth, to courtship, to making mistakes—or even committing sin—to inflicting pain, on others and herself', 186).[40]

My final line of enquiry addresses the relationship of the political to the personal histories, quests, desires, and suffering that take centre stage in this novel. As I have suggested, it is Madou's death that finally unifies and partly resolves distinct stories, the family drama and the political story. Yet even as the two faces of the novel are kept somewhat distinct from each other on a narrative level, we have seen how they inform each other throughout. The resurfacing of personal memories that pervades the characters' preoccupations within the narrative takes place during, and is triggered by, the period of Madou's visit on official governmental business, the content of which indirectly leads to his death. What is to be made of the official, political occasion providing the frame for the return of familial traumas, for the repetitions, duplications, and reduplications of archetypal models of guilt that I have shown to structure personal relationships, memories, and the struggle with identities? And what of the way in which both the political and the personal stories are brought to a violently single end?

I have been arguing that the over-abundance and repetition of archetypes—most specifically archetypes that recall the myth of an originary familial curse and of crimes that lead to others—are symptomatic of the deferred search for roots that pervades the character's lives. The roots of present exile and misery, of guilt, of identity, are sought by looking to the past. The lost mother is an organizing point that figures the origin, and she is the site of trauma that must return and be returned to. Madou's assassin, the young Victor, 'était né avec les indépendances et cependant, il n'avait jamais connu que la misère, les injustices et les humiliations' (102). He is compelled to come to Rihata to avenge the capture of the guerrilla movement's matriarch Muti, 'mother'. Hence the loss of the mother comes to organize not only the personal narrative strand as exemplified by Christophe's quest, but also the political story of Victor's revenge. It is at this point, then, that one may be tempted to offer some kind of allegorical reading involving 'mother Africa', her violation in the

---

[40] The disintegration of an Antillean woman in living in Africa with her African husband is also the subject of an Antillean novel of the same period, Warner-Vieyra's *Juletane*. The outlet for the protagonist's alienation is madness, which may also lie in wait for Marie-Hélène.

post-independence African state, and her avenging by the younger Africa reclaiming its 'victorious' moment of independence.

My attention here, however, is rather to whether the text's various uses of archetypes, origins, and the figure of the mother might have something broader to tell us about allegory. The close association of mother and homeland appears in Marie-Hélène's ruminations concerning her own exile from Guadeloupe and how she had looked to Africa as an adoptive mother:

> Retourner à la Guadeloupe ne signifiait guère pour Marie-Hélène que retourner vers sa mère. L'île et la mère était la même chose, utérus clos dans lequel blottir sa souffrance, yeux fermé, apaisée par la pulsation du sang. Mais la mère était morte. Alors la douleur de l'avoir perdu à jamais, de n'avoir même pas assisté à ses derniers moments, se changeait en haine de l'île, à présent stérile, matrice désertée qui n'envelopperait plus de foetus. Restait l'Afrique, mère aussi, proche par l'espoir et l'imaginaire. (77)[41]

Returning to Guadeloupe had meant little more for Marie-Hélène than going back to her mother. The island had symbolised one thing: her mother; a womb in which she could retreat from her suffering, eyes closed, fists clenched, soothed by the throbbing blood circulating round her. But her mother was dead. The grief of having lost her for ever, of not having been near at the last moment, had made her hate the island and it had become like a sterile womb, never to nurture a foetus again. So Africa, Mother Africa, had appealed to her imagination and raised her expectations. (63)

Through the quests of the characters Christophe and Victor, the mother—whether allegorizing Guadeloupe or Africa, whether in the play of distance and longing or in the mourning of the destruction of an anterior state—is the lost object in need of recuperation, and short of that, substitution. On the verge of death, Madou's last thoughts are about a return to the mother's body:

> Il reposait dans le ventre de sa mère, loin des bruits et de la fureur que cet attentat déclenchait. Depuis longtemps il n'avait pas connu cette paix, cette douceur. C'était le retour au temps d'avant l'enfance, d'avant la création du monde, d'avant les désirs et le péché. C'était l'Eden... (178)

He was lying in his mother's womb, far from the sound and the fury that the assassination attempt had triggered. He had not experienced such peace and quiet for a long time. He had returned to a time before childhood, before the creation of the world, before desire and sin. It was Eden. (158)

---

[41] The connection of the imagined return to the maternal womb and death recurs throughout Condé's oeuvre: see e.g. her play *Pension Les Alizés* (Paris: Mercure de France, 1988), 85; *Pays mêlé* (Paris: Hatier, 1985), 74; *Traversée de la Mangrove* (Mercure de France, 1989), 163. See my discussion of *Moi, Tituba* in Ch. 5.

That Madou's death, which I have argued is in effect a punishment for the rupture with an anterior life, is also presented as a return to the womb, to Eden, may speak to the relationship between the political and the personal, which are unified in this resolution. The sheer proximity in this resolution, of the 'return of the repressed' in the form of ritual punishment, to the desired return to the mother's body, is suggestive. The personal and the political—familial miseries and the horrors of post-independence Africa—are figured as having the same traumatic root. The political frame becomes the occasion for the return of personal ghosts because they are symptomatic of the same rupture.

Incest, the loss of the mother, African independence, diaspora, exile: all point to and articulate together a quasi-mystical, Fall-like break that may be the precondition for any notion of a relationship of reference between the personal and the political. That a novel set in a troubled African society in the direct aftermath of independence—in a state that is struggling to negotiate between old and new, that is unnamed and inescapably allegorical or representative—should evince such an obsession with original sin and the transgression of taboo can be understood through Derrida's reading of the prohibition of incest, 'loi sacrée entre toutes', as the foundation of all social order:[42]

> La société, la langage, l'histoire, l'articulation, en un mot la supplémentarité naissent donc en même temps que la prohibition de l'inceste. Celle-ci est la brisure entre la nature et la culture. . . . L'âge des signes d'institution, l'époque du rapport conventionnel entre le représentant et son représenté appartient au temps de cet interdit.[43]

> Society, language, history, articulation, in a word supplementarity, are born at the same time as the prohibition of incest. This last is the hinge [brisure] between nature and culture. . . . The age of the signs of the institution, the epoch of the conventional relationships between the representer and its represented belongs to the time of this interdict.[44]

The traumatic root may then be seen as precisely the moment of the interdict that establishes the rupture that makes society, representation, and history possible. In the wake of a break that reinstitutes the necessity and possibility of history and writing, Condé's post-

---

[42] Jacques Derrida, *De la grammatologie* (Paris: Minuit, 1967), 374.
[43] Ibid. 375.
[44] Id., *Of Grammatology*, trans. Gayatri Chakravorty Spivak (Baltimore: Johns Hopkins University Press, 1976), 265.

independence Africa becomes the stage for the enactment of anxieties about discontinuity through the preoccupation with origins, most prominent among them the incest taboo and the mother. Derrida points to the paradoxical relationship between the point of rupture and origin:

> Le déplacement du rapport à la mère, à la nature, à l'être comme au signifié fondamental, telle est certes l'origine de la société et des langues. Mais peut-on désormais parler d'origine? Le concept d'origine, ou de signifié fondamental, est-il autre chose qu'une fonction, indispensable mais située, inscrite, dans le système de signification inauguré par l'interdit?[45]

> The displacing of the relationship with the mother, with nature, with being as the fundamental signified, such indeed is the origin of society and languages. But can one speak of origins after that? Is the concept of origin or of the fundamental signified, anything but a function, indispensable but situated, inscribed, within the system of signification inaugurated by the interdict?[46]

What makes the concept of origin possible is the rupture. An important function of the interdict is to establish a 'before' and an 'after' the interdict, a point that is the basis for the 'post-' in 'postcolonial'. The question of roots, as Derrida suggests, expresses a nostalgia that is a function of the discontinuity. It is a question that can only appear when it has already become impossible.

> On est toujours en-deçà ou au-delà de la limite, de la fête, de l'origine de la société, de ce présent dans lequel simultanément l'interdit se donne(rait) avec la transgression: ce qui (se) passe toujours et (pourtant) n'a *proprement* jamais lieu. C'est toujours *comme si* j'avais commis un inceste.
> Cette naissance *de la société* n'est donc pas un passage, c'est bien un point, une limite pure, fictive et instable, insaisissable. On la franchit en l'atteignant. En elle la société s'entame et se diffère. En commençant, elle commence à se dégrader.[47]

> We are always short of or beyond the limit of the festival, of the origin of society, of that present within which simultaneously the interdict is (would be) given with the transgression: that which passes (comes to pass) always and (yet) never *properly* takes place. It is always *as if* I had committed incest.
> This *birth of society* is therefore not a passage, it is a point, a pure, fictive and unstable, ungraspable limit. One crosses it in attaining it. In it society is broached and is deferred from itself. Beginning, it begins to decay.[48]

[45] Id., *De la grammatologie*, 376.
[46] Id., *Of Grammatology*, 266.
[47] Id., *De la grammatologie*, 377.
[48] Id., *Of Grammatology*, 267.

The pervasive presence of past sin and guilt in *Saison* may have to do with this paradoxical point at which a new society is born. This point implicates everyone in the transgression of the law that could never have been transgressed. This point, which makes possible the fact of being 'post-independence' or 'postcolonial', is the would-be destination of the nostalgia and guilt that are ways of gesturing toward the breach that both establishes a beginning and defers it. In this context, then, the 'personal' and the 'political', as another version of the two sides of the divide, also become terms that designate a decay that the new beginning entails. What comes into focus in the moment of being postcolonial is also the now possible condition of asking what becomes the impossible question of allegory.

5

ALLEGORY, SORCERY, AND HISTORICAL REWRITING: *MOI, TITUBA, SORCIÈRE . . . NOIRE DE SALEM*

In this chapter, I address Condé's most widely-read and perhaps most ambitious work, a historical fiction which addresses ideas of origin, discontinuity, exile, and return, within a powerful allegorical framework provided by sorcery. Gayatri Spivak reminds us that 'the general mode for the post-colonial is citation, re-inscription, re-routing the historical'.[1] *Moi, Tituba, sorcière . . . Noire de Salem* (1986) presents a counter-history that seeks to fill the gap in history produced by the displacement of slavery and by the recording of history from the colonizing perspective.[2] The Salem witch trials of 1692–3 provide the historical frame for this novel, which rewrites the life of Tituba, a slave from Barbados who was accused of witchcraft. This chapter examines the relationship between allegorical and historical rewriting, in order to explore how sorcery's allegorical ways of knowing and telling illuminate the possibility of historical truth refracted through a 'vérité du délire'.[3] I shall suggest in what follows that the relationship of psychoanalytic modes of knowledge to modernity has a resonant analogue in the relationship of Tituba's sorcery to postcoloniality.

ORIGINS AND DISCONTINUITY

Maryse Condé's novel *Moi, Tituba* presents a useful occasion for the investigation of postcolonial allegory. It is not difficult to make a case for the allegorical relationship between the story of Tituba, a black slave from Barbados accused and convicted of witchcraft in the Salem witch trials, and Maryse Condé, postcolonial writer. This reading is imposed upon the reader even before the book is opened. The layout of the cover of the first edition, published by Mercure de

[1] 'Reading *The Satanic Verses*', *Third Text*, 11 (1990), 41–60: 41.
[2] Maryse Condé, *Moi, Tituba, sorcière . . . Noire de Salem* (Paris: Mercure de France, 1986). All references will be given in the text.
[3] Jacques Derrida, *Mal d'Archive: Une impression freudienne* (Paris: Galilée, 1995), 136.

France, produces a telling juxtaposition of the title and the author's name. The words '*Moi, Tituba, sorcière*' are printed in white, framed in between 'Maryse Condé' above, and '*Noire de Salem*' below, both printed in orange. As one critic has noted, the visual correspondence between 'Maryse Condé' and '*Noire de Salem*'—which together form a frame for *Moi, Tituba, sorcière*—endorses an equivalence between the black woman author and the eponymous black woman title-character.[4]

This visualization is perhaps a 'paratextual device' that 'prefigures' Condé's epigraph:[5] 'Tituba et moi, avons vécu en étroite intimité pendant un an. C'est au cours de nos interminables conversations qu'elle m'a dit ces choses qu'elle n'avait confiées à personne. Maryse Condé' ('Tituba and I lived on the closest of terms. During our endless conversations, she told me things she had confided to nobody else.').[6] The writer presents herself as listener and transcriber of the true story that is to follow.[7] This language appears to arrange a relationship of reciprocity and identification between Condé and Tituba: it is not merely that Condé tells Tituba's story, but that the novel arises out of a mutual exchange in which Condé's novel is the written counterpart of Tituba's oral narrative. By implicit extension, an equivalence between Tituba the witch in the fictional frame and Condé the writer is suggested. Through the confluence of cover and epigraph, the allegorical relation between Condé's realm of writing and Tituba's realm of sorcery is suggested pre-emptively.

Condé responds to an absence of historical archive in telling Tituba's previously marginalized, excluded story. Because the authorial first person of the epigraph gives way to Tituba's autobiographical first person in the main text, several critics have interpreted the epigraph as 'showing clearly the shift of power and speech from Condé's side to Tituba's'.[8] This withdrawal of authorial power, it is

[4] Lillian Manzor-Coats, 'Of Witches and Other Things: Maryse Condé's Challenges to Feminist Discourse', *World Literature Today*, 67/4 (1993), 737–44: 737.
[5] Ibid.
[6] Maryse Condé, *I, Tituba, Black Witch of Salem*, trans. Richard Philcox (Charlottesville, Va.: University Press of Virginia, 1992). All references will be given in the text.
[7] This epigraph winks at the tradition of the African-American slave narrative, in which an epigraph or other external source typically vouches for the story's authenticity.
[8] Elisabeth Mudimbe-Boyi, 'Giving a Voice to Tituba: The Death of the Author?', *World Literature Today*, 67/4 (1993), 751–6: 752. 'With the epigraph, Condé excises herself from the text that follows, . . . effacing herself and leaving the entire textual space and a full voice to her character. In textualizing Tituba as an "I", a subject, the writer withdraws her own authority from the narrative' (751).

argued, is a self-effacement that allows Tituba's voice to arise.[9] The epigraph's supposed transfer of authority, authorship, and authenticity raises the question of the supposed empowerment of the formerly voiceless Tituba and voluntary self-erasure of Condé. The celebratory critical emphasis on the process of giving Tituba a 'full voice' that 'restores her to history'[10] invites analytic pressure in terms that Gayatri Spivak has made familiar through her seminal discussion of the possibility of speaking of and for 'the historically muted subject of the subaltern woman' in the context of postcolonial Indian historiography.[11] If Condé's project is one of 'letting Tituba speak',[12] we might ask, with what 'voice-consciousness'[13] can Tituba speak?

Elisabeth Mudimbe-Boyi places enthused emphasis on Condé's unveiling of the 'power and presence', and the preservation of the 'integrity and authenticity', of Tituba's voice.[14] In her view, this is enabled by Condé's ceding of authorial control directly to Tituba.[15] Spivak's critique of the project of recovering the subaltern warns against the nostalgic 'assumption that there *is* a pure form of consciousness' to be retrieved.[16] Before celebrating the 'victory over voicelessness and erasure'[17] purportedly proclaimed by the author's giving up of the textual space to the historically voiceless Tituba, we might reflect on Spivak's observation that 'the subject of exploitation cannot know and speak the text of female exploitation, even if the absurdity of the nonrepresenting intellectual making space for her to speak is achieved'.[18] The grasping of the subaltern voice-consciousness is the product of an appropriation and reinscription of an Other whose subjectivity is 'irretrievably heterogeneous'.[19]

[9] 'Through this signed epigraph, Condé establishes the authority of Tituba's voice, which narrates the rest of the fictional autobiography in the first person, by destabilizing Condé's own authorial position' (Manzor-Coats, 'Of Witches and Other Things', 737).
[10] Mudimbe-Boyi, 'Giving a Voice to Tituba', 753.
[11] 'Can the Subaltern Speak?', 295.
[12] Mudimbe-Boyi, 'Giving a Voice to Tituba', 751.
[13] Spivak, 'Can the Subaltern Speak?', 285.
[14] 'Giving a Voice to Tituba', 752. On the importance of 'voice', see also Carole Boyce Davies and Elaine Savory Fido, 'Introduction: Women and Literature in the Caribbean: An Overview', in eid. (eds.), *Out of the Kumbla: Caribbean Women and Literature* (Trenton: African World, 1990), 1–24: 1: 'The concept of voicelessness necessarily informs any discussion of Caribbean women and literature.'
[15] Mudimbe-Boyi goes so far as to state that Condé 'giv[es] up her position of power as a member of the ruling class, only to become what Antonio Gramsci characterizes as a subaltern' ('Giving a Voice to Tituba', 752)
[16] 'Can the Subaltern Speak?', 286.
[17] Mudimbe Boyi, 'Giving a Voice to Tituba', 756.
[18] 'Can the Subaltern Speak?', 288.
[19] Ibid. 284.

If the epigraph establishes authority, it is not through the author's destabilization. Just as the cover's layout instructs the reader to read the identity of 'Moi, Tituba, sorcière' in light of the author's surrounding persona, the epigraph, I would argue, constitutes an assertion of authorial presence and power rather than an act of absenting and self-disempowerment. It is an imposition of Condé's authorial presence ('moi') where otherwise we would proceed directly to the first-person narrative of ('Moi') Tituba. Enacting a shift of the identity of 'moi' from the title's Tituba to Condé, the epigraph's equivalence and identification between 'Tituba et moi' suggests that Tituba's story be read as a proxy for the author's. The authorial absention is in effect an appropriation of Tituba's voice to stand for the 'absent' author. As Spivak observes about 'people whose consciousness we cannot grasp', 'to confront them is not to represent (*vertreten*) them but to learn to represent (*darstellen*) ourselves'.[20] It is effectively Tituba who is absented through the epigraph and the author who represents, is represented, and becomes representative.

The epigraph tells us of Condé's privileged access and indispensable role ('elle m'a dit ces choses qu'elle n'avait confiées à personne'). In dividing Tituba's oral from Condé's written word, the epigraph suggests that the 'shift of power and speech' that gives voice to Tituba and makes possible the telling of her previously untold story coincides with a process of making Tituba and her story refer allegorically.[21] Angela Davis takes up and applies the allegorical status of Tituba's story to the situation of blacks in America: 'Tituba looked for her story in the history of the Salem witch trials and could not find it. I have looked for my history in the story of the colonization of this continent and I have found silences, omissions, distortions, and fleeting, enigmatic insinuations.'[22] The silences and omissions themselves take on a representative, allegorical character. Bringing Tituba's voice out of silence, it seems, is a matter of allegory, a matter of speaking otherwise.

This play of authorial presence/absence and empowerment/disempowerment, casts light on the violence of the opening sentences of the novel:

Abena, ma mère, un marin anglais la viola sur le pont du Christ the King,

---

[20] 'Can the Subaltern Speak?', 288.
[21] 'Tituba, in reconstructing one individual's story, also allegorizes the collective history of the Caribbean' (Mudimbe-Boyi, 'Giving a Voice to Tituba', 755).
[22] Foreword to Condé, *I, Tituba, Black Witch of Salem*, p. xi.

ALLEGORY, SORCERY, HISTORICAL REWRITING 121

un jour de 16** alors que le navire faisait voile vers la Barbade. C'est de cette agression que je suis née. De cet acte de haine et de mépris. (15) Abena, my mother, was raped by an English sailor on the deck of Christ the King one day in the year 16**, while the ship was sailing for Barbados. I was born from this act of aggression. From this act of hatred and contempt. (3)

The beginning—of the story, Tituba's origin—is constituted by an act of rape on a slave ship during the middle passage. The image is explicitly emblematic: 'l'humiliation de cette enfant symbolisait celle de tout son peuple, défait, dispersé, vendu à l'encan' (17; 'this child's humiliation symbolized the condition of his entire people: defeated, dispersed, and auctioned off', 5). Consider the initial ambiguity and confusion about the subject in the first sentence. We are initially under the impression that Abena is the subject. The next few words leave the reader hanging and offer several candidates for the subject: 'Abena, ma mère, un marin anglais'. It is only with the words 'la viola' that the reader suddenly understands what is occurring. In the process of shifting from subject to object in this sentence, Abena is raped: the process of grammatical decoding coincides with her rape. In this sentence, the withdrawal of Abena's status as subject on the level of grammar functions as the linguistic enactment of rape.

What is the significance of rape *as* a violent appropriation of subjectivity and a beginning? Abena's subjectivity gives way to the rapist's in what we can indeed call a shift of power and speech. The extremity of sexual violence demonstrates the shift achieved with grammar. The story and Tituba are born of 'cette agression', which is both grammatical and physical. Using this lens to reread Condé's epigraph reveals a similar move from cover to epigraph: 'Tituba et moi, avons vécu en étroite intimité pendant un an. C'est au cours de nos interminables conversations qu'elle m'a dit ces choses qu'elle n'avait confiées à personne.' Tituba's self-proclaiming 'Moi, Tituba' of the title becomes, in the epigraph, 'Tituba et moi'. The subject shifts from explicit 'moi' to the implied 'nous'. The first-person plural claims Tituba's subjectivity as part of a 'nous' that articulates a relationship of differential power.

Presence and absence map on to a relationship of allegorical reference, as one subject is appropriated to stand for the other. The result of the manipulation of subjectivity here is not the equality that the 'nous' at first seems to imply; rather a shift of subject coincides with a shift of power. What the epigraph shares with the opening sentence of the novel is impregnation: the 'étroite intimité', possibly a relationship of lovers, over the approximate period of carrying a child, or writing this novel. Condé even claims privileged access by subtly evoking the exclusivity of sexual conquest: 'elle m'a dit ces choses qu'elle n'avait confiées à personne'. If the opening sentence of the novel is an explicit instance of sexual violence, the epigraph's 'étroite intimité' is a more subtle act of possession out of which this novel is born. It is of course possible to read the authorial legitimacy that is at stake in the epigraph as a question of impregnation or 'possession' by Tituba's spirit, in keeping with the relationship to ancestral spirits and the supernatural that is present in the fictional narrative. Condé has spoken of the references to spirits and the occult in *Moi, Tituba* as ironic pastiche of the black female heroic novel.[23] The importance of the notion of supernatural 'possession' to a postcolonial writer's project will become clearer in what follows.

SORCERY AND FIGURES

The violent instance of the mother ('Abena, ma mère' and Tituba as Condé's spiritual mother) being made absent constitutes the beginning and enables birth. After giving birth to Tituba, Abena dies very shortly, only a few pages later. In effect, the death of the mother gives birth to the story. Although Tituba is born of rape by a white man, Yao, a slave and Abena's lover, adopts Tituba as his own. Yao also gives Tituba her name, not an Ashanti name but an invented one: 'Sans doute, Yao en l'inventant, voulait-il prouver que j'étais fille de sa volonté et de son imagination. Fille de son amour' (19; 'Yao probably invented it to prove that I was the daughter of his will and imagination. Daughter of his love', 6). This act is the first assertion of imaginary parentage and lineage, made necessary by the trauma of rape.[24]

When Abena is hanged for fighting off the master's sexual advances, Tituba is adopted and raised by Man Yaya, an old woman who teaches her the art of sorcery. The death of the mother and the consequent adoptive parentage is an important point of departure

---

[23] See Pfaff, *Entretiens*, 90; Ann Scarboro, Afterword to *I, Tituba, Black Witch of Salem*, 175–225: 212.
[24] Rape also figures importantly in Simone Schwarz-Bart's representation of women's exploitation in the cane-fields in her novel *Pluie et vent sur Télumée Miracle* (Paris: Seuil, 1972).

for Tituba's creative trajectory. Compare the following passages, the first taking place before and the second after Abena's death:

Les premières années de ma vie furent sans histoires. Je fus un beau bébé, joufflu, car le lait de ma mère me réussissait bien. Puis j'appris à parler, à marcher. Je découvris le triste et cependant splendide univers autour de moi. Les cases de boue séchée, sombres contre le ciel démesuré, l'involontaire parure des plantes et des arbres, la mer et son âpre chant de liberté. (19)

The first years of my life were spent peacefully. I was a beautiful baby, and my mother's milk did wonders for me. Then I learned to talk and walk. I discovered the sad, yet wonderful universe around me. The slave cabins made of dried mud, silhouetted against the huge sky, the haphazard arrangement of plants and trees, the sea and its bitter song of freedom. (6)

Man Yaya m'apprit les plantes.
Celles qui donnent le sommeil. Celles qui guérissent plaies et ulcères.
Celles qui font avouer les voleurs.
Celles qui calment les épileptiques et les plongent dans un bienheureux repos. Celles qui mettent sur les lèvres des furieux, des désespérés et des suicidaires des paroles d'espoir.
Man Yaya m'apprit à écouter le vent quand il se lève et mesure ses forces au-dessus des cases qu'il se prépare à broyer.
Man Yaya m'apprit la mer. Les montagnes et les mornes. (23)

Mama Yaya taught me about herbs. Those for inducing sleep. Those for healing wounds and ulcers. Those for loosening the tongues of thieves. Those that calm epileptics and plunge them into blissful rest. Those that put words of hope on the lips of the angry, the desperate, and the suicidal.
Mama Yaya taught me to listen to the wind rising and to measure its force as it swirled above the cabins it had the power to crush.
Mama Yaya taught me the sea, the mountains, and the hills. (9)

Sorcery is born out of the loss of Tituba's mother: Tituba learns the craft from her adoptive mother. Man Yaya herself cultivates the art in response to the loss of her family, also a result of the cruelty of whites. She finds in sorcery an alternative to an order imposed by the structure of domination: 'En réalité, elle avait à peine les pieds sur notre terre et vivait constamment dans leur compagnie, ayant cultivé à l'extrême le don de communiquer avec les invisibles' (22; 'In fact, she was hardly of this world and lived constantly in their company. She had cultivated to a fine art the ability to communicate with the invisible', 9). When sorcery appears for the first time in the novel, it is explicitly presented as a process of rereading and transformation. Man Yaya teaches Tituba a systematic reinterpretation and reordering of the world around her. The phenomena of nature, which before seemed to Tituba unmotivated, are now assigned meanings according to how they can be used to cure and to bring comfort. In Man Yaya's division of 'notre terre' and 'les invisibles', the realm of the invisible is the realm of an alternative set of meanings to the power of the colonizer: 'Que l'homme n'est pas un maître parcourant à cheval son royaume' (23; 'That man is not the master riding through his kingdom on horseback', 9). When Man Yaya teaches Tituba what is to be gleaned from plants, the wind, and the sea, it is an education in the figurative reading of the world.[25] At the end of the novel, this figurative function becomes more evident when Tituba teaches sorcery to her own adopted daughter:

Je lui révèle les secrets permis, la force cachée des plantes et le langage des animaux. Je lui apprends à découvrir la forme invisible du monde, le réseau de communications qui le parcourt et les signes-symboles. (270)

I tell her the secrets I'm allowed to share, the hidden power of herbs and the language of animals. I teach her to look for the invisible shapes in the world, the crisscross of communications, and the signs and the symbols. (177)

The world is a network of sign-symbols that must be read figuratively in order to reveal the deeper, hidden 'forme invisible du monde', and sorcery is the art that engages that reading.

Tituba's first years are characterized as 'sans histoires' (19). Sorcery supplements a lack through rewriting.[26] Yao feels this lack when he turns toward the sea and sees in it the hope of returning to Africa: 'Yao tournait mon visage vers le large et me murmurait à l'oreille: —Un jour, nous serons libres et nous volerons de toutes nos ailes vers notre pays d'origine' (19; 'Yao turned my face toward the open sea and whispered in my ear: "One day we shall be free and we shall fly back to the country we came from"', 6). In Tituba's education in the meaning of the sea ('Man Yaya m'apprit la mer'), the healing and transformative functions of sorcery suggest the effort to respond to and recuperate a loss. The loss of the 'pays d'origine', the

---

[25] Recall the lines, 'cette ville plate ... en rupture de faune et de flore', in Cesaire, *Cahier*, 72. Man Yaya's teaching of the natural phenomena can be seen as a passing on of 'techniques d'existence' (Glissant, *Discours*, 29) that make possible the 'prise en compte de la terre nouvelle' (ibid. 31).

[26] The notion of the construction of history through magic is central to Glissant's *Le Quatrième Siècle* (Paris: Seuil, 1964). Tituba's other major Antillean antecedent is the *sorcier* of Césaire's *Cahier*, 116: 'donnez-moi la foi sauvage du sorcier | donnez à mes mains puissance de modeler | donnez à mon âme la trempe de l'épée'.

death of the mother, and the absence of history all constitute versions of the lack that makes both possible and necessary the cultivation of Tituba's sorcery, her entry into the symbolic order.[27]

If sorcery is figurative rereading and rewriting, it is simultaneously a site of the possibility of textual ambiguity, of the multiplicity of interpretations, and of systematic misreading and misnaming. In all of the instances in which Tituba is accused of being a 'sorcière'— by John Indien, Susannah Endicott, the people of Salem, and Christopher—she feels that she is misunderstood, that the word is 'mal interpreté' (101). Christopher asks: 'Es-tu sorcière? Oui ou non?' ('Are you a witch? . . . Yes or no!'). She responds: 'Chacun donne à ce mot une signification différente. Chacun croit pouvoir façonner la sorcière à sa manière afin qu'elle satisfasse ses ambitions, ses rêves, ses désirs . . .' (226; 'Everyone gives that word a different meaning. Everyone believes he can fashion a witch to his way of thinking so that she will satisfy his ambitions, dreams, and desires', 146). Thus sorcery becomes an incarnation of the instability of figures; this indeterminacy coincides with the functioning of 'sorcière' as the repository of various peoples' and communities' anxieties, fears, and desires. The Salem trials of 1692–3 lend themselves to interpretation as an outstanding historical event during which the figure of the witch became such a repository of Puritan society's repressed fears,[28] causing women to become scapegoats and martyrs.[29]

Jules Michelet's 1862 text *La Sorcière* explores a theory of witches in Europe as both victims of and rebels against religious and patriarchal authority. Michelet reads the burning of witches for their collusion with nature as punishment for and expression of anxieties about women's uncontainable transgressive potential vis-à-vis masculine

---

[27] My analysis here is informed by the Lacanian notion of death as intrinsic to the transition from the Imaginary to the Symbolic order and the notion of that transition as a kind of trauma. See esp. Jacques Lacan, 'Fonction et champ de la parole et du langage en psychanalyse', in *Écrits* (Paris: Seuil, 1966), 237–322 and 'Tuché et automaton', in *Le Séminaire*, bk. xi. *Les Quatre Concepts fondamentaux de la psychanalyse*, ed. Jacques-Alain Miller (Paris: Seuil, 1973), 53–62.

[28] For useful accounts, see Elaine G. Breslaw, *Tituba, Reluctant Witch of Salem: Devilish Indians and Puritan Fantasies* (New York: New York University Press, 1996); Winfried Nevins, *Witchcraft in Salem Village in 1692: Together with Some Accounts of Other Witchcraft Prosecution in New England and Elsewhere* (Boston: Lee and Shepard, 1982); Bernard Rosenthal, *Salem Story: Reading the Witch Trials of 1692* (Cambridge: Cambridge University Press, 1993).

[29] Arthur Miller's *The Crucible* (New York: Viking, 1953), also based on the Salem trials, is an allegory for the hysteria of the McCarthy era, during which anxieties about communism were manifested in the witch-hunts of the 1950s.

systems (the Church, medical science, sexual norms).[30] The witch in Michelet embodies an excessive craving threatening to break loose.[31] The witch conceives Nature and cannot be contained within culture. Drawing upon Michelet, feminist mythology has given a central place to the witch, who has become an important icon of female subversion on the basis of her combination of dangerous appetite, forbidden knowledge, and powerful acts.[32] The witch, at once cruelly victimized by, and wildly free of, repressive authority, is an embodiment of the contradictions of femaleness, and of the dangerous elements on whose repression social order depends: 'Innocente, folle, pleine de souvenirs mal remémorés, coupable de fautes inconnues' ('She is innocent, mad, full of badly remembered memories, guilty of unknown wrongs').[33] The witch's extremity and excess of appetite overstep acceptable boundaries, threatening the stability of the symbolic system in place:

Les sociétés ne parviennent pas à offrir à tous la même insertion dans l'ordre symbolique; ceux qui sont, si l'on peut dire, entre les systèmes symboliques, dans les interstices, hors-jeu, ceux-là sont affligés d'une dangereuse mobilité symbolique. Dangereuse pour eux, puisque c'est cela qu'on appelle folie, anomalie, perversion. . . . Et, plus que tous ceux-là, les femmes incarnent bizarrement ce groupe d'anomalies qui montre les failles d'un système d'ensemble.[34]

Societies do not succeed in offering everyone the same way of fitting into the symbolic order; those who are, if one may say so, between symbolic systems, in the interstices, offside, are the ones who are afflicted with a dangerous

[30] For a historical orientation of witchcraft in Europe, see Robin Briggs, *Witches and Neighbours: The Social and Cultural Context of European Witchcraft* (London: Harper Collins, 1996).
[31] 'Elle a une *envie* de femme. Envie de quoi? Mais du Tout, du grand Tout universel. Satan n'a pas prévu cela, qu'on ne pouvait l'apaiser avec aucune créature. . . . A ce désir profond, vaste comme une mer, elle succombe, elle sommeille, . . . elle a rêvé. . . . C'est que le monstre merveilleux de la vie universelle chez elle s'était englouti; que désormais vie et mort, tout tenait dans ses entrailles, et qu'au prix de tant de douleurs elle avait conçu la Nature' (Jules Michelet, *La Sorcière: Nouvelle édition critique avec introduction, variantes et examen du manuscrit*, ed. Walterus Kusters (Nijmegen: Kusters, 1989), 192.
[32] According to Marguerite Duras, Michelet's *La Sorcière* is 'a text that has been assimilated by many new French feminist writers, particularly Clément and Gauthier. It is part of their canon'. See Isabella Courtivron and Elaine Marks (eds.), *New French Feminisms: An Anthology*, (Sussex: Harvester Press, 1981), 175. Xavière Gauthier created a feminist literary review in 1976 called *Sorcières*. See her essay in the first issue, 'Why Witches?', trans. Erica M. Eisinger, in Courtivron and Marks (eds.), *New French Feminism*, 199–203.
[33] Hélène Cixous and Catherine Clément, *La Jeune Née* (Paris: Union générale d'éditions, 1975), 14; trans. Betsey Wing as *The Newly Born Woman* (Theory and History of Literature, 24; Minneapolis: University of Minnesota Press, 1986), 6.
[34] Cixous and Clément, *La Jeune Née*, 17–18.

symbolic mobility. Dangerous for them, because those are the people afflicted with what we call madness, anomaly, perversion. . . . And more than any others, women bizarrely embody this group of anomalies showing the cracks in an overall system.[35]

The repeated misdefinitions of the word 'sorcière' by men in *Moi, Tituba* suggest that Tituba's own threatening uncontainability and transgression—as an orphan living outside the plantation system in Barbados, as a black woman slave in Salem—are manifested in the very indeterminacy of signification itself.[36]

The witch as a political and poetic figure in Condé's literary project, embodies an appetitive transgression, on the part of the colonized subject. Tituba's sorcery, which includes memories of European witchcraft and its location within Christianity, also recalls elements of African religions' transgression with regard to Christianity and European colonialism. Condé writes in *La Parole des femmes:*

Les esclaves arrivaient aux Antilles avec tout un tissu de croyances et de pratiques qui tant bien que mal s'intégraient à la religion catholique imposée. En Haïti, cela donne le vodou. Dans les petites Antilles, le quimbois. . . . L'Antillais, si catéchisé qu'il soit, garde au fond de lui le besoin d'une approche du surnaturel qui ne soit pas celle qu'édicte la religion officielle.[37]

Consisting of animistic practices such as communication with ancestors' spirits, the use of herbs to cure, and magic spells, Tituba's *Détour*-like sorcery contains Caribbean traces of African traditional practices.[38] Sorcery becomes an allegory for Condé's project by bringing to light a notion of writing or rewriting as transgression, an exploration of new kinds of appetite and appropriateness, with a power of absorption raging beyond the symbolic confines set by the colonizer. *Moi, Tituba* constitutes a rereading and a rewriting 'in the interstices' of received historical narrative, which is mostly characterized by Tituba's absence from the accounts of an event in which she was central. Her only mention in the historical archives reads, according to Condé: 'Tituba, une esclave de la Barbade et prati-

[35] *Newly Born Woman,* 7.
[36] I also read the pointedness with which the text insists on Tituba's immense sexual appetite as a version of her transgression of acceptable symbolic boundaries.
[37] *La Parole des femmes: Essai sur des romancières des Antilles de langue française* (Paris: Harmattan, 1979; repr. 1993), 48–9.
[38] On practices of magic in the French Caribbean, see Simonne Henry-Valmore, *Dieux en exil* (Paris: Gallimard, 1988).

quant vraisemblablement le hodoo' (231; 'Tituba, a slave originating from the West Indies and probably practicing "hoodoo"', 149). Condé's project of writing the history of Tituba is allegorized by Tituba's sorcery, and in turn shows writing to be the allegorical rewriting of symbolic boundaries.

EXILES

While Yao looks to Africa as utopian origin, Tituba's utopia is Barbados itself in the wake of her real and adoptive mothers' deaths. The narrative is aware that she is about to lose her home: 'Je m'en aperçois aujourd'hui, ce furent les moments les plus heureux de ma vie. Je n'étais jamais seule puisque mes invisibles étaient autour de moi, sans jamais cependant m'oppresser de leur présence' (25; 'Today I realize that these were the happiest moments of my life. I was never alone, because my invisible spirits were all around me, yet they never oppressed me with their presence', 11). It is after the death of her parents that Tituba is happiest, when they are around her in invisible form.[39] Tituba's utopia already depends upon a distance from origins. At the same time, however, it is characterized by a unity with nature.

The loss of the blissful state immediately following her mother's death precedes Tituba's initiation into heterosexual love. When Tituba meets John Indien and asks her parents' spirits to make him fall in love with her, her mother sighs, 'Pourquoi les femmes ne peuvent-elles se passer des hommes? Voilà que tu vas être entraînée de l'autre coté de l'eau' (33; 'Why can't women do without men? ... Now you're going to be dragged off to the other side of the water', 15). Tituba's desire for John Indien is juxtaposed with the idea of crossing. The trope of crossing and of consequent exile, which will become Tituba's central preoccupation, has heterosexuality as its first referent. Tituba's love for John Indien prefigures later exile from her island home. This association arises because the pivotal moment of meeting John Indien changes everything for Tituba, beginning with the way she sees her utopian home: 'Pour la première fois, je vis ce lieu qui m'avait servi d'abri et il me parut sinistre' (31; 'I saw the

---

[39] The theme of the supernatural is explored in many Antillean novels, including Condé, *La Vie scélérate*, (Paris: Sehers, 1987); Gisèle Pineau, *La Grande Drive des esprits* (Paris: Le Serpent à plumes, 1993); Chamoiseau, *Chronique des sept misères*, (Paris: Gallimard 1986); Confiant, *Eau de café* (Paris: Grasset, 1991); Schwarz-Bart, *Pluie et vent sur Télumée Miracle*.

place I called home with new eyes and it looked sinister', 14). It is the first time that she sees her body as an alien object: 'Jusqu'alors, je n'avais songé à mon corps. Étais-je belle? Étais-je laide? Je l'ignorais. Que m'avait-il dit?' (32; 'Up until now I had never thought about my body. Was I beautiful? Was I ugly? I had no idea. What had he said?', 15). Even her sexual feelings are characterized for the first time by self-alienation: 'brusquement il sembla que ce n'était plus moi, mais John Indien qui me caressait ainsi' (32; 'it seemed that it was no longer me but John Indian who was caressing me', 15). Despite the pleasure she associates with John Indien, she wonders whether this new awareness of her sexual self as other shares something in common with the extreme violation and disempowerment of her mother's rape: 'Était-ce ainsi que malgré elle, ma mère avait râlé quand le marin l'avait violée?' (32; 'Was that how my mother had moaned in spite of herself when the sailor had raped her?', 15).[40] Because of John Indien, Tituba is struck for the first time by the strangeness of the natural surrounding in which she lives, in a shack on the outskirts of the plantation:

Les planches, grossièrement équarries à coups de hache étaient noircies par pluies et vents. Une bourgainvilée géante, adossée à son flanc gauche, ne parvenait pas à l'égayer, malgré la pourpre de ses fleurs . . . un calabassier noueux, des roseaux. Je frémis. (31)

The planks, roughly squared off with an axe, were blackened by wind and rain. The purple flowers of a giant bougainvillea growing against the left side of the cabin did little to brighten it up . . . a gnarled calabash tree and some reeds. I shuddered. (14)

By contrast, Bridgetown is suddenly appealing:

Une forêt de mâts obscurcissait la baie et je vis flotter des drapeaux de toutes nationalités. Les maisons de bois me parurent gracieuses avec leurs vérandas et leurs énormes toits où les fenêtres s'ouvraient toutes grandes, commes des yeux d'enfant. (33)

A forest of masts hid the bay and I could see flags of all nationalities flying. The wooden houses looked elegant to me with their verandas and enormous roofs, their windows open wide like the eyes of a child. (16)

The 'forêt de mâts' in the bay of Bridgetown not only mark its commercial international importance as a seaport, but is a reminder

[40] For a discussion of the use of sex to figure a circular, repetitive history, see Michelle Smith, 'Reading in Circles: Sexuality and/as History, in *I, Tituba, Black Witch of Salem*', *Callaloo*, 18/3 (1995), 602–7.

of the act of crossing that has taken place.[41] Tituba's desire for heterosexual love coincides with her crossing into culture: she cuts off tangled hair and puts on a dress and earrings. All of this prefigures the central oceanic crossing of this novel, Tituba's exile to America.[42] At the level of plot, it is Tituba's love of John Indien that results in her actual exile. John Indien's mistress sells them to a clergyman bound for America. Consequently her mantra becomes:

Enjambez l'eau, ô, mes pères!
Enjambez l'eau, ô, mes mères!
Je suis si seule dans ce lointain pays!
Enjambez l'eau (112)

Cross the waters, O my fathers, Cross the waters, O my mothers,
I'm so alone in this distant land! Cross the waters (69)

Reminiscent of the 'prière virile' of the *Cahier*, Tituba's prayer is an incantation that figures sorcery's art as the power to bring about a crossing of the ocean.

The tight association of crossing the water with sexuality is continued in Tituba's sexual relationships with her later lovers, Hester Prynne and Benjamin Cohen d'Azevedo.[43] These sexual relationships are also textualized as crossings. Tituba dreams of a ship making its way to shore:

Cette nuit-là, j'eus un rêve.
Mon bateau entrait au port, la voile gonflée de toute mon impatience. J'étais sur le quai et je regardais la coque enduite de goudron fendre l'eau. Au pied d'un des mâts, je distinguai une forme que je ne pouvais nommer. Pourtant je savais qu'elle m'apportait joie et bonheur. (188)

That night I had a dream.
My ship was entering the harbor, its sails swelling with all impatience. I was on the wharf watching the tarred prow cut through the water. At the foot of one of the masts I could make out a shape that I was unable to name, but I knew it was bringing me joy and happiness. (121)

This shadowy figure is Hester's spirit who comes and makes love to Tituba:

Cette nuit-là, Hester vint s'étendre à côté de moi. Doucement le plaisir

---

[41] See in my discussion in Ch. 1 of the 'mâts' as indicators of metaphorical crossing in Baudelaire's 'Parfum exotique' and Mallarmé's 'Brise marine'.
[42] Condé's focus on Tituba's exile in America can be seen as a kind of *Détour* that follows the *Retour* of her African novels.
[43] Nathaniel Hawthorne's heroine of his 1850 text *The Scarlet Letter* appears anachronistically in *Moi, Tituba* as a white contemporary feminist with separatist ideals. Through Hester, Condé explores ironic correspondences between religious Puritan and contemporary feminist attitudes toward sexuality.

m'enhavit, ce qui m'étonna. Peut-on éprouver du plaisir à se serrer contre un corps semblable au sien? . . . Hester m'indiquait-elle le chemin d'une autre jouissance? (188) That night Hester lay down beside me, as she did sometimes. I laid my head on the quiet water lily of her cheek and held her tight. Can you feel pleasure from hugging a body similar to your own? . . . Was Hester showing me another kind of bodily pleasure? (122) Hester's spirit brings her sexual happiness, likened to a boat's arrival. In yet another association of sex and crossing, Tituba imagines the act of making love to Benjamin as a sea voyage: 'Quand tu me rejoignais dans le grand lit du galetas, nous tanguions comme en un bateau ivre sur une mer démontée. Tu me guidais de tes jambes de rameur et nous finissions par atteindre la rive' (218; 'When you joined me in my big bed in the attic, we used to pitch and plunge like a drunken boat on a choppy sea. We rowed together under your guidance and finally reached the shore', 140). If Tituba's love of John Indien is the cause of the first crossing and exile, the latter two crossings are both arrivals, two versions of imagined recuperation. Despite the text's connection of heterosexuality with exile and enslavement, Tituba affirms heterosexual love. By contrast, her relationship with Hester offers a hint of an alternative that the text implies may be a true return, a recuperation from exile. The theme of crossing the sea persists in the text as the hope for recovering an alienated self:

La mer, c'est elle qui m'a guérie.
Sa grande main humide en travers de mon front. Sa vapeur dans mes narines. Sa potion amère sur mes lèvres. Peu à peu, je recollais les morceaux de mon être (184)

It was the sea that healed me.
Her great, wet hand pressed against my forehead. Her salts filled my nostrils. Her bitter potion moistened my lips. Gradually I pieced myself together. (119)

The loss of the mother is the central and originary trauma with which the remainder of the narrative struggles to cope. When Abena is hanged for fighting off the master's sexual advances, the narrative repeats several times, 'On pendit ma mère' (21–2; 'They hanged my mother', 8). This traumatic discontinuity recurs in the repeated images of hanged women, juxtaposed with discontinued pregnancies.[44] Tituba witnesses the public hanging of Goody Glover, an old

[44] On this point, see Mara Dukats, 'A Narrative of Violated Maternity: *Moi, Tituba, sorcière . . . Noire de Salem*', *World Literature Today*, 67.4 (1993), 745–50.

woman accused of being a witch. In this Tituba experiences the return of Abena's hanging:

> C'était comme si j'avais été condamnée à revivre l'exécution de ma mère! Non, c'était pas une vieille femme qui balançait là! C'était Abena dans la fleur de son âge et la beauté de ses formes! Oui, c'était elle et j'avais à nouveau six ans! Et la vie était à recommencer depuis ce moment-là! (83)
>
> It was as if I had been sentenced to relive my mother's execution. No, it wasn't an old woman hanging there. It was Abena in the flower of her youth and at the height of her beauty. Yes, it was she and I was six years old again. And my life had to begin all over again from that moment! (49)

Immediately she decides to abort the foetus she is carrying. This juxtaposition of her mother's hanging and the abortion of her unborn child presents the abortion as a necessary and voluntary repetition of her mother's murder. There is an identification between the hanged mother and the unborn child:

> Par une étrange aberration, il me semblait que le cri qu'avait poussé la femme Glover en s'engageant dans le corridor de la mort, venait des entrailles de mon enfant, supplicié par la même société, condamné par les mêmes juges. (87)
>
> By a strange aberration it seemed to me that the cry uttered by Goody Glover setting off along the corridor of death came from the bowels of my child, tortured by the same society and sentenced by the same judges. (52)

Tituba's decision brings out the tight connection between traumatic repetition and discontinuous beginning. This is also the case with Hester's suicide by hanging while pregnant. On learning of Hester's death, Tituba's voice merges with the voice of Hester's unborn child.

> Je fracturai en hurlant la porte du ventre de ma mère. Je défonçai de mon poing rageur et désespéré la poche de ses eaux. Je haletai et suffoquai dans ce noir liquide. Je voulus m'y noyer. . . . Mère, notre supplice n'aura-t-il pas de fin? Puisqu'il en est ainsi, je ne viendrai jamais au jour. Je resterai tapie dans ton eau, sourde, muette, aveugle, laminaire sur ta paroi. Je m'y accrocherai si bien que tu ne pourras jamais m'expulser et que je retournerai en terre avec toi sans avoir connu la malédiction du jour. (173)[45]

---

[45] Note the reference to Césaire's *moi, laminaire* . . . (Paris: Seuil, 1982). For a discussion of the use of the *Cahier* intertext in *Moi, Tituba*, see Mara Dukats, 'The Hybrid Terrain of Literary Imagination: Maryse Condé's Black Witch of Salem, Nathaniel Hawthorne's Hester Prynne, and Aimé Césaire's Heroic Voice', *College Literature*, 22/1 (1995), 51–61.

I screamed down the door of my mother's womb. My fist broke her bag of waters in rage and despair. I choked and suffocated in this black liquid. I wanted to drown myself.... Mother, will our torture never end? If this is how things are, I shall never emerge into the light of day. I shall remain crouched in your waters, deaf, dumb, and blind, clinging like kelp to your womb. I shall cling so tightly you'll never expel me and I shall return to dust without you, without ever having known the curse of day. (111)

These deaths form a chain of identification between women along the mother–child relationship: Abena, Goody Glover, Tituba, and Hester are identified as mothers, while Tituba is Abena's, her own, and Hester's child. These substitutions are made in moments of violent discontinuity.[46] In all these repetitions, the discontinuity is in some important part an act of will: Abena's decision to fight back leads to her hanging; Tituba aborts her foetus upon seeing Goody Glover hanged; Hester hangs herself and in doing so aborts her foetus. These are also instances of women exercising control over their bodies and their maternity at the cost of death.[47]

Literal maternity is substituted with metaphorical maternity. All the mother–child relationships are substitutions, all of them bonded by the workings of sorcery: Man Yaya, Betsey, Hester, Iphigène, Samantha. Tituba imagines her healing of Betsey in a ritual bath as an act of purification for her child's murder. Iphigène, her 'fils-amant', is also a substitute for her dead child. Tituba realizes that the child to whom she denied life has nevertheless come to be central to her life, having 'donné à mon existence saveur et signification' (235; 'given my existence a meaning and a purpose', 152). Motherhood repeatedly produces meaning, beginning with Tituba's surrogate mother Man Yaya's education in figural rereading. Out of discontinuous maternal beginnings, the narrative produces substitutive relationships between women in its effort to recuperate the initial loss.

---

[46] Caroline Rody argues that the mother–daughter relationship can be read as an allegory of historiographic desire in Caribbean and African-American women's texts. See *The Daughter's Return: African-American and Caribbean Women's Fictions of History*, (Oxford: Oxford University Press, 2000).

[47] Compare to the infanticide in Toni Morrison, *Beloved* (London: Chatto and Windus, 1987). For a discussion of the two novels and the necessity of looking for ties between Antillean and African American literature, see Carla Peterson, 'Le Surnaturel dans *Moi, Tituba, sorcière... Noire de Salem* de Maryse Condé et *Beloved* de Toni Morrison', in *L'Œuvre de Maryse Condé* (Paris: Harmattan, 1996), 91–104.

RECAPITULATION OF PAST DISCOURSES

The exile from the motherland also occasions substitutions of another kind, when Tituba finds that the elements necessary for practising the art of sorcery are no longer available: 'Je décidai d'user de subterfuges' (78; 'I decided to make substitutions', 45). In a Glissantian *Détour*, she uses as substitutes the plants that she finds in America. Her desire to regain her native land is manifested in several instances of imagined return. In remembering her island, she experiences nostalgia for the oppressive and cruel plantation life she left:

Je revoyais la plantation de Darnell Davis, la hautaine Habitation et ses colonnades au sommet du morne, les rues cases-nègres, grouillantes de souffrances et d'animation, enfants au ventre balloné, femmes vieillies avant l'heure, hommes mutilés, et ce cadre sans joie que j'avais perdu me devenait précieux tandis que des larmes coulaient sur mes joues. (82)

I could see Darnell Davis's plantation, the arrogant Great House with its columns at the top of the hill, the black shack alleys seething with suffering and life, children with bloated stomachs, women wizened before their time, crippled men; and those cheerless surroundings I had lost suddenly meant so much that tears streamed down my cheeks. (48)

In this first instance of yearning, which contains a reference to Joseph Zobel's *La Rue Cases-Nègres*, it becomes evident that the life of the island is so inextricable from the horrors of slavery that even Tituba's longing for return cannot be separated from the unhappy memories of slavery that form the content of her nostalgia for home. The nostalgia for an anteriority is a problem to which contemporary West Indian writers must respond in their narratives of return. Below, I argue that in the following five instances of imagined return placed throughout the novel, one can trace the evolution of Antillean literature.

The first of these instances of imagined return is expressed in the language of exoticism associated with the West Indies:

la houle des champs de canne à sucre prolongeant celle des vagues de la mer, les cocotiers penchés du bord de mer et les amandiers-pays tout chargés de fruits rouges ou vert sombre. (102)

the swell of the sea merging into the waves of the sugarcane fields, the leaning coconut palms on the seashore, and the almond trees loaded with red and dark green fruit. (62)

The exotic landscape is evoked in a borrowed language of nostalgia, having little in common with Tituba's former descriptions of her island home.[48] Remarkably, in a manner reminiscent of earlier poetry in French written by bourgeois West Indian poets, this picture effectively wants to erase the presence of the slave, even while depending for its readability upon the traces of slavery:

> Si je distinguais mal les hommes, je distinguais les mornes, les cases, les moulins à sucre et les cabrouets à boeufs que fouettaient des mains invisibles. Je distinguais les habitations et les cimetières des maîtres. (102)
>
> Although I had trouble making out the inhabitants, I could see the hills clearly, the cabins, the sugar mills, and the ox carts whipped by invisible hands. I got a glimpse of the Great Houses and the masters' graveyards. (62)

Tituba is then quick to point out the difference between the nostalgia of the colonized and the nostalgia of the colonizer, even as they are informed by the same exotic vision. Tituba contrasts her nostalgia with that of Betsey and Mistress Parris:

> Ce qu'elles regrettaient, c'était la douceur d'une vie plus facile, d'une vie de Blanches, servies, entourées par des esclaves attentionnés. . . . Les jours qu'elles y avaient coulés, avaient été faits de luxe et de volupté. Moi, qu'est-ce que je regrettais? Les bonheurs ténus de l'esclave. (103)
>
> What they yearned for was the sweetness of a gentler life, the life of white women who were served and waited on by attentive slaves. . . . The life they had spent there was composed of luxury and voluptuousness. And what did I yearn for? The subtle joys of being a slave. (63)

The reference to the famous mantra, 'Là, tout n'est qu'ordre et beauté, | Luxe, calme, et volupté', of Baudelaire's 'L'Invitation au voyage' notes the ability of the slave to take on a French poet's exotic idiom in speaking of her own home, in a vision that depends upon her presence in the picture as a slave.

The second instance of return is an explicit reference to Césaire:

> Alors, mon esprit pourrait-il retrouver le chemin de la Barbade? Et même s'il y parvenait, serait-il condamné *à errer*, impuissant et sans voix? . . . Mon esprit délivré reprendrait-il le chemin du *pays natal?* J'aborde à la terre que j'ai perdue. *Je reviens vers la hideur désertée de ses plaies.* Je la reconnnais à son odeur. Odeur de sueur, de souffrance et de labeur. Mais paradoxalement odeur forte et chaude qui me réconforte. (110, *emphasis added*)
>
> Would my soul find its way back to Barbados? And even if it did, would be condemned to wander helplessly, without a voice? . . . Would my soul, once delivered, set off back to my native land? I'm reaching the land I lost. I'm

---

[48] See my discussion in Ch. 1 of the trope of travel, return, and the role of the exotic.

returning to the forsaken hideousness of its sores. I recognize it by its smell. The smell of sweat, suffering, and labor. But paradoxically a warm, strong smell that reassures me. (67)

This *Cahier* intertext ('J'ai longtemps erré et je reviens vers la hideur désertée de vos plaies', 86) embraces the nostalgia for the native land while rejecting the exoticism. Return is envisioned as an active embracing of the hideousness, suffering, and the ugliness of the island.

The third instance of nostalgia imagines the landscape of the island through the lens of motherhood: 'Le calebassier exhibitait des rotondités, pareilles à ventre de femme enceinte. La rivière Ormonde gazouillait comme un nouveau-né. Pays, pays perdu? Pourrais-je jamais te retrouver?' (129; 'The calabash tree was showing swellings like the womb of a pregnant woman. The River Ormond was gurgling like a newborn baby. Will I ever find my way back to you, my lost beloved country?', 79). The mother–child relationship informs this image of the natural landscape, as is particularly characteristic of West Indian women's writing.[49] What is striking about this passage is its doubt about the possibility of return, and more, the questioning of the basic premiss that the land is to be seen as lost in the first place. Along with all the problems of discontinuous maternity in the narrative, this ambivalent vision of the lost land as maternal in character seems to problematize a simple notion of loss and recuperation.

The fourth passage is affirmative: 'Je la retrouve, cette île que j'avais crue perdue!' (161; 'I am back on the island I thought I had lost!', 102). It seems to respond to both the exoticism and the stark Césairean vision. It does not deny the natural splendour of the island landscape: 'Pas moins fauve, sa terre. Pas moins verts, ses mornes. Pas moins violacées, ses cannes Congo, riches d'un suc poisseux. Pas moins satinée, la ceinture émeraude de sa taille' (161; 'No less rust-colored, her soil! No less green, her hills. No less mauve, her sugar-cane, sticky with juice. No less satiny the emerald belt around her waist', 102). It simultaneously functions as a reminder of the continued misery of the people:

> Mais les hommes et les femmes y souffrent. Ils sont dans l'affliction. On vient de pendre un nègre au faîte d'un flamboyant. La fleur et le sang se confondent. Ah oui, je l'oubliais, notre esclavage n'est pas terminé. (161)

---

[49] Examples include Françoise Ega, *Le Temps des madras* (Paris: Éditions maritimes d'outre-mer, 1966) and Schwarz-Bart, *Pluie et vent sur Télumée Miracle*.

ALLEGORY, SORCERY, HISTORICAL REWRITING 137

But the men and women are suffering. They are in torment. A slave has just been hung from the top of a flame tree. The blossom and blood have merged into one. I have forgotten that our bondage is not over. (102)

This passage, which refers to the importance of realism and landscape in Glissant's writing, juxtaposes the natural beauty and resources of the island ('fleur'), and the bitter suffering ('sang') of the island's people.[50]

The final passage contains a verbatim repetition of part of the passage just cited ('Pas moins fauve, sa terre . . . ', 211) which serves to mark that the landscape may not have changed, but that the willingness of the slaves to accept their enslavement will not continue for long: 'Mais les temps ont changé. Les hommes et les femmes n'acceptent plus de souffrir' (211; 'But the times have changed. The men and women are no longer prepared to put up with suffering', 136).

The potential for bringing about a change in the lives of her people gives Tituba a new sense of revolutionary purpose, and it is this purpose that informs the final imagined return, which takes place on a ship during Tituba's actual return to Barbados after her long exile:

> Je commençai d'imaginer un autre cours pour la vie, une autre signification, une autre urgence.
> Le feu ravage le faîte de l'arbre. Il a disparu dans un nuage de fumée, le Rebelle. Alors c'est qu'il a triomphé de la mort et que son esprit demeure. Le cercle apeuré des esclaves reprend courage. L'esprit demeure.
> Oui, une autre urgence. (210)

> I began to imagine another course for my life, another meaning, another motive. The fire engulfs the top of the tree. The Rebel has disappeared in a cloud of smoke. He has triumphed over death and his spirit remains. The frightened circle of slaves regains its courage. The spirit remains.
> Yes, another motive for life. (136)

Tituba imagines herself as the 'Rebelle', the hero of Césaire's plays, who incites the slaves to revolt.[51] This passage completes the evolution of the various strategies of literary return, from exoticism, *négritude*, women's writing, the focus on realism and landscape, to a vision of revolutionary potential through literature. These imagined returns have been the workings of Tituba's substitutive art. The

[50] For Glissant's views on the importance of landscape in literature, see his interview with Wolfgang Bader, 'Poétique antillaise, poétique de la relation', *Komparatistische Hefte*, 9–10 (1984), 83–100: 92–3.

[51] The 'Rebelle' is a reference to the hero of Césaire's *Et les chiens se taisaient* (Paris: Présence africaine, 1956), who is, to some degree, the main character in all of Césaire's plays.

evolution of sorcery's content traces the evolution of Antillean literature. Tituba identifies her ultimate return to Barbados as having a revolutionary purpose. Simultaneously, this final return functions as a comment on the potential role of literature in bringing about change. Return, which has been the preoccupation of West Indian literature from its inception, has a revolutionary goal.

Most notably the recapitulation of past discourses in this text brings out a notion of Antillean literature as a site of the layering, nestling, and entanglement of discourses, black and white, Antillean and French. This recapitulation functions as an exemplary Glissantian 'point d'intrication'. It is a series of *Détours* that return to an 'always already' saturated textual space.

WRITING, NEUROSIS, PERFORMANCE: LITERATURE AND POLITICS

Tituba repeatedly insists on limiting her powers of sorcery. She confines them to healing and comforting rather than to eradicating the oppression of her people. The question whether the writerly project has a political goal is contested. The men in Tituba's life mark the distinction between politics and sorcery along the divide between male and female, between acts and words. When Tituba asks Christopher to let her join in the fight against the white masters, he laughs and says 'Te battre? Comme tu y vas. Le devoir des femmes, Tituba, ce n'est pas de se battre, faire la guerre, mais l'amour!' (234; 'Fight? You're going too fast. A woman's duty, Tituba, is not to fight or make war, but to make love!', 151). This attitude is also exemplified by Iphigène's distinction between sorcery and political acts: 'je respecte tes talents de guérisseuse. N'est-ce pas grace à toi que je suis en vie à respirer l'odeur du soleil? Mais fais-moi grâce du reste. L'avenir appartient à ceux qui savent le façonner et crois-moi, ils n'y parviennent pas par des incantations et des sacrifices d'animaux. Ils y parviennent par des actes' (252; 'I respect your talents as a healer. Isn't it thanks to you that I am alive and breathing? But please spare me the rest. The future belongs to those who know how to shape it and believe me, you won't get anywhere with incantations and animal sacrifices. Only through actions' 164). Both men must acknowledge the vital necessity of sorcery to their well-being: Christopher hopes that Tituba will find a way to make him invincible, and Iphigène owes his life to her healing power. Yet

ALLEGORY, SORCERY, HISTORICAL REWRITING 139

when it comes to political struggle, Iphigène's distinction privileges concrete, material acts, as opposed to sorcery's incantations. But the text does not accept this distinction between acts and words, between politics and writing. It is the very character of sorcery to efface that distinction, for throughout the text words function as acts. Words possess the performative power to conjure spirits and even to navigate the sea (214–15). Words comfort against adversity: 'De mots. Rien parfois ne vaut les mots. Souvent menteurs, souvent traîtres, ils n'en demeurent pas moins des baumes irremplaçables' (137; 'With words. Sometimes nothing can replace words. Often deceitful, often treacherous, they nevertheless have an invariable soothing effect', 84). The end of the novel suggests that the 'chanson de Tituba' (267; 'song of Tituba', 175) that remains in the imagination of the people of her country plays a fundamental role in political acts: 'Pas une révolte que je n'aie fait naître. Pas une insurrection. Pas une désobéissance' (268; 'I have been behind every revolt. Every insurrection. Every act of disobedience', 175). Sorcery is the root of revolt and resistance. As a commentary on the potential of literature to bring about political change, sorcery questions the notion of writing as distinct from politics. But does sorcery's role in political life lie in its actual power to change the material world, or rather in its usefulness as performance that serves symbolically to focus the group's concerns—in the manner of spectacle? This question becomes important in exploring the allegorical relationship between sorcery and writing.

In his compelling comparison of shamanism and psychoanalysis in *Anthropologie structurale*, Lévi-Strauss locates the power of sorcery in collective consensus about its effectiveness, rather than in the sorcerer's actual pattern of success in healing the ill.[52] The basic structure central to both shamanism and psychoanalysis is the relationship of the sick patient and the powerful healer; practices of sorcery are 'thérapeutiques psychologiques plus anciennes et plus répandues'.[53] The effectiveness of shamanism is constituted not by actual cures but instead by the feeling of security that the community derives from the myth that constructs their world.[54] The public participates in the cure, and each curing act of the shaman confirms the group's belief-

---

[52] 'Le Sorcier et sa magie', in *Anthropologie structurale I* (Paris: Plon, 1958), 183–203.
[53] Ibid. 202.
[54] On the worldwide phenomenon of shamanism in the history of religions, see Mircea Eliade, *Le Chamanisme et les techniques archaïques de l'extase* (Paris: Payot, 1951).

system, which in turn is needed for the cure to be effective. Similarly in psychoanalysis, the treatment consists precisely of the reorganization of the patient's universe according to psychoanalytic interpretation. Moving from sickness to health entails the putting into place of an organizing myth that issues the explanation and constitutes the cure.

For this process a neurotic is needed: 'la pensée normale souffre toujours d'un déficit de signifié, tandis que la pensée dite pathologique . . . dispose d'une pléthore de signifiant' ('Normal thought continually seeks the meaning of things which refuse to reveal their significance. So-called pathological thought, on the other hand, overflows with emotional interpretations and overtones, in order to supplement an otherwise deficient reality').[55] Lévi-Strauss reads the sorcerer as a neurotic who provides such an abundance of meaning: 'Dans le problème de la maladie, que la pensée normale ne comprend pas, le psychopathe est invité par le groupe à investir une richesse affective, privée par elle-même de point d'application' ('Normal thought cannot fathom the problem of illness, and so the group calls upon the neurotic to furnish a wealth of emotion heretofore lacking a focus').[56] Through his performance, the shaman infuses with meaning that which the community finds incomprehensible. The unreadable sickness is expelled through the intense spectacle of neurosis:

En soignant son malade, le shaman offre à son auditoire un spectacle. . . . Ce spectacle est toujours celui d'une répétition, par le shaman, de 'l'appel' c'est-à-dire la crise initiale qui lui a apporté la révélation de son état. . . . Il les revit dans toute leur vivacité, leur originalité et leur violence. . . . Nous pouvons dire, empruntant à la psychanalyse un terme essentiel, qu'il abréagit. . . . Le shaman est un abréacteur professionnel.[57]

In treating his patient the shaman also offers his audience a performance. . . . It always involves the shaman's enactment of the 'call,' or the initial crisis which brought him the revelation of his condition. . . . He actually relives them in all their vividness, originality, and violence. . . . we can say, borrowing a key term from psychoanalysis, that he abreacts. . . . The shaman is a professional abreactor.[58]

---

[55] Lévi-Strauss, 'Le Sorcier et sa magie', 200; trans. as 'The Sorcerer and his Magic', in *Structural Anthropology I*, by Claire Jacobson and Brooke Grundfest Schoepf (Garden City NY: Anchor, 1967), 175–6.
[56] Id., 'Le Sorcier et sa magie', 200; 'The Sorcerer and his Magic', 176.
[57] Id., 'Le Sorcier et sa magie', 199.
[58] Id., 'The Sorcerer and his Magic', 175.

The shaman, as neurotic, experiences and performs, publicly and symbolically on behalf of the collectivity, the cathartic reactivation of 'la crise initiale' that is at the root of the illness. The moment of abreaction is the moment of cure. The illness itself seemingly has the character of neurosis, of repression and return. The public performance by the sorcerer fills the gap in meaning from which the community suffers:

> Car seule, l'histoire de la fonction symbolique permettrait de rendre compte de cette condition intellectuelle de l'homme, qui est que l'univers ne signifie jamais assez, et que la pensée dispose toujours de trop de significations pour la quantité d'objets auxquels elle peut accrocher celles-ci. Déchiré entre ces deux systèmes de références, celui du signifiant et celui du signifié, l'homme demande à la pensée magique de lui fournir un nouveau système de référence, au sein duquel des données jusqu'alors contradictoires puissent s'intégrer.[59]

> For only the history of the symbolic function can allow us to understand the intellectual condition of man, in which the universe is never charged with sufficient meaning and in which the mind always has more meanings available than there are objects to which to relate them. Torn between these two systems of reference—the signifying and the signified—man asks magical thinking to provide him with a new system of reference, within which the thus-far contradictory elements can be integrated.[60]

The shaman forges the rupture between signifier and signified, between the dearth and plenitude of explanations, neurotically performing the collective trauma and curing through reactivation.

Cixous and Clément explore the connections between (Michelet's) sorceress and (Freud's) hysteric, two exemplary women figures:

> Poids subversif du retour du refoulé, évaluation du pouvoir de l'archaïque, puissance ou non de l'imaginaire sur le symbolique et sur le réel, c'est là le cœur de l'histoire qui lie ensemble la figure de la sorcière et celle de l'hystérique.[61]

> The heart of the story linking the figures of the sorceress and hysteric lies in the subversive weight attributed to the return of the repressed, in the evaluation of the power of the archaic.[62]

The sorceress is reviled, feared, and invested with power because she is a 'porteuse du passé' ('bearer of the past'), an embodiment of the

---
[59] Id., 'Le Sorcier et sa magie', 202–3.
[60] Ibid., 'The Sorcerer and his Magic', 178.
[61] Cixous and Clément, La Jeune Née, 22.
[62] Eaed., Newly Born Woman, 9.

'return of the repressed' of culture, society, and community.[63] Reading the sorceress as mother of the hysteric, Clément sees in this woman's fate the structure of a neurosis. In her suffering, Clément sees a public expiation of a repressed guilt that is forced upon her:

> Ces femmes pour échapper au malheur de leur exploitation—économique, familiale—ont choisi de souffrir spectaculairement devant un public d'hommes: du spectacle, de la souffrance, c'est la crise; or la crise est aussi une fête, une fête de la culpabilité retournée comme une arme, une histoire de séduction.... Dans la sorcellerie et l'hystérie, du côté du spectacle, il faut un public, prêt à satisfaire son merveilleux désir.[64]
>
> These women, to escape the misfortune of their economic and familial exploitation, chose to suffer spectacularly before an audience of men: it is an attack of spectacle, a crisis of suffering. And the attack is also a festival, a celebration of their guilt used as a weapon, a story of seduction.... But an audience, ready to satisfy its fantastic desire, is necessary for the spectacular side of sorcery and hysteria.[65]

The public spectacle takes the form of a forcing out of a traumatic, repressed event: a confession of satanic possession, a memory of family seduction: 'Un corps étranger, réel ou métaphorique, doit sortir du corps' ('A foreign body, real or metaphorical, must leave the body');[66] 'Il sortira, cet acte, en mots ou en larmes, en voix de diable, en déjection, en rire: mais il sortira' ('It will come out, this act, in words or in tears, in devil's voice, in excrement, in laughter; but it will come out').[67]

Lévi-Strauss and Clément provide a model for understanding the writer/sorceress in *Moi, Tituba* as neurotic. On such a reading, Condé's epigraph may function as a confession of her possession by the spirit of Tituba. The novel constitutes a spectacle wherein the writer abreacts for her collectivity by performing her possession with their ancestor's spirit. The 'crise initial' that is reactivated and needs curing is the absence of history that troubles the collective consciousness. *Moi, Tituba* poses sorcery as a return, as a means of recuperating a traumatic history. The text's central historical event, the Salem witch trials of 1692–3, has barely left any record of the role of Tituba: 'Je cherche mon histoire dans celle des Sorcières de Salem et ne la

---

[63] Eaed., *La Jeune Née*, 20; *Newly Born Woman*, 9.
[64] Eaed., *La Jeune Née*, 22–3.
[65] Eaed., *Newly Born Woman*, 10.
[66] Eaed., *La Jeune Née*, 31; *Newly Born Woman*, 14.
[67] Eaed., *La Jeune Née*, 34; *Newly Born Woman*, 16.

trouve pas. . . . De moi, on ne parle pas' (231; 'I can look for my story among those of the witches of Salem, but it isn't there. . . . not a word about me', 149); 'Aucune, aucune biographie attentionnée et inspirée recréant ma vie et ses tourments!' (172; 'There would never, ever, be a careful, sensitive biography recreating my life and its suffering!', 110). It is this absence within the history of the Salem witch trials to which this novel responds. As Bhabha puts it, 'The colonial space is the *terra incognita* or the *terra nulla*, the empty or waste land, whose history has to be begun, whose archives must be filled out.'[68] In the process of this 'filling' of the historical record, the figure of sorcery itself is textualized as a response to the absence of history. With respect to history, the collectivity suffers from a deficit of meaning, and the writer cures through the spectacle of her neurotic performance of the 'return of the repressed'.

The narrative itself suffers from traumatic repetitions. The symptoms of the gap in history are manifested in the repetition of traumatic events that cannot be assimilated into a normal understanding. Tituba has a dream on the night that Benjamin's house is burned down, and she awakes to find the room in flames (206). She wakes from the same dream ('Je voulais entrer dans une forêt . . .') when the revolt that she has planned with Iphigène is ambushed by traitors (261). In writing, a traumatic history, repetitive or non-existent, could be recuperated. But even writing is structured by the symptoms of trauma, as suggested by the exact repetition of passages. Of her story, Tituba says: 'Et puis, à la raconter, est-ce que je n'en revis pas, une à une, les souffrances? Et dois-je souffrir deux fois?' (255; 'And then by telling it, I shall be reliving my suffering over and over again. And must I suffer twice?', 166). In the act of writing as return, the interaction between undesired repetition and desired return is negotiated. If writing is a way to recuperate traumatic or missing events into a history, writing as a form of return must confront the force of the unexpected return of unassimilated traces. Hence postcolonial writing is always rewriting.

The writer as neurotic may perform a symbolic function for the collectivity by repeating its suffering. In doing so, she provides the collectivity with a system of reference that restructures its universe. But does writing as neurotic repetition undo the distinction between words and acts, between literature and politics? In Clément's account of abreaction, the terrible past that has left its archaic traces

[68] *The Location of Culture* (London: Routledge, 1994), 246.

on the sorceress/hysteric is expelled through a discharge that is 'entre langage et acte' ('between language and act').[69] The distinction between word and act is effaced at the very moment of abreaction: the discharge of the word constitutes a reactivation, a return of the act, while the act also comes into being at the moment of the discharge. The inquisitions of witch-hunts produce archives and they also produce witches. The sorceress herself is an embodiment of the word as act. Similarly in writing, the question of whether the word actually changes the material world is not the relevant question about the relationship of words and acts.[70] Rather, it is the in-betweenness of writing that emerges as the writer abreacts collective neurosis, in which the borderlines of word and act, literature and politics lose their edge.

THE CONCLUSORY POLITICS OF RETURN

At the end of the main text of the novel, Tituba's revolt is foiled by internal divisions and she is hanged by the whites: a repetition of her mother's hanging. She dies misunderstood and misrepresented, as lies about her life are told at the scene of her death. That is the end—but not quite. There is another exergue to this novel, an epilogue. The epilogue is remarkable in the confidence of its assertions of success, in contradistinction to Tituba's failure in the main ending. The epilogue asserts that recuperation is achieved:

Oui, à présent je suis heureuse. Je comprends le passé. Je lis le présent. Je connais l'avenir. A présent, je sais pourquoi il y a tant de souffrances, pourquoi les yeux de nos nègres et négresses sont brillants d'eau et de sel. (271)

Yes, I am happy now. I can understand the past, read the present, and look into the future. Now I know why there is so much suffering and why the eyes of our people are brimming with water and salt. (178)

All is understood. Rather than the traumatic repetition that we have seen as structuring the narrative, Tituba's story is now assimilated

---

[69] Cixous and Clément, *La Jeune Née*, 33; *Newly Born Woman*, 16.

[70] The relevant question, according to Celia Britton, is about the way in which discourse, magical or political, makes possible a collective relationship to the past: 'There is thus no difference between the magic and the political interpretations of the past in so far as their status as "histoire" or "discours" is concerned' ('*Discours* and *histoire*, Magical and Political Discourse in Edouard Glissant's *Le Quatrième Siècle*', *French Cultural Studies*, 5 (1994), 151–62: 161–2.

into the simple linear temporality of the past, the present, and the future. This recuperation is figured as a very literal reunion with the land itself: 'Et puis, il y a mon île. Je me confonds avec elle' (270; 'And then there is my island. We have become one and the same', 177). The recuperative moment is located in the convergence with the land and in the relation to her daughter. I have argued for the figurative, allegorical function of Tituba's sorcery, which both marks breaks in level and effaces them. The recuperative moment, however, seems to depend upon a union with the land. Sorcery itself suddenly seems to become, in the epilogue, the means to the literal and the essential. Paradoxically, while the book has been an instance of rewriting, Tituba's epilogue claims not to need writing at all:

Je n'appartiens pas à la civilisation du Livre et de la Haine. C'est dans leurs cœurs que les miens garderont mon souvenir, sans nul besoin de graphies. C'est dans leurs têtes. Dans leurs cœurs et dans leurs têtes. (268)

I do not belong to the civilization of the Bible and Bigotry. My people will keep my memory in their hearts and have no need for the written word. It's in their heads. In their hearts and in their heads. (176)

The 'chanson de Tituba' by implication is passed on through the oral tradition.

The epilogue opens, 'Voilà l'histoire de ma vie. Amère. Si amère. Mon histoire véritable commence où celle-là finit et n'aura pas de fin' (267; 'And that is the story of my life. Such a bitter, bitter story', 175). What is the relationship of the epilogue to the rest of the novel, and why is it presented separately and not just as part of the novel? As the 'histoire véritable', the authentic story, the epilogue provides an inspirational resolution of the severe doubts, pessimism, and doomed repetition endemic to the story. What makes the epilogue the 'histoire véritable' is the regaining of 'authenticity' in the final six pages, however disingenuously, through a neat resolution of what the entire novel has gone to great lengths to problematize.

I would argue that the novel appends an epilogue after Tituba's death because the epilogue itself fulfils the recuperative, *heroic* function with respect to the novel that Tituba does in the novel:

Car, vivante comme morte, visible comme invisible, je continue à panser, à guérir. Mais surtout, je me suis assigné une autre tâche.... Aguerrir le cœur des hommes. L'alimenter de rêves de liberté. De victoire. Pas une révolte que je n'aie fait naître. Pas une insurrection. Pas une désobeissance. (268)

For now that I have gone over to the invisible world I continue to heal and

146 ALLEGORY, SORCERY, HISTORICAL REWRITING

cure. But primarily I have dedicated myself to another task. . . . I am hardening men's hearts to fight. I am nourishing them with dreams of liberty. Of victory. I have been behind every revolt. Every insurrection. Every act of disobedience. (175)

Even though she dies in a failed revolt, Tituba continues to be important to the revolutionary struggle, giving hope to her people's dreams of freedom and victory. This text assigns writing the same role, to effect political change: that is the ultimate desired return. The epilogue of this novel serves as the written counterpart to Tituba's role in her people's struggle after her death and defeat. Without it, would its readers feel the novel as a performative contradiction, as undercutting its hope and vision of return?

Regarding recuperation or lack thereof, two passages, one an exact repetition of the other, stand out in the text. They both consist of the following song:

> La pierre de lune est tombée dans l'eau
> Dans l'eau de la rivière
> Et mes doigts n'ont pu la repêcher,
> Pauvre de moi!
> La pierre de lune est tombée.
> Assise sur la roche au bord de la rivière
> Je pleurais et je me lamentais.
> Oh! pierre douce et brillante,
> Tu luis au fond de l'eau.
> Le chasseur vint à passer.
> Avec ses flèches et son carquois
> Belle, Belle, pourquoi pleures-tu?
> Je pleure, car ma pierre de lune
> Gît au fond de l'eau.
> Belle, Belle, si ce n'est que cela,
> Je vais t'aider.
> Mais le chasseur plongea et se noya.
>
> (91 and 177–8)
>
> The moonstone dropped into the water,
> Into the waters of the river,
> And my fingers couldn't reach it,
> Woe is me!
> The moonstone has fallen.
> Sitting on a rock on the riverbank
> I wept and I lamented.
> Oh, softly shining stone,

ALLEGORY, SORCERY, HISTORICAL REWRITING 147

> Glimmering at the bottom of the water.
> The hunter passed that way
> With his bow and arrows.
> 'Why are you crying, my lovely one?'
> 'I am crying because my moonstone
> Lies at the bottom of the water.'
> 'If it is but that, my lovely,
> I will help you.'
> But the hunter dived and was drowned.
>
> (55 and 113)

Tituba sings this lament for her unborn child. It alludes to the well-known Psalm 137, the archetypal psalm of exile. I quote from the King James version:

> By the rivers of Babylon, there we sat down, yea, we wept, when we remembered Zion.
> We hanged our harps upon the willows in the midst thereof.
> For there they that carried us away captive required of us a song; and they that wasted us required of us mirth, saying, Sing us one of the songs of Zion.
> How shall we sing the Lord's song in a strange land?

Tituba's song for her unborn child tells of a loss that is never recuperated: it associates discontinuous maternity with the loss of origins. This song—about an irretrievable 'pierre de lune' and the drowning of a chivalrous would-be hero who tries to rescue it—is one instance of many in the novel that are dissonant with the novel's conclusion, in which Tituba claims that the mother–child reunion is regained, and that recuperation is achieved. It seems altogether possible that the epilogue's 'chanson de Tituba', which Tituba claims remains in the hearts of her people, is precisely this lament, which tells of the writer-hero's failure. This reading subverts the optimism of the epilogue and its ambition to unite politics and literature as inspiration for collective political struggle.

I would venture to suggest that the secret of the book lies in its desire both to be political and yet to transcend politics as literature. This quandary is expressed poignantly in Patrick Chamoiseau's *Texaco* when the character of Aimé Césaire, mayor of Fort-de-France, poses a question to the unlettered Marie-Sophie Laborieux, who has just quoted an inspiring passage from the *Cahier* to him:

> —Dites-moi, madame Laborieux, vous avez lu le *Cahier* ou c'est juste une citation que . . .

—Je l'ai lu, monsieur Césaire...
Il ne dut pas me croire.[71]
—Tell me, Madame Laborieux, have you read the Notebook or is it just a quotation that...
—I read it, Monsieur Césaire...
He must not have believed me.[72]

The contradictions and denials of *Moi, Tituba* express the desire to be read and valued beyond political efficacy even as politics and literature continue to be thought inseparable in the postcolonial context. The paradoxical, unexpressed nature of this aspiration makes it a fitting counterpart to the novel's central figure of sorcery, which strives simultaneously to allegorize literature and to transcend allegory.

[71] *Texaco* (Paris: Gallimard, 1992), 403.
[72] *Texaco*, trans. Rose-Myriam Réjouis and Val Vinokurov (New York: Pantheon, 1997), 368.

6

REPRESENTING CARIBBEAN CROSSINGS: *TRAVERSÉE DE LA MANGROVE*

Since Aimé Césaire's bold assertion in the *Cahier* that 'ma bouche sera la bouche des malheurs qui n'ont point de bouche' (88; 'my mouth will be the mouth of those griefs which have no mouth', 89), the individual as representative of the collectivity has been a central trope in Antillean literature. In the *Cahier*, this statement coincides with the return journey, the taking on of representativeness allegorized in the success of the oceanic crossing. Césaire's crossing presents a paradigm for Antillean writers. Fifty years later, having herself undertaken—both experientially and novelistically—the crossings of departure, exile, and return, Maryse Condé wrote her first novel entirely conceived and set in Guadeloupe, *Traversée de la Mangrove* (1989).[1] Françoise Lionnet has suggested in an influential work on this novel that 'we can see the irony and cautious distance of the 1970's giving way to a "rootedness", to a focus on Antillean specificity'.[2] In this chapter, I question this characterization of Condé's trajectory and this novel's place in it, especially given the extent to which the text challenges the impulse to represent in the terms prescribed by literary movements. I shall argue that this novel allegorizes its own contested representativeness with respect to *créolité*, and in doing so, goes to the struggle for the soul of *créolité* by putting pressure on its gender politics and its privileging of the collectivity.

Appropriate to Condé's arrival 'home', the central site of crossing is no longer the sea, but is internal to the island. The indigenous mangrove swamp, with its gnarled tangle of roots, trunks, and branches intertwined and extending in all directions, provides a rich metaphor on many different levels.[3] Challenging Lionnet's sugges-

---

[1] Maryse Condé, *Traversée de la Mangrove* (Paris: Mercure de France, 1989). All references will be given in the text.

[2] *Postcolonial Representations: Women, Literature, Identity* (Ithaca NY: Cornell University Press, 1995), 78.

[3] The image of a network of entangled roots as a metaphor for Antillean identity is formulated in the 'identité-rhizome' of Glissant's *Poétique de la relation* (Paris: Gallimard, 1990), 23–4. This is inspired by the notion of rhizome developed by Gilles Deleuze and Félix Guattari in *Mille plateaux* (Paris: Minuit, 1980). See also Leah Hewitt's discussion of

tion to the contrary, I shall suggest that for Condé, the Antillean situation is not one of 'rootedness', but of further irony, distance, and renewed departure.

CRÉOLITÉ: CONTESTING REPRESENTATION

Introducing *Traversée* to the public, Patrick Chamoiseau claims: 'Maryse Condé foresees that in our countries, the "we" takes precedence over the "I" and that the protagonist is an entire people who has managed to survive.'[4] In the major Antillean literary movements, one way the question of the relationship of the individual to the collective has been posed is through the relationship of the writer to her people. The *créolité* movement was launched with the publication of *Éloge de la créolité* (1989) by Martinicans Jean Bernabé, Patrick Chamoiseau, and Raphaël Confiant in the same year as the publication of *Traversée*. Like its antecedents *négritude* and *antillanité*, *créolité* has as one of its primary concerns the question of collective identity and literary production. The rhetoric of collective representation in *Éloge* assigns to the Antillean writer a fundamental task: 'parachever la voix collective', to bring about 'l'inévitable cristallisation d'une consciente commune'.[5] However, when asked by Condé to speak as a representative for the *créolité* movement about her novel, Chamoiseau, one of the movement's leaders, protests that 'the act of reading is a personal, even intimate affair', which emerges from 'personal preoccupations, interests, anxieties, questions, and desires'. He proposes that his reading constitutes a set of 'highly personalized' reflections, and comments pointedly that he will keep his actual *créolité*-driven aesthetic judgement to himself.[6] Having himself refused the yoke of representativeness urged by Condé, he proceeds to lay this yoke on Condé's novel by reading it as an allegory for an entire people.

This exchange between Condé and Chamoiseau regarding the personal and the collective is symptomatic of processes of prescrip-

the metaphor of the mangrove, 'Inventing Antillean Narrative: Maryse Condé and Literary Tradition', *Studies in 20th Century Literature*, 17/1 (1993), 79–96: 85–6.

[4] 'Reflections on Maryse Condé's *Traversée de la Mangrove*', trans. Kathleen Balbutansky, *Callaloo*, 14/2 (1991), 389–95: 392. In the French Caribbean, a book is introduced to the public by a 'public reader', who is often a prominent writer. This piece was broadcast in Guadeloupe on radio at the time of the publication of *Traversée*.

[5] Jean Bernabé, Patrick Chamoiseau, and Raphaël Confiant, *Éloge de la créolité*, bilingual edn. trans. M. B. Taleb-Khyar (Paris: Gallimard, 1989), 40.

[6] Ibid. 389.

tion, imposition, and refusal of the injunction to represent extending from a debate about the roles of Antillean writers and texts to the nature of literary interpretation itself. Condé locates 'a crisis, a malaise' affecting West Indian literature in the history of cultural commands imposed by the dominant literary movements, of which *créolité* is the most recent incarnation.[7] In the evolution from *négritude* to *créolité*, one thread of continuity is the connection between masculinist rhetoric and the imperative to represent the collectivity. Condé points out that women writers have not obeyed these commands, and consequently have been devalued by West Indian male writers and theorists. James Arnold has argued that in the French Antilles today there exist two literary cultural groups divided along gender: the theoretically driven and linguistically constrained male writers of the *créolité* movement, and the women writers—not deemed true *créolistes* by the male writers—who nevertheless better express *créolité*'s ideals of openness and freedom in their disregard of linguistic, sexual, and spatio-temporal boundaries.[8] The interaction between Chamoiseau and Condé usefully demonstrates this overall gendered dynamic.

Éloge opens:

Ni Européens, ni Africains, ni Asiatiques, nous nous proclamons Créoles. Cela sera pour nous une attitude intérieure, mieux: une vigilance, ou mieux encore, une sorte d'enveloppe mentale au mitan de laquelle se bâtira notre monde en pleine conscience du monde.

Neither Europeans, nor Africans, nor Asians, we proclaim ourselves Creoles. This will be for us an interior attitude—better, a vigilance, or even better, a sort of mental envelope in the middle of which our world will be built in full consciousness of the outer world.[9]

Inspired by Glissant, the authors of *Éloge* take the Antillean reality of racial, ethnic, cultural, and linguistic creolization and complexity as the basis for their theory of *créolité*. They define *créolité* as the 'agrégat interactionnel ou transactionnel' ('interactional or transactional aggregate') of the various elements that have characterized the history

---

[7] Maryse Condé, 'Order, Disorder, Freedom, and the West Indian Writer', *Yale French Studies*, 83/2 (1993), 121. She argues that in the face of a restrictive order, women writers introduce an element of creative disorder that looks forward to a future of freedom in West Indian literature.
[8] 'The Erotics of Colonialism in Contemporary French West Indian Literary Culture', *New West Indian Guide*, 68/1–2 (1994), 5–22.
[9] Bernabé, Chamoiseau, and Confiant, *Éloge*, 13, 75.

of the region.[10] *Créolité* therefore emphasizes diversity over 'la fausse universalité, monolinguisme, et . . . pureté' ('false universality, . . . monolingualism, and . . . purity').[11] Rather than looking to Africa or Europe, the authors turn inward toward the Antilles. They privilege above all a literature created out of oral Creole culture and language as the authentic expression of the region's *créolité*.[12] Even the opening words of this text suggest a certain contradiction. They carve out creoleness from an oppositional enumeration of what it is not. The principle of contact and relation is rhetorically negated, and a sense of parochial insulation from the world is implied ('enveloppe mentale'), even as the idea of *créolité* itself embodies the combination of many diverse cultures.

This contradiction is played out in the gendered dynamics of *créolité*. The logic of *Éloge* operates on a set of binary oppositions that align along the male–female hierarchy. Most prominent of these are interiority–exteriority and Self–Other; expression authentic to *créolité* presupposes 'l'exorcisme de la vieille fatalité de l'extériorité' ('exorcising the old fatality of exteriority'),[13] 'vision intérieure' ('interior vision'),[14] and 'une descente en soi-même . . . sans l'Autre, sans la logique aliénante de son prisme' ('descending in ourselves, but without the Other, without the alienating logic of his prism').[15] Sartrean echoes of Orphic descent inform the opposition of interiority, the self, and authenticity against exteriority, the Other, and alienation.[16] The language of creoleness and authenticity comes to depend on

[10] Bernabé, Chamoiseau, and Confiant, *Éloge*, 26, 87. In the French Antilles, the term and concept *créole* at first included all people born on the islands, but soon came to designate only white Europeans born on the islands. The contemporary emphasis on mixture and multiple origins in a sense represents a reappropriation. For an informative discussion of the historically diverse uses of the term, see Robert Chaudenson, *Des îles, des hommes, des langues créoles—cultures créoles* (Paris: Harmattan, 1992). For a discussion of the meanings of the term *créole* in relation to the *créolité* movement, see Mary Gallagher, 'Whence and Whither the French Caribbean "Créolité" Movement', *ASCALF Bulletin*, 9 (1994), 3–18.

[11] Ibid. 28, 90.

[12] The leading figures in the effort to rehabilitate Creole language through literature, Raphaël Confiant and Patrick Chamoiseau, now write in an experimental style that is neither Creole nor standard French. Confiant has written a number of novels entirely in Creole. Both have produced transcriptions of oral tales: Chamoiseau, *Au temps de l'antan: Contes du pays martinique* (Paris: Hatier, 1998); Confiant, *Contes créoles des Amériques* (Paris: Stock, 1995).

[13] Bernabé, Chamoiseau, and Confiant, *Éloge*, 23, 85.

[14] Ibid. 26, 87.

[15] Ibid. 41, 102.

[16] See Jean-Paul Sartre, 'Orphée Noir', Preface to Léopold Sédar Senghor (ed.), *Anthologie de la nouvelle poésie nègre et malgache de langue française* (Paris: Presses universitaires de France, 1948), pp. ix–xliv.

maleness. Declaring proudly 'Nous sommes à jamais fils d'Aimé Césaire' ('We are forever Césaire's sons'),[17] the authors recall that *négritude*—which itself deployed a masculinist rhetoric—'a mis fin à l'amputation qui générait un peu de la superficialité de l'écriture par elle baptisée doudouiste' ('put an end to the amputation which generated some of the superficiality of the so called doudouist writing').[18] The authors read pre-Césairean Antillean literature as having been castrated by colonialism, and restored to manhood by *négritude*. Later in the text, the anxiety of castration is made explicit: 'le drame de beaucoup de nos écrivains provient de la castration dont, linguistiquement, ils ont été victimes au temps de leur enfance' ('the tragedy lived by many of our writers comes from the castration which, linguistically, they were victims of during their childhood').[19] The repression of the Creole language is 'l'agenouillement d'une cathédrale' ('the kneeling of a cathedral'), 'une amputation culturelle' ('a cultural amputation'), a betrayal of the phallus.[20] The *créolité* theorists situate themselves as inheritors of a lineage dedicated to remasculinizing their culture and literature.[21]

[17] Bernabé, Chamoiseau, and Confiant, *Éloge*, 18, 80. One of the co-authors of *Éloge*, Confiant, has attacked the literary father Césaire precisely for his neglect and contempt of Creole throughout his literary and political career. See Confiant's polemical *Aimé Césaire*. Jonathan Monroe attempts to read Césaire's work as already anticipating the movement from *négritude* to an emphasis on creolization. See '*Mischling* and *Métis*: Common and Uncommon Languages in Adrienne Rich and Aimé Césaire', in Gustavo Perez Firmat (ed.), *Do the Americas Have a Common Literature?*, (Durham, NC: Duke University Press, 1990), 282–315.
[18] Bernabé, Chamoiseau, and Confiant, *Éloge*, 17, 79.
[19] Ibid. 44, 105. Childhood experiences of Creole culture, its vibrancy and its suppression, are portrayed in the memoirs of Chamoiseau, *Antan d'enfance* (Paris: Gallimard, 1990) and *Chemin-d'école* (Paris: Gallimard, 1994), and Confiant, *Ravine du devant-jour* (Paris: Gallimard, 1993). The first and best-known work of this genre is Joseph Zobel, *La Rue Cases-Nègres* (Paris: Frossart, 1950).
[20] Bernabé, Chamoiseau, and Confiant, *Éloge*, 43, 104. We recall that Césaire's evocation of *négritude* in the *Cahier* actually negated the image of the cathedral ('ma négritude n'est ni une tour ni une cathédrale') in its reliance on a language of penetration and plunging: 'elle plonge dans la chair rouge du sol | elle plonge dans la chair ardente du ciel | elle troue l'accablement opaque de sa droite patience' (115).
[21] Confiant claims that 'Refouler le créole c'est donc refouler formidablement le sexuel' (*Aimé Césaire: Une traversée paralloxale du siecle* (Paris Stock, 1993), 78). Hyper-male sexuality is a theme in several of the *créolistes*' novels, in which exaggerated depictions of male sexual potency abound: Chamoiseau's *Chronique des sept misères* (Paris: Gallimard, 1986) and *Texaco* (Paris: Gallimard, 1992); Confiant's *Le Nègre et l'amiral* (Paris: Grasset, 1992) and *Eau de café* (Paris: Grasset, 1991); and René Depestre, *Hadriana dans tous mes rêves* (Paris: Gallimard, 1988). For an intriguing discussion of the representation of sexuality in Antillean novels, see Thomas Spear, 'Jouissances carnavalesques: Représentations de la sexualité', in Maryse Condé and Madeleine Cottenet-Hage (eds.), *Penser la créolité* (Paris: Karthala, 1995), 135–52.

If, in the rhetoric of *Éloge, créolité* is gendered masculine, it confronts the feminine in the form of a traumatic space:

> la vision intérieure et l'acceptation de notre créolité nous permettront d'investir *ces zones impénétrables du silence où le cri s'est dilué*. C'est en cela que notre littérature nous restituera à la durée, à l'espace-temps continu, c'est en cela qu'elle s'émouvra de son passé et qu'elle sera historique.
>
> interior vision and the acceptance of our Creoleness will allow us to invest these impenetrable areas of silence where screams were lost. Only then will our literature restore us to duration, to the continuum of time and space; only then will it be moved by its past and become historical.[22]

It is the unreadable space that poses an obstacle to penetration and history. The traumatic repressions and discontinuities characterizing the problem of historical (non)understanding that I have discussed in Chapter 3 are interpreted here tellingly as 'zones impénétrables' to be recuperated. It is by assimilating these unknown spaces that the 'durée' of historical narrative continuity can be established. The taming of zones of unreadable silence suggests an undiluted potency already familiar from the language of penetration in the *Cahier*.

In previous chapters, I have explored various in-between spaces—oceanic, allegorical, traumatic—each of which serve as both medium and obstacle to crossing, reference, knowledge, and meaning. The in-between space at issue in *créolité* is richly metaphorized in the figure of the mangrove:

> La Créolité est notre soupe primitive et notre prolongement, notre chaos originel et notre mangrove de virtualités. Nous penchons vers elle, riches de toutes les erreurs et forts de la nécessité de nous accepter complexes.
>
> Creoleness is our primitive soup and our continuation, our primeval chaos and our mangrove swamp of virtualities. We bend toward it, enriched by all kinds of mistakes and confident of the necessity of accepting ourselves as complex.[23]

The figure of the mangrove, as intertwined, tangled, and inextricable as Antillean racial, linguistic, ethnic, and cultural roots and branches, is used to celebrate *créolité*'s valorization of diversity, complexity, and *métissage*. Elsewhere in *Éloge*, however, the image of the mangrove

---

[22] Bernabé, Chamoiseau, and Confiant, *Éloge*, 38, 99. The italicized phrase is from Glissant, who is footnoted in the text of *Éloge*. Compare to Luce Irigaray: 'En dehors de ce volume déjà circonscrit par la signification articulé dans le discours (du père) rien n'est: *l'afemme. Zone de silence*', in *Ce sexe qui n'en est pas un* (Paris: Minuit, 1977), 111.

[23] Bernabé, Chamoiseau, and Confiant, *Éloge*, 28, 90.

may be associated with the alienation resulting from acceptance of the colonizer's values: 'D'où le dénigrement de la langue créole et de la mangrove profonde de la créolité. D'où . . . notre naufrage esthétique' ('Hence the defamation of the Creole language and the deep mangrove swamp of Creoleness. Hence . . . our aesthetic shipwreck').[24] The link here between the mangrove and the shipwreck implicitly suggests the failure of an unknown, perhaps unknowable space.[25] *Créolité* in *Éloge* becomes at once the overcoming of the impenetrability of such zones, while itself constituting an impenetrable zone that it tries to overcome. The complexity of the mangrove is the condition for both power and impotence: the inclusion of the colonizer in *créolité*'s complexity renders the mangrove an image both of desired diversity and potential threat. I mean to suggest that the ambivalence occasioned by the mangrove can be read as an ambivalence regarding *créolité*'s gender identity. The mangrove disrupts the gender division set up in the text: while it is a metaphor for a remasculinized *créolité*, it embodies female unreadability. The danger of the mangrove, in its open-ended and indeterminate boundarilessness, is distinctly a feminine danger inextricably linked to the properties of *créolité* itself.

Créolité occupies the peculiar position of having within it the imperative to write within certain authentic themes and linguistic styles that are truly representative of the Antillean collectivity's *créolité*, and also the potential for infinite openness to diverse cultural elements. *Éloge* underlines the gendered character of the question of representativeness within Antillean discourse. Critics have tended to consider *Traversée* to be text celebratory of *créolité*. But *Traversée* challenges the very possibility of representing the Caribbean multiplicity and diversity to which *créolité* lays claim, and *Traversée* ironically presents the challenge by way of allegory.

THE WRITER AS OUTSIDER

A site of ambivalence about the gender identity of *créolité* in *Éloge*, the mangrove becomes another layer of an already rich metaphor when Condé entitles her novel *Traversée de la Mangrove*. The impenetrable zone that forms the structural centre of this novel is the life and death

---
[24] Ibid. 51, 111.
[25] See my discussion of shipwrecks and crossing in Ch. 1.

of Francis Sancher. The *habitants* of a small village, Rivière au Sel, are gathered around his corpse during a wake that spans the novelistic space located in between dusk and dawn. The details of Sancher's life and death are mysterious.[26] In each chapter, through a different individual's narrative, we glimpse pieces of information regarding Sancher's past, his preoccupations, his interactions with the characters, and the changes he brought about in their lives. These pieces in aggregate do not form a fully coherent explanation of his death, but rather reveal a multiplicity of competing perspectives and meanings that contribute to an incomplete, contradictory, and fragmented story engendered from Sancher's relation to each narrator.[27] In 'an anthropology of everyday life in Guadeloupe',[28] the novel draws its characters from the diverse social groupings of Guadeloupe, as well as from lone marginal figures: blacks, light-skinned bourgeois, East Indians, a Chinese-Caribbean postman, a healer, a *conteur*, a spinster schoolteacher, a Haitian migrant worker. In each narrative, memories of Sancher intertwine with stories of past pain, anxiety, regret, and plans for the future. The characters' testimonies form the jumble of intersecting branches of the novelistic mangrove.

Francis Sancher/Francisco Sanchez is first and foremost an outsider to Guadeloupean society. He has travelled the world and could be Cuban, Colombian, African, European, North American.[29] He arrives one day and takes over a haunted house in Rivière au Sel. He claims to have ancestors who were *béké* slave owners from Guadeloupe. He is a figure of opacity: his racial, ethnic, and geographical identity are unclear. The same is true of his past, what he seeks in coming to Guadeloupe, the nature of his ancestor's sins and

---

[26] An interesting parallel is found in Chamoiseau's novel *Solibo Magnifique* (Paris: Gallimard, 1988), which begins with the death of the storyteller Solibo, who represents the oral creole culture of the Antilles. Both *Traversée* and *Solibo Magnifique* are structured, in the style of a 'whodunit', around the mysterious death of a representative figure of 'Créolité'.

[27] Critics of this novel have made much of the multiple-voiced, decentred nature of the narrative technique deployed. On the question of gender and narrative structure, see Suzanne Crosta, 'Narrative and Discursive Strategies in Maryse Condé's *Traversée de la mangrove*', *Callaloo*, 15/1 (1992), 147–55. Christophe Lamiot discusses how the novel's privileged 'rhetoric of viewpoint' shows how literature engages in 'the complex procedure of endless interrogation' as 'various narrators successively come to speech, neither of them providing a final word, or even a decisive word, about anything'. See 'A Question of Questions through a Mangrove Wood', *Callaloo*, 15/1 (1992), 138–46: 139, 142.

[28] Lionnet, *Postcolonial Representations*, 85.

[29] Several hints in the text suggest his similarity with Che Guevara: his places of travel, medical training, work as a liberator, repeated references to Cuba and also Africa.

the curse that is upon him, why he lives in fear, and the meaning of his strange utterances. He has multiple sexual relationships and children with several women. There are rumours that he may be 'makoumé' (homosexual) and in a relationship with Moïse the postman, another outcast. Even as opacity, complexity, marginality, and deviance mark him as an outsider, they also render him an archetypal Antillean. As Chamoiseau puts it, 'Who among us can claim an unspoiled personal genesis without absences? What Creole person possesses a transparent past that would authorise certainty? . . . Francisco Sanchez inscribes himself in the anthropological reality of our countries.'[30]

One of the first things the curious villagers of Rivière au Sel learn about Sancher is that he is a writer.[31]

Ecrivain? Qu'est-ce qu'un écrivain?

La seule personne à qui on donnait ce titre était Lucien Évariste et c'était en grande partie par moquerie. Parce que depuis son retour de Paris, il ne perdait pas une occasion de raconter qu'il travaillait à un roman. Un écrivain, est-ce donc un fainéant, assis à l'ombre de sa galerie, fixant la crête des montagnes des heures durant pendant que les autres suent leur sueur sous le chaud soleil du Bon Dieu? (38)

Writer? What's a writer?

The only person they gave that title to was Lucien Evariste, and that was mainly a joke, because ever since he had returned from Paris he didn't miss a single opportunity to talk about the new novel he was working on. Was a writer then a do-nothing, sitting in the shade on his veranda, staring at the ridge of mountains for hours on end while the rest sweated it out under the Good Lord's hot sun? (21)

The villagers take offence at writing's frivolity and remove from the daily reality of their lives. Lucien Évariste, the only other member of their community who is a writer (apparently unpublished), has come to be known as a writer only since his return from Paris. The villagers perceive the activity of writing as coming from the *métropole*. Hence being a writer is tied to Sancher's bearing of the taint of foreign places, other lands, and colonial influence.

Lionnet writes that through the figure of Sancher, the novel reflects upon 'the role of the writer as outsider, and of the outsider as

---

[30] Chamoiseau, 'Reflections', 39?.
[31] Lydie Moudileno has done a thorough study of the 'personnage d'écrivain' in Antillean literature, *L'Écrivain antillais au miroir de sa littérature*. See esp. her discussions of *Traversée*, *La Vie scélérate*, and *Les Derniers Rois mages* as metaliterary discourses, pp. 141–71.

catalyst or *pharmakon*, both poison and antidote, dangerous supplement, chronicler, and *aide-mémoire* of the community'.[32] Condé herself has compared Sancher's situation as outsider in Rivière au Sel to her own upon her return to Guadeloupe in 1986. After her intercontinental wanderings, Condé settled in the small town of Montebello: 'I was interested in the character of the stranger—me, for instance, in Montebello, or Francis Sancher in Rivière au Sel—how people react to him, how they define themselves in relation to him, how he influences them, how they affect him.'[33] The character of Sancher, who forces people of the town to confront, through their reaction to and interaction with him, their relationship to themselves and the outside world, is a figure for Condé, who found herself an outsider to Guadeloupe, as a writer and a wanderer. The novel ironizes the marked absence of Antillean writers in their own cultures, and pointedly, Condé's own tendency to spend long periods of time abroad at foreign universities:

> Lucien bondit, songeant à Alejo Carpentier et José Lezama Lima et se voyant déjà discutant style, technique narrative, utilisation de l'oralité dans l'écriture! En temps normal, pareilles discussions étaient impossibles, les quelques écrivains guadeloupéens passant le plus clair de leur temps à pérorer sur la culture antillaise à Los Angeles où à Berkeley. (219)

> Lucien jumped, thinking of Alejo Carpentier and José Lezama Lima, and already saw himself discussing style, narrative technique, and the use of oral tradition in writing. Usually such a discussion was impossible, since the few Guadeloupean writers who did exist spent most of their time holding forth on Caribbean culture in Los Angeles or Berkeley. (182)

Through the character of Sancher, Condé explores her role as the Other in Guadeloupean society. Sancher's status as Other is underlined by his belief that his ancestors were white slave owners. Condé remarks: 'Although he is not a symbolic character, I believe Francis Sancher portrays the European vis-à-vis the West Indian world. The European is responsible for slavery, the slave trade, and for all sorts of wrongdoings during the colonial period.'[34] Sancher's otherness with regard to the West Indies is tied to the history of European slavery and the responsibility that he bears for that history. It is striking that in the same breath that she describes the character as

---

[32] *Postcolonial Representations*, 75.
[33] Françoise Pfaff, *Conversations with Maryse Condé* (Lincoln, Neb: University of Nebraska Press), 71.
[34] Ibid. 72.

allegorizing European colonialism, she both claims that he is not a 'symbolic' character and renders Sancher's otherness in Guadeloupe an allegory of her own remove from the island.[35] In referring to each other, Sancher's and Condé's otherness also allegorize the desire not to be allegory.

DEPARTURES AND CROSSINGS

All the villagers in *Traversée* are in a state of imprisonment of some kind. Sancher has a liberating effect upon the lives of the people with whom he comes into contact.[36] Several of the characters' narratives evince a language of confinement, from which Sancher delivers them. Mira, one of Sancher's lovers, describes a recurrent dream in which she is trapped inside a house without doors or windows: 'Soudain, quelqu'un frappait à une cloison qui se lézardait, tombait en morceaux et je me trouvais devant un in-connu, solide comme un pié-bwa et que me délivrait' (54; 'Suddenly someone knocked on a wall that cracked and crumbled and I came face to face with a stranger, as solid as a tree, who rescued me', 36). Sancher comes to be her emancipator, and she goes to him and finds comfort simply because he is not from the island:

> Sans doute parce qu'il venait d'Ailleurs. D'Ailleurs. De l'autre côté de l'eau. Il n'était pas né dans notre île à ragots, livrée aux cyclones et aux ravages de la méchanceté du cœur des Nègres. (63)

> Probably because he came from Elsewhere. From over there. From the other side of the water. He wasn't born on our island of malice that has been left to the hurricanes and the ravages caused by the spitefulness in the hearts of black folks. (43)

Sancher represents for Mira the freedom and possibilities of Elsewhere as opposed to the constraints and insularity of Guadeloupe.

---

[35] As a case in point, Condé has said that when she was on the radio upon her return, listeners telephoned to ask if this French-speaking Maryse Condé were white. See Vèvè Clark, 'Je me suis réconciliée avec mon île: Une interview de Maryse Condé', *Callaloo*, 12/1 (1989), 86–132: 110–112.

[36] Ellen Munley uses a Kohutian paradigm of psychoanalytic self-psychology to examine how 'Francis Sancher functions as a catalyst for psychic healing' for the various characters in the novel, arguing that Sancher liberates the characters by enabling them to extend the boundaries of the self and to see their interconnectedness to the community. See Munley, 'Mapping the Mangrove: Empathy and Survival in *Traversée de la mangrove*', *Callaloo*, 15/1 (1992), 156–66: 159.

Many of the characters feel the island as a prison and through their contact with Sancher are inspired to look outward for new beginnings. Sancher's death leads to the resolutions of these characters to undertake departures for other shores. Oceanic crossing is a recurrent trope in the characters' narratives. Several of the narratives reflect the Césairean intertext: three of the male characters echo the *Cahier* passage that sets up my discussion of crossing in Ch. 1. Faced with the depressing possibility of spending his life trapped in the island's unkindness and solitude, Moïse the postman contemplates leaving:

Partir. Oui, mais cette fois vers quelle Amérique?
Souvent des camarades de la poste se faisaient muter en métropole. On les voyait aux congés annuels, une blonde au bras, un lac de tristesse au fond des prunelles et les houles amères de l'exil labourant les commissures de leurs lèvres.
Partir. Mais à en croire Francis Sancher qui avait parcouru la terre, pas un coin sous le soleil qui ne porte son lot de désillusions. Pas une aventure qui ne se solde par l'amertume. Pas un combat qui ne se conclue par l'échec. Alors, vivre à Rivière au Sel à perpétuité? Finir ses jours, solitaire comme un mâle crabe dans son trou? (49)

Leave. Yes, but this time in the direction of which American dream?
His colleagues at the post office often got themselves transferred to French France. You would see them on their annual leave, trailing along a blonde, a lake of sadness at the back of their eyes and the bitter swell of exile furrowing the corners of their mouths.
Leave. But if you were to believe Francis Sancher, who had traveled all over the world, there's not a place under the sun that does not have its share of disillusions. Not a single adventure that doesn't end in bitterness. Not a fight that doesn't finish up a failure. So live in Rivière au Sel forever? End one's days as lonely as a male crab in its hole? (29)

Since Césaire's 'Partir' in the *Cahier*, the model of departure, exile, and return has been an archetypal Antillean literary trajectory. Moïse's question 'mais cette fois vers quelle Amérique?' indicates that the 'retour au pays natal' that followed Césaire's exile is now to be followed by yet another departure, another exile, perhaps to a new elsewhere. Even before departing, however, Moïse has already been disabused of the anticipation of arrival and recuperative return. His intimation that the failed voyage and exile are inescapable, at home or elsewhere, is indicative of a post-Césairean existential awareness.

Yet the world outside beckons, especially for characters who, like

Moïse (who is born of a Chinese mother), occupy the margins of Guadeloupean society because of prejudices that abound. Émile Étienne envisions his departure as escape from the harsh colour hierarchy that subjected him to mockery as a dark-skinned schoolboy ('Sirop Batterie', 239; 'Black Treacle', 199) and limited his opportunities:

> Partir. Respirer un air moins confiné. Il lui sembla soudain qu'il étouffait sous les grands arbres et il rêva d'une terre où l'œil ne se cognerait pas aux mornes, mais suivrait la courbe illimitée de l'horizon. Une terre où quoi qu'on en dise la couleur de la peau n'importerait pas. Une terre-terre fertile à labourer. (239)
> Leave. Breathe a less rarified air. He suddenly seemed to be suffocating under the tall trees, and he dreamed of a land where the eye would not be blackened by the hills but could follow the unlimited curve of the horizon. A land where, despite what they say here, the color of one's skin doesn't matter. A homeland where the soil would be rich for plowing. (199)

The departure represents the limitless possibilities that may accompany the freedom from narrow social constraints. Aristide, who had been in an incestuous sexual relationship with his sister Mira before she leaves to go live with Sancher, also decides to leave:

> Lui, qu'avait-il fait? Rien, sinon bêcher un corps proche du sien. . . . Il n'avait quitté le pays que pour de brefs séjours, toujours pressé de revenir vers une couche. Il ne s'était jamais soucié de ce qui passait de l'autre côté de l'horizon, en l'autre bord du monde, et soudain ce désir se levait en lui, impérieux comme celui d'une femme. (79)
> What had he done? Nothing, except sap a body that was close to his. . . . He had spent only very brief periods away from the island and was always in a hurry to return home to his lovenest. He had never given a thought to what was happening beyond the horizon, on the other side of the world, and suddenly there was this pressing desire inside him, like that for a woman. (57–8)

Partir, comme ses deux frères avant lui, très tôt las des coups de gueule et des coups de pied de Loulou et qui faisaient leurs vies, l'un en métropole, l'autre à La Pointe.
Partir. Oh, cela ne se ferait pas sans mal. . . .
Oui, il quitterait cette île sans ampleur où, hormis les dimensions de son pénis, rien ne dit à l'homme qu'il est homme. . . . Alors Amérique? Europe? L'immensité de son choix l'étourdit. Dans le fond, est-ce qu'il ne devrait pas

être reconnaissant à Francis Sancher puisqu'il lui avait donné la liberté, le délivrant de Mira? (79)

Leave, like his two brothers before him, who had quickly tired of Loulou's cussing and kicking and made a life for themselves, one in French France and the other in La Pointe.
Leave. Oh, it wouldn't be easy. . . .
Yes, he would leave this island without a future where, except for the size of his penis, nothing tells a man he's a man. . . . So, to America? To Europe? The immense possibilities open to him made him feel dizzy. In fact, perhaps he should be grateful to Francis Sancher for having given him his freedom, for having delivered him from Mira. (58)

The incest of the siblings Mira and Aristide represents the extent to which they experience their lives as stifling and literally insular. Both are freed by their contact with Sancher. The subsequent coupling of Mira and Sancher suggests a freedom that awaits outside. For Aristide, leaving the island becomes possible only when Mira leaves him for Sancher. In *Moi, Tituba*, as discussed in Ch. 5, crossing represents sexual coupling. Mira becomes pregnant, and Aristide's newfound desire to explore the possibilities of other lands is compared to a renewed sexual desire for other women. The departure represents for Aristide a rechannelling of a frustrated masculinity, or rather, a broadening of the limited way that he has expressed his sexuality thus far.

Each narrative in *Traversée* can be seen as individualized agon with Césaire's 'Partir'. Chamoiseau reads these various characters' feelings of imprisonment and desire to leave the island as signs of 'alienation that stifles one in one's own country'.[37] One of the ways the authors of *Éloge* seek to undo this alienation from oneself is to valorize certain 'authentic' island themes. In a section entitled 'la thématique de l'existence', they enumerate certain topics that are 'true' expressions of Antillean creole culture. Condé responds, 'Are we condemned *ad vitam æternam* to speak of vegetable markets, story tellers, "dorlis", "koutem". . . ? Are we condemned to explore to saturation the resources of our narrow islands? We live in a world where, already, frontiers have ceased to exist.'[38] Her works accordingly take place on several continents, and her characters travel and

---

[37] 'Reflections', 393.
[38] 'Order, Disorder, Freedom', 130. Note that Condé's comment is a barely veiled reference to Chamoiseau's novels. His *Chronique des sept misères* is a novel about the old market in Fort-de-France, a novel whose hero is fathered by a *dorlis*, a spirit that can penetrate through locked doors at night. Chamoiseau's second novel, *Solibo Magnifique*, is

grapple with their identities in forced or voluntary confrontation with different cultures:

> I don't really see what I could say about the owner of the local bar-grocery store next door, who has never left Montebello, who was born here and will die here. She may be fascinating, but she would interest me only to the extent that she had been in contact with the Other. What interests me is cultural encounters and the conflicts and changes that come from them.[39]

The departures that Condé takes in literature have their counterpart in her own life. Having left Guadeloupe at 16, she returned in 1986, only to depart again: 'I returned, telling myself that I was going to write and settle down once and for all. But I realized very quickly that this was not possible, and right away I wanted to leave again.'[40] For Condé, this desire to travel and resistance to settling in one place are strongly tied to her activity as a writer: 'I believe now that it's this wandering that engenders creativity. In the final analysis, it is very bad to put down roots. You must be errant and multifaceted, inside and out. Nomadic.'[41] In contrast to the *Éloge*'s proponents of 'l'enracinement dans l'oral', Condé sees desire to depart as not merely symptomatic of alienation but an impulse toward creativity.

REPRESSED CROSSINGS: THE SEA, SEXUALITY, AND DEATH

The close connection between wandering and creativity is explored tragically in the character of Léocadie Timothée, an elderly spinster who has put down roots and spent all her years as a schoolmistress on the island. Having observed the social and political evolution of the island since 1920 when she opened the first school in Rivière au Sel, she is the voice of a past time. She has seen the changing nature of Guadeloupe's relationship to the rest of the world: 'Dans le temps, nous n'avions pas connaissance du monde et le monde n'avait pas connaissance de nous' (139; 'In times gone by, we knew nothing about the world and the world knew nothing about us', 112). From a time when few people travelled off the island at all, she has seen the

about a storyteller. Richard Burton has made the controversial suggestion that the *créolistes*' excessive orientation toward a past life is not relevant to contemporary Martinique, which he deems to now be a 'post-Creole' society. See 'Modernité et Créolité: Une manière de réponse', *Antilla*, 620 (1995), 29.

[39] Pfaff, *Conversations*, 28–9.
[40] Ibid. 24.
[41] Ibid. 28.

world become 'aussi microscopique qu'une tête d'épingle' (140; 'as microscopic as a pinhead', 112), with Guadeloupeans living in all different parts of the world and moving back and forth, and people from all continents living in Guadeloupe. She has observed with dismay the modern diminishing importance of geographical boundaries, in contrast to which she has devoted her whole life to Guadeloupe and has never left the island.

She is at once afraid of and drawn to the sea, which represents the call of the world outside.

Je ne savais pas nager. Aussi, je me tenais loin de la mer qui me hélait de sa voix de femme folle:
—Approche-toi près, tout près. Arrache tes vêtements. Plonge. Laisse-moi te rouler, te serrer, frotter ton corps de mes algues. Tu ne sais pas que c'est de moi que tu es née? Tu ne sais pas que tu me portes en toi? Sans moi, ta vie n'existerait pas.

Une fois, je suis tombée sur un homme et une femme qui faisaient l'amour sous un amandier-pays. Pas gênés, ils m'ont jeté des paroles si grossières que je me suis mise à courir. (140–1)

I didn't know how to swim. So I stayed far from the sea who called to me with the voice of a madwoman:
'Come nearer, nearer. Tear off your clothes. Plunge in. Let me roll over you, squeeze you and rub your body with my seaweed. Don't you know this is where you came from? Don't you know I'm part of you? Without me, you wouldn't be alive.'

Once I came across a man and a woman making love under an almond tree. Not at all embarrassed, they shouted such obscenities I started to run. (113)

Léocadie Timothée's narrative associates her tortured relation to the sea with repressed sexuality. Just as she has never left the island, she has never had a romantic relationship. Just as others experience the island as imprisoning, she describes her desexualized body as 'la prison dans laquelle j'étais condamnée à vivre' (144; 'the prison I had been sentenced to live in', 116). The personified sea speaks in an overtly sexualized language, teasing her to tear off her clothes and come into physical contact with it. In describing itself as necessary to birth and life, the sea here brings together the notions of crossing, sexuality, and creativity.

The passage quoted also suggests the originary role that crossing the sea has played in the black diaspora ('c'est de moi que tu es née'). This dramatizes the other-within-the-self ('tu me portes en toi') that is a constitutive part of Creole Antillean identity. Léocadie Timothée bitterly asks herself why she had chosen to bury herself in the island her whole life. Her answer, 'C'est que je voulais travailler pour ma race' (141; 'Because I wanted to work for my race', 113), suggests that she has developed and promoted a notion of identity apart from contact with others. Her repression of racial and cultural hybridity and exchange is textually associated with her desexualization and avoidance of the world beyond her home.

While Léocadie Timothée has spent her life rooted in the same place, Francis Sancher has been errant and nomadic. In contrast to her complete absence of sexual activity, Sancher has had many and varied romantic attachments. While she is childless, he has many children who are all over the world. She has devoted her life to working on behalf of blacks, and his *errance* has been in part an attempt to transcend his whiteness. In many ways, Léocadie Timothée and Francis Sancher can be seen as type and antitype, their lives inverted mirrors of each other. It is appropriate then that at the outset of the novel it is she who discovers his dead body while she is walking through the forest. When she begins her narrative with 'Ce mort-là est à moi' (139; 'That corpse is mine', 111), the ambiguity inspires several different readings. It is an acknowledgement that in Sancher she encounters her double, and that his dead body is a reflection of her moribund spirit. Also, in claiming the corpse as her own, she assumes responsibility for his death. It is an admission of guilt: 'Ce n'est pas hasard si c'est moi qui l'a trouvé. . . . Je suis devenue sa maîtresse et sa complice. Je ne le quitterai qu'au moment où les premières pelletées de terre tomberont sur le bois de son cercueil' (139; 'It's no coincidence that I was the one to find him. . . . I have become his mistress and his accomplice. I won't leave him until the first shovelfuls of earth fall on his wooden coffin', 111). Even if she does not admit to having killed him, she has wished for and brought about his demise. At the same time, she intimates that a romantic and criminal partnership perhaps existed between them.

I have pointed to how the themes of crossing and sexual fertility converge in several instances in this novel to figure a way out of the imprisonment that the characters experience. Sancher, whose contact with the villagers has a liberating effect on their lives, himself has undertaken many crossings in his life and has fathered several offspring. Yet he is no less imprisoned than the villagers who become inspired by his voyages, and he sees his crossing as having failed. The failure of the voyages that he has undertaken haunts his nightmares:

Ses sommeils n'étaient pas des voyages en paradis, mais des combats avec des invisibles qui, à en juger par ses cris, enfonçaient des pointes rougies à la braise dans les recoins de son âme. (40)

His sleep was not filled with voyages to paradise, but struggles with invisible spirits who, judging from his shouts, stuck their red-hot irons into every corner of his soul. (23)

When light-skinned Loulou Lameaulnes suggests that they think of themselves as being on the same side of the black–white divide, Sancher protests:

Nous ne sommes plus du même camp et je vais te dire que je n'appartiens plus à aucun camp. . . . Au début, c'est vrai, nous étions du même camp. C'est pour cela que je suis parti de l'autre côté du monde. Je ne peux pas te dire que ce voyage-là s'est bien terminé. Je suis naufragé, échoué sur la grève (127)

You're mistaken. We're no longer on the same side and what's more I don't belong to any side. And yet, to a certain extent, you're right. To start off with, it's true, we were on the same side. That's why I left for the other side of the world. I can't say the journey ended successfully. I was shipwrecked, washed up on the shore (101)

Sancher understands his *errance* and accompanying involvement in the political struggles in several countries as a process of trying to undo his identity as a white colonizer. The various crossings that he has undertaken figure his attempt to change from one side to the other of the colonized–colonizer divide. However, the crossing has resulted in a shipwreck, and rather than succeeding in changing sides, he has forsworn the idea of belonging to sides altogether. The shipwreck here not only figures failure, but also the in-between space of simultaneous belonging and non-belonging that Sancher self-consciously occupies. If the voyage figures Sancher's attempt to transcend the limitations of his white ancestors' crimes, the shipwreck is a figure for his state of imprisonment in the impossibility of erasing that aspect of his ancestral past. In many ways, the failed voyage as captured by the figure of the shipwreck represents Sancher's unwitting *créolité*, the ambivalent and painful multiplicity of his uneasily coexisting ancestries.

Sancher's dying belief is that despite his lifetime of trying to undo the crimes of his ancestors, his blood is his destiny, and his past is irrevocable:

On ne peut pas mentir à son sang! On ne peut pas changer de camp! Troquer un rôle pour un autre. Rompre la chaîne de galère. J'ai essayé de le faire et tu vois, cela n'a rien changé. . . . Toi, tu crois que nous naissons le jour où nous naissons? . . . Moi, je te dis que nous naissons bien avant cela. A peine la première gorgée d'air avalée, nous sommes déjà coupables de tous les péchés originels, . . . commis par des hommes et des femmes retournés depuis longtemps en poussière, mais qui laissent leurs crimes intacts en nous. J'ai cru que je pouvais échapper à la punition! Je n'y suis pas arrivé! (41–2)

One can't lie to one's flesh and blood! One can't change sides! Swap one role for another. Break the chain of misery. I've tried and you see, nothing's changed. . . . You, do you believe we are born the day we are born? . . . I'm telling you we're born well before that. Hardly have we swallowed our first breath of air than we already have to account for every original sin . . . committed by men and women who have long returned to dust, but leave their crimes intact within us. I believed I could escape punishment! I couldn't! (24)

He has come to Guadeloupe after his wandering, resigned finally to meet what he sees as his unavoidable fate, his punishment for his ancestor's crimes. His ancestors before him have died mysteriously at a similar age due to the curse on his lineage. Despite his efforts to choose his own fate, he must be held accountable for the sins of those before him. The determinism of blood lineage renders him already, irrevocably guilty from birth. His descendants will similarly inherit his guilt. His voyages to other lands constitute his effort to be reborn: 'Cuba, c'est le pays que j'avais choisi pour ma re-naissance. Vois-tu, là j'étais naïf. C'est impossible. On ne re-naît jamais. On ne sort jamais deux fois du ventre de sa mère' (155; 'Cuba is the country I chose for my rebirth. You see, I was naïve about that. It's impossible. You are never born again. You never come out twice from your mother's womb', 125). The choice of Cuba as the place of rebirth is telling. Because Cuba is a Caribbean island in which a successful revolution was waged, Sancher's efforts could be read as a Glissantian *Détour*.[42] Yet even after his attempted *Détours* in Cuba, Africa, and South America, he is convinced of his inability to escape his ancestral original sin.

Sancher has come to Guadeloupe to die and to put an end to his lineage along with its curse. He lives in constant fear of pursuit by his avenger, real or supernatural. Ironically, however, despite his belief that rebirth is impossible, his presence in Rivière au Sel, or rather his

---

[42] See Glissant's mention of Moncada in *Discours*, 132 and my discussion in Ch. 3 above.

death, has precisely the effect of rebirth for many of the villagers with whom he comes into contact. Mira, having given birth to his child, says 'Ma vraie vie commence avec sa mort' (231; 'My real life begins with his death', 193), and Dodose says 'Voici venu le temps de mon re-commencement' (214; 'Now is the time for me to start over again', 177). At the wake, Moïse, Aristide, Émile Étienne l'Historien, Lucien Évariste, Dodose Pélagie, and Dinah each make the decision to leave their lives in Rivière au Sel to seek new possibilities in other lands. Dodose Pélagie resolves to travel in order to seek better medical care for her ill son. Rosa resolves to repair her relationship with the daughter she neglected to love. Lucien Évariste and Émile Étienne are both inspired with ideas for new literary and historical projects, for which they will also have to travel. Mira's son Quentin, one expects, will wander the world in search of his identity. All these characters are given a new beginning by Sancher's death, in most cases accompanied by a decision to leave the island.

The familiar Christian themes of original sin, martyrdom, and redemption render Sancher a Christlike figure whose death gives others new life.[43] But what is the nature of his involuntary martyrdom, and of the redemption his death allows? The 'original sin' for which the Sancher line bears guilt is slavery. On this level, we can understand Sancher's extraordinary terror of Xantippe and belief that he is pursuing him to his death to be tied to Xantippe's role as the archetypal black man of the island.

> Il m'a suivi partout. Quand je traversais les rivières à gué, il était là. Quand j'enfonçais jusqu'à mi-corps dans les marais. Il ne m'a jamais lâché d'une semelle. Une nuit, j'ai plaidé avec lui: 'Est-ce que tu ne connais pas le pardon? La faute est très ancienne. Et puis, je n'en suis pas l'auteur direct. Pourquoi faut-il que les dents des enfants toujours soient agacées?' (118)

> He's followed me everywhere. When I forded the rivers he was there. When I was up to my waist in the swamps, he stuck to me like a leech. One night I pleaded with him: 'Don't you know the meaning of forgiveness? The fault is a very ancient one. I'm not the one to be blamed directly. Why do the children's teeth always have to be on edge?' (91)

Xantippe is a mythical, representative West Indian archetype. It is precisely the problem of representativeness that seems to be pursuing Sancher. Even though it was not in fact he who committed the crime of slavery, he is made to stand and be accountable for ancient crimes

---

[43] See my discussion in Ch. 4, above, of Christophe in *Saison*, who bears the sins of the older generation.

committed; the punishment is not only that he must die but that he must carry with him the crimes of his ancestors. His martyrdom is in effect that of having to bear the burden of an already-guilty and inescapable past.

The theme of blood-lines and transgenerational haunting of past guilt that we have seen in the discussion of *Saison* in Ch. 4 also informs the narratives of the villagers. Dinah, Mira's stepmother, says, 'Personne ne sait que je suis la cause du drame qui vient de trouver sa conclusion. . . . Les malheurs des enfants sont toujours causés par les fautes cachées des parents' (104; 'Nobody knows that I am to blame for the tragedy that has just drawn to a close. . . . The misfortunes of the children are always caused by the secret sins of the parents', 79). Rosa, Vilma's mother, echoes: 'C'est moi qui suis coupable, responsable de tout ce malheur. Car, il ne faut pas chercher, le malheur des enfants est toujours causé par les parents' (166; 'I am the one to blame for all this unhappiness. For you don't need to look very far; a child's misfortunes can always be traced to the parents', 136). The belief in the transmission of guilt across generations expressed by these two mothers can be juxtaposed with the theme of motherhood that runs through the novel. The daughters, Mira and Vilma, are both Sancher's lovers and each becomes pregnant with his child. They share in common their abandonment by their mothers, for whom Sancher becomes a substitute: Mira's mother died in childbirth, and Vilma's mother does not love her. Several of the other characters are also not loved by their mothers: Loulou, for example, and Sonny. The theme of motherlessness or the absence of a mother's love, can be read, as we have seen in Ch. 5, along the lines of exile from one's homeland:[44] 'la Guadeloupe marâtre ne nourrit plus ses enfants et que tant d'entre eux se gèlent les pieds en région parisienne' (37–38; 'Guadeloupe, that cruel stepmother, no longer nurtures her children, so many of them are forced to freeze to death in the Paris suburbs', 21).[45] However, the absent mother is also simultaneously too present in the form of the transgenerational transmission of guilt that burdens the daughters.

[44] Rosa also associates the reunion with her lost child with India, her *pays d'origine*.
[45] Marie-Agnès Sourieau uses the psychoanalytic language of 'le traumatisme originel' and 'le retour à la mère/terre' to read the theme of the mother in *Traversée*: 'Ce manque maternel fondamental, tant dans le cadre familial que communautaire, entraîne des déséquilibres relationnels dont témoigne *Traversée de la Mangrove*, un monde empreint d'une violence extrême, un monde dans lequel l'agressivité tend à la négation mortelle de l'autre et de soi-même'. See 'Traversée de la mangrove de Maryse Condé: Un champ de pulsions communes', *Francofonia*, 24 (1993), 109–22.

TWO HAUNTS: HISTORY AND REPRESENTATION

Similarly, Sancher's martyrdom can be read as the result of a past that haunts by being at once too absent and too present. As for his knowledge of his ancestors' history, he possesses only scraps of information in the form of old documents whose contents' veracity is dubious. He has only a sketchy idea of his past. In Guadeloupe his search proves to be still more deferred, as he cannot find any definite confirmation for any of his beliefs about his ancestors' presence and activities on the island. Yet this history is overwhelming. It haunts his nightmares and follows him around the world, and finally hounds him to his death. Its meaning remains elusive yet determinate.

Sancher's predicament, 'L'histoire, c'est mon cauchemar' (235; 'History's my nightmare', 196), an echo of Joyce and Marx,[46] seems to capture the paradox of being at once without history and chained to it.[47] It is at this point that the comparison between Sancher and Condé may again be made. The central allegorical relation in this text, as Condé herself has suggested, is that between Sancher and the postcolonial writer. While literally the original sin is slavery, Sancher's martyrdom lies in his obligation to be representative: what kills him is the burden of the past, and he dies on behalf of the villagers who find redemption in his death. Despite his wanderings, he cannot be free of this burden. This allegorizes the predicament of the writer: she is called upon to represent her people and their collective history. The original sin that haunts and drives Sancher to his grave can be read as the force of a collective history that underlies the referential demands and expectations placed on postcolonial writing.

When Condé compares her situation as a writer returning to Guadeloupe to Sancher's situation in Rivière au Sel, this implicitly draws attention to the ways in which her return also constitutes a similar martyrdom in literary terms. After having travelled the world both physically and novelistically, she, like Sancher, returns to

---

[46] 'History, Stephen said, is a nightmare from which I am trying to awake', James Joyce, *Ulysses* (1922); 'The tradition of all the dead generations weighs like a nightmare on the brain of the living', Karl Marx, *The Eighteenth Brumaire of Louis Bonaparte* (1852).

[47] The theme of the familial haunting is also explored in a different way in *Les Derniers Rois mages*, in which Spéro's knowledge of his royal African ancestry makes his life in the present unlivable. The memory of Béhanzin, last king of Dahomey, deposed by the French and exiled to Martinique at the end of the 19th cent., is also the subject of Glissant's *La Case du commandeur*.

Guadeloupe to write. *Traversée* is Condé's first novel to be written and to take place exclusively in Guadeloupe. For this reason, its reception by Antilleans had special significance for debates about Antillean literature. Chamoiseau comments about *Traversée:*

> Another reflection concerns the contemporary nature of the novel, which takes place here and now, as if to break from the past of our literatures. In spite of this effort, however, the narrative carries an ancestral essence with profound meanings that transcend time ... because the essential reality of a people and a country can signify its truth without the feeble artifice of contemporaneity. Our past is so much alive in our daily cares and problems that this contemporary novel speaks with the voice of the old Guadeloupean mabos telling our true story.[48]

Chamoiseau's comments indicate that the stakes are very high for reading *Traversée* as a certain kind of representative Antillean work, even as he points to the text's desire *not* to be read that way. He accuses the novel of wanting, in its contemporaneity, to 'break from the past of our literatures'. He reads Condé's choice to portray modern Guadeloupean life to be a gesture of resistance to history. But regardless of this resistance, he claims, an 'ancestral essence' prevents the break with the past from being successful. Thus through the novel, he claims, the 'essential reality' of the Antilles can 'signify its truth'. The realm of the personal is so inevitably and deeply infused with the preoccupation with 'our past' that the personal narrative inevitably becomes the collective narrative. Chamoiseau imposes a reading of the novel as an Antillean novel, in which the writer's desire to break free comes up against her state of being chained inescapably to history and to collective life. Chamoiseau plays the role of taskmaster, disapproving the unruliness of trying to evade the burden placed on writers.

Chamoiseau invokes the 'voice of the old Guadeloupean mabos'. Not only does Condé's novel refer to the collective past, but she speaks with its folkloric voice. This particular comment in Chamoiseau's text might be read as a pointed response to Condé's character Cyrille, the *conteur*. The theorists of the *créolité* movement have made the *conteur* their central male figure, the repository of Creole culture and the agent of its transmission from life on the plantation.[49] In

---

[48] 'Reflections', 393.
[49] Confiant's glossy photo-anthology *Les Maîtres de la parole créole* (Paris: Gallimard, 1995), consisting of profiles of actual Antillean *conteurs* and transcriptions of their tales, notably does not include a single woman.

Traversée, the *conteur* is an incoherent buffoon and serves as little more than comic relief. This jab at the ancestor claimed by *créolité* signals a larger critique of the *créolité* movement undertaken by the novel. In an article published the same year as her novel, Condé reflects upon how her return to Guadeloupe has shed light on her role as a writer:

> To live in this land is to speak of it in the present. It is to write of it in the present.
> And this leads me to reflect upon this question: what should we say in our books? ...
> This is something very difficult: to find a way of speaking about this land as it is, to take account of its modernity and perhaps to integrate its modernity with its memories, the shreds of a past without which the present would have no vitality, no flavour.[50]

Condé's emphasis on speaking and writing in the present seems to be a self-consciously coded wresting away of literary freedom from the iron grip of imposed prescriptions. Yet she is aware of the meaning that 'the shreds of a past' bear on the present in the Antilles, and she sees herself in the role of creative *bricoleuse*, drawing upon incomplete pieces of the past to open up the present and the future.

With the character of Lucien Évariste, Condé parodies the Guadeloupean writer's situation. Like the character Jean Louis, author of *La Guadeloupe inconnue*, who is ridiculed in *La Vie scélérate* for writing a book that nobody will read, Lucien Évariste is an independence activist educated in France and enamoured of the revolutionary potential of writing. He is under pressure from his patriotic circle to write in Creole but is ashamed to admit that he barely knows the language.[51] He is unsure about whether to write a historical novel about the heroism of the maroons or about a nineteenth-century slave revolt. His friendship with Sancher, however, inspires him to depart from these ideas altogether:

> Au lieu, enfant d'aujourd'hui et de la ville, de traquer des nèg mawon ou des paysans du XIX siècle, pourquoi ne pas mettre bout à bout souvenirs et bribes de confidences, écarter les mensonges, reconstituer la trajectoire et la personnalité du défunt? ... Il lui faudrait refuser le vertige des idées reçues. Regarder dans les yeux de dangereuses vérités. Déplaire. Choquer.[52] ...

---

[50] 'Habiter ce pays, la Guadeloupe', *Chemins critiques*, 1 (1989), 11, 13, as cited in Lionnet, *Postcolonial Representations*, 72–3.

[51] Condé herself is not adept at Creole, as she admits in Françoise Pfaff, *Entretiens avec Maryse Condé* (Paris: Karthale, 1993), 112.

Europe. Amérique. Afrique. Francis Sancher avait parcouru tous ces pays. Alors ne devrait-il pas en faire autant? (227)

Instead of hunting down Maroons or nineteenth-century peasants, why not, as an urban son of the twentieth century, put together Sancher's memories end to end, as well as snatches of his personal secrets, brush aside the lies and reconstitute the personality of the deceased? . . . He would have to reject the power of generally accepted ideas. He would have to look dangerous truths in the face. He would have to displease. He would have to shock. . . .
Europe. America. Africa. Francis Sancher had traveled all these lands. So shouldn't he do the same? (188–9)

Putting aside the heroic historical novel about the maroons and foregoing the approval of his cohorts, Lucien Évariste decides to write a modern novel about Francis Sancher by putting together fragments of memories and secrets. Of course the author's own *Moi, Tituba* could be described as a book of the heroic genre of *marronage*. Although Condé has described her Tituba as a 'mock-epic character' and Tituba's encounter with the maroons as a parody of the genre,[53] *Traversée* perhaps represents a move away from the heroic genre, albeit a rewriting of it, and toward a different kind of history. Similarly, at the end of *La Vie scélérate*, Coco describes the book that she will write:

Peut-être faudrait-il que je la raconte, cette histoire? Avec risque de déplaire et de choquer, peut-être faudrait-il que moi, à mon tour, je paie ma dette? Ce serait une histoire de gens très ordinaires qui à leur manière très ordinaire n'en avaient pas moins fait couler le sang. . . . Un livre bien différent de ceux ambitieux qu'avait rêvés d'écrire ma mère: 'Mouvements révolutionnaires du monde noir' et tutti quanti. Un livre sans grands tortionnaires ni somptueux martyrs. Mais qui pèserait quand même son poids de chair et de sang. Histoire des miens.[54]

Would I perhaps have to recount this story? At the risk of displeasing and shocking, would I in my turn, perhaps have to pay my debt? It would be a story of very ordinary people who in their very ordinary way had nonetheless made blood flow. . . . A book quite different from those ambitious ones my mother had dreamed of writing: *Revolutionary Movements of the Black World* and all the rest. A book with neither great torturers nor lavish martyrdoms.

[52] According to Condé, her own playful ridicule of Guadeloupean independence activists in *La Vie scélérate* offended many of her politically committed friends. See Condé's anecdotal account in Clark, '"Je me suis réconciliée"', 106.

[53] See Ann Scarboro, Afterword to Maryse Condé, *I, Tituba, Black Witch of Salem*, trans. Richard Philcox (Charlottesville: University Press of Virginia, 1992), 201; Pfaff, *Entretiens*, 90.

[54] (Paris: Seghers, 1987), 340.

But one that would still be heavy with its weight of flesh and blood. The story of my people.[55]

Émile Étienne, l'Historien resolves to forego history to explore the 'lieux de mémoire' of the island:

Je voudrais écrire une histoire de ce pays basée sur les souvenirs gardés au creux des mémoires, au creux des curs. Ce que les pères ont dit aux fils, ce que les mères ont dit aux filles. Je voudrais aller du Nord au Sud, de l'Est à l'Ouest recueillir toutes ces paroles qu'on n'a jamais écoutées (237)

I'd like to write a history of this island that would be based solely on the memories kept in the hollow of our minds and the hollow of our hearts. What fathers told their sons and mothers told their daughters. I'd like to travel north and south, east and west, collecting all those words that have never been listened to (198)

The shift from the ambition to write 'histoire' to the writing of 'mémoire' that Condé, after Pierre Nora, has noted in her own oeuvre, is marked in these characters' crucial moments of recognition of their roles as writers.[56]

These resolutions draw attention to the necessity of departure for writing. They closely associate the rejection of the writing of predictable and programmatic texts with the decision to travel to other lands. Literary freedom is associated with *errance*. On the other hand, the text self-consciously remarks on some of the ambivalences of such literary cosmopolitanism. The writer's distance from local readers, as well as a tendency to be oriented toward a French/European audience:

Il se vit édité par une grande maison de la Rive Gauche, salué par la presse parisienne, mais affrontant la critique locale:
—Lucien Évariste, ce roman-là est-il bien guadeloupéen?
—Il est écrit en français. Quel français? As-tu pensé en l'écrivant à la langue de ta mère, le créole?
—As-tu comme le talentueux Martiniquais, Patrick Chamoiseau, déconstruit le français-français? (228)

He saw his book published by a leading publisher on the Left Bank in Paris, acclaimed by the press, but coming up against local critics.
'Is this novel really Guadeloupean, Lucien Evariste?'
'It's written in French. What kind of French? Did you ever think of writing in Creole, your mother tongue?'

[55] Conde, *Tree of Life*, trans. Victoria Reiter (New York: Ballantine, 1992), 357.
[56] Pfaff, *Entretiens*, 99; Pierre Nora, *Les Lieux de mémoire*, i. *Entre Mémoire et Histoire: La Problématique des Lieux* (Paris: Gallimard, 1984), pp. xvii–xlii.

'Have you deconstructed the French-French language like the gifted Martinican writer Patrick Chamoiseau?' (189)

While it may be necessary to be elsewhere and an outsider to write, this location and identity bring the writer's authenticity into question, especially since the writer becomes 'other' by association with the colonial *métropole*. Through Lucien Évariste, the novel parodies some of the ambivalences plaguing the postcolonial writer, who is called upon to answer to the vanguards of authenticity and held accountable to a notion of representativeness. The ironic insertion of Chamoiseau into this passage is Condé's pointed characterization of the *créolité* movement as such a source of literary constraint that applies standards of authenticity to Antillean texts with reference to Creole culture.[57]

Perhaps in response to her playful parody, Chamoiseau writes: 'in reading this title, *Traversée de la mangrove*, I hear and would certainly have written: *Tracée dans la mangrove*, in order to evoke both the path of the runaway slave and the Creole act of crossing'.[58] Ironically, he invokes the very same maroons that Lucien Évariste abandons as the subject of his novel.[59] Remarkably, Chamoiseau reinstates the primacy of the maroon as the referent of the narrative, changing the title in order to make his point. Of course, 'the Creole act of crossing' is well evoked by Condé's title and there is no need to change it to give it that resonance. However, Chamoiseau wants to associate the maroon and *créolité*, asserting their coexistence as referents of his rewriting of Condé's title.

This leads us directly to Sancher's comment about the title of the book that he has come to Guadeloupe to write:

Tu vois, j'écris. Ne me demande pas à quoi ça sert. D'ailleurs, je ne finirai

---

[57] 'I fear that Creole might become a prison in which the Caribbean writers run the risk of being jailed', Condé, interviewed in Scarboro, Afterword to *I, Tituba*, 207.

[58] 'Reflections', 390. Note the title of Chamoiseau and Confiant's *Lettres créoles: Tracées antillaises et continentales de la littérature— Haiti, Guadeloupe, Martinique, Guyane, 1635–1975* (Paris: Hatier, 1991).

[59] In contrast to the critical consensus about *Traversée*'s celebration of *créolité*'s communal orientation, Kathleen Balbutansky points out that Chamoiseau overlooks the 'ironic impact of the novel's title. Indeed, the title, which also serves as a signifier for the novel, is not so much an echo of the optimistic view of the "mémoire collective" of *Éloge* as it is an intertextual pun, a sober warning'. She rightly observes that 'the fundamental irony of Condé's novel is that its dead Caliban lays bare the impossibility of ever recovering a "conscience commune" and the danger of pursuing it'. See '*Créolité* in Question: Caliban in Maryse Condé's *Traversée de la mangrove*', in Condé and Cottenet-Hage (eds.), *Penser la créolité*, 101–11: 103–5.

jamais ce livre puisque, avant d'en avoir tracé la première ligne et de savoir ce que je vais y mettre de sang, de rires, de larmes, de peur, d'espoir, enfin de tout ce qui fait qu'un livre est un livre et non pas une dissertation de raseur, la tête à demi fêlée, j'en ai trouvé le titre: 'Traversée de la Mangrove'. (192) You see, I'm writing. Don't ask me what's the point of it. Besides, I'll never finish this book because before I've even written the first line and known what I'm going to put in the way of blood, laughter, tears, fears and hope, well, everything that makes a book a book and not a boring dissertation by a half-cracked individual, I've already found the title: 'Crossing the Mangrove.' (158)

The nature of a creative work that explores the vicissitudes of pain, fear, hope, pleasure, and 'the exigencies of the human heart', is threatened by a determinacy implied by the titling of a book in advance.[60] This is precisely what Chamoiseau does in titling Condé's novel to fit his expectation that it be authentically Guadeloupean. Sancher points to the necessity of textual freedom for literary endeavours to be 'successful'. However, even the possibility of this success is undercut. Vilma responds, 'On ne traverse pas la mangrove. On s'empale sur les racines des palétuviers. On s'enterre et on étouffe dans la boue saumâtre' (192; 'You don't cross a mangrove. You'd spike yourself on the roots of the mangrove trees. You'd be sucked down and suffocated by the brackish mud', 158), and Sancher confirms: 'C'est ça, c'est justement ça' (192; 'Yes, that's it, that's precisely it', 158).

Chamoiseau claims that 'Maryse Condé foresees that in our countries, the "we" takes precedence over the "I" and that the protagonist is an entire people who has managed to survive.'[61] We must note that the protagonist of *Traversée* rather saliently fails to survive in the literal sense. Indeed, Francis Sancher's mysterious death in the forests of Guadeloupe—one that he predicted and feared—is the occasion for this novel-as-wake. Rather than foresee a survival, does Condé foresee some kind of inevitable death befalling the collectivity? Is Antillean literary culture as doomed as Francis Sancher? The allegorical relationship of 'I' to 'we' does indeed preoccupy this novel. Chamoiseau identifies the collectivity as the surviving protagonist of Condé's novel. Yet the national allegory that Chamoiseau proposes might be paradoxically undercut if one reads Sancher's

---

[60] Condé, 'Habiter', 13, cited in Lionnet, *Postcolonial Representations*, 73.
[61] 'Reflections', 292.

death as a failure to cross the mangrove of representativeness. Rather than see the protagonist as an allegorical representative of Antilleans, we might instead read Sancher's death as an allegory of the failure or refusal of representativeness.

What can it mean that Sancher's title, which overdetermines his novel, also describes an impossibility, a manifestation of what Glissant calls 'opacité': the act of crossing the mangrove?[62] Michael Lucey writes that *Traversée* 'is perhaps finally a novel about the possibility of failure, . . . the failure, for example, to account for a death; or the failure to write a past for Guadeloupe which could somehow unite its present or foresee its future; the failure also of finally ever writing a novel which could be "guadeloupéen".'[63] I mean to suggest that the failure of ever writing an authentically Guadeloupean novel, underscored by Sancher's inability to write the novel we are reading, may have something to do with the 'opacité' of allegory. Sancher's title, of course, also refers to the title of the novel that we are reading, and so his comments about his own novel invite the *mise-en-abîme* of the allegorical frame. Perhaps we could say that Condé's novel too is doomed to failure as a literary text because its meaning is overdetermined. But it is *precisely* this sort of allegorical decoding that is the cause of the overdetermination of both texts, Sancher's and Condé's. Even as we read the impossibility of crossing the mangrove as being 'about' the failure of reading allegorically, to do so we must rely on the allegorical frame that is set up by the text itself. Even while the concept of crossing the mangrove provides a rich interpretive framework, to read is to undermine interpretation. We are left within the vertiginous performative contradiction of the allegorical mangrove. This then, is the nature of Sancher's fatality: being caught in the back and forth of determinacy and indeterminacy that allegory underwrites.

Death and its productive potential are central to the contradictory logic of *Traversée*. Sancher comes to Guadeloupe to die and intends to put an end to his entire lineage. This mission coincides with his quest for his roots, his search for his Guadeloupean *béké* ancestors. He wants to terminate the pregnancies of Mira and Vilma in order to break the chain of his lineage and end its curse. The text associates the

---

[62] See Glissant, *Poétique de la relation*, (Paris: Gallimard, 1990), 203–9: 205–6: 'L'opaque ... est le non-réducible, qui est la plus vivace des garanties de participation et de confluence'.
[63] 'Voices accounting for the Past: Maryse Condé's *Traversée de la Mangrove*', in Condé et al. (eds.), *L'Héritage de Caliban* (Guadeloupe: Jasor, 1992), 123–32: 132.

quest for ancestral origin with a death impulse, a 'mal d'archive'.[64] The drive to ascertain the meaning of his past proves fatal. The novel begins, as it were, in the wake of Sancher's death, a gap that engenders the narratives that we have been reading.[65] As I have previously argued, his death is a martyrdom of representativeness that frees others from the burden of history. While some have seen Condé's return to Guadeloupe as evidence of a 'new-found humility' with regard to Guadeloupean culture,[66] I read this novel as an esoteric testament to a literary freedom ever more threatened by the expectation of authenticity because of the tendency of postcolonial literature to be haunted by the burden of history.[67]

My final points concern the character of Xantippe, with whose phantasmal narrative Condé chooses to conclude her novel. Xantippe is Condé's parody of the archetypal *uber*-male of *négritude*. Set apart from the other characters' narratives, his narrative has the air of myth. He is a maroon and a representative of the African element of Antillean identity. He is the Adamic originator and namer:

> J'ai nommé des ravines, sexes grands ouverts, dans le fin fond de la terre. J'ai nommé les roches au fond de l'eau et les poissons, gris comme les roches. En un mot, j'ai nommé ce pays. Il est sorti de mes reins dans une giclée de foutre. . . . Je n'aimais que le sable noir, noir comme ma peau et le deuil de mon cœur. (241–2)

> I named the gullies, gaping vaginas at the bottom of the earth. I named the rocks at the bottom of the water, and the fish, as gray as the rocks. In a word, I named this land. It spurted from my loins in a jet of sperm. I loved the black sand, black as my skin and the mourning in my heart. (202)

We recall Tituba's lament about the moonstone lost at the bottom of the water. Xantippe's naming of what lies in the (feminine) depths perhaps hopes to put to rest anxieties about loss, failure, and indeterminacy of the mangrove, with a claim to ownership of land by way of possessory ejaculation. Xantippe's description of his wife is

---

[64] Derrida, *Mal d'Archive: Une impression freudienne* (Paris: Galilée, 1995).
[65] Priska Degras uses Glissantian language to discuss the novel's preoccupation with lost history in 'Maryse Condé: L'Écriture de l'Histoire', *L'Esprit créateur*, 33/2 (1993), 73–81: 'Le Drame de "l'impossibilité" de l'Histoire donne ainsi naissance à une multiplicité de récits' (81).
[66] Lionnet, *Postcolonial Representations*, 72.
[67] One could postulate that Condé too 'departs' after this novel. Her next three works resume her literary *errance*, taking her characters to Cuba, Dominica, Colombia, and North America.

reminiscent of Senghor's poetic depiction of the hyper-sexualized black woman: 'Dans le temps d'autrefois, j'ai vécu avec Gracieuse. Gracieuse. Négresse noire. Canne Kongo juteuse. Malavois à écorce brodée. Tu fondais sous le palais de ma bouche' (242; 'Long ago I lived with Gracieuse. Gracieuse. My ebony-black woman. My juicy Kongo cane. My embroidered malavois, melting under the palate of my mouth', 202).[68] The relationship between naming, masculinist rhetoric and sexuality, and the privileging of unity with nature and the land present in Xantippe's monologue, parodies Antillean literary discourse—its origins in *négritude* and its contemporary incarnation in *créolité*.

Xantippe is the one by whom Sancher feels he is being pursued to his death. He is the one holding Sancher accountable for his ancestry and his past. Xantippe is the self-proclaimed repository of the island's history:

Rivière au Sel j'ai nommé ce lieu.

Je connais toute son histoire. C'est sur les racines en béquilles de ses mapous lélé que la flaque de mon sang a séché. Car un crime s'est commis ici, ici même, dans les temps très anciens. . . . Je sais où sont enterrés les corps des suppliciés. . . . Personne n'a percé ce secret, enseveli dans l'oubli. (244–5)

Rivière au Sel I named this place.

I know its entire history. It was on the buttress roots of its manjack trees that the pool of my blood dried. For a crime was committed here, on this very spot, a long, long time ago. . . . I know where the tortured bodies are buried. . . . Nobody has pierced this secret, buried and forgotten. (204–5)

Unearthing the buried, piercing secrets, penetrating, and naming the depths, are versions of allegory's will to unveil. In light of the correspondences between Sancher and Condé, Xantippe's haunting of the island can be read as the force of an archetype that continues to haunt Antillean literary endeavours. The maroons that Lucien Évariste decides to abandon in his literary project make their appearance here in the archetypal form of Xantippe, as if to imply that his novel, which is also Sancher's as well as the one we are

---

[68] *Poèmes* (Paris: Seuil, 1984), 16–17: 'Femme nue, femme obscure | Fruit mûr à la chair ferme, sombres extases du vin noir, bouche qui fait lyrique ma bouche | Savane aux horizons purs, savane qui frémis aux caresses ferventes du Vent d'Est | Tamtam sculpté, tamtam tendu qui grondes sous les doigts du vainqueur | Ta voix grave de contralto est le chant spirituel de l'Aimée.'

reading, is ultimately unable to escape that determinacy and expectation. Xantippe's claim to know all the island's history, in contrast to the fragmented, incomplete patchwork of history—or memory— that forms the novel's structure, provides an answer to the mystery of Sancher's death. Xantippe's final pseudo-resolution of the questions raised throughout the novel tolls the bell of Sancher's doom: the burden of hermeneutic constraint placed on a literature, in which successful unearthing and unveiling is also a failure to cross.

EPILOGUE

Throughout this book, I have been concerned with the question of exemplarity: what does it mean to claim that a text, a character, an author, or a crossing is representative?[1] Now I pose again the question of representativeness, this time with respect to the book itself. This study began with Aimé Césaire and closed with Maryse Condé. Through its most salient shifts, from poetry to prose fiction, from a male to a female figure, from a senior to a relatively junior figure in twentieth-century French Antillean literature, this book registers the extent to which an Antillean sensibility initially formulated in poetry has been inherited, challenged, revised, and reinvigorated by prose fiction, especially with the emergence of writing by women.

The *Cahier*, the founding and most influential text of this literature, is a poem of grand, even epic, tone and scope. Yet the text with which I close, *Traversée*, is a prose fiction of quotidian existence, a 'poetic of daily life' that self-consciously prioritizes the vicissitudes of individual itineraries.[2] On the one hand, Condé's fiction seems to facilitate the ironic questioning of the possibility and desirability of the representativeness that hallmarks the grand sweep of the poetic ur-text. On the other hand, ambivalence about representativeness is, as we have seen, already present in the founding text's encounter with its allegorical modes. From the interlacing of a complex of problems in Chapters 1–3, to the engagement of one artist's attempt to work out these patterns in her evolving oeuvre and in the hurly-burly of her career in Chapters 4–6, the route that this book has travelled has become both more singular and more representative at the same time.

My argument has relied to some extent on the particularity of Condé, whose position vis-à-vis her fellow writers is unique. The distinctive triangular and self-critical trajectory of her life and her fiction uniquely facilitates the exploration of dynamics of *Retour*,

---

[1] For an exploratory overview of the concept of exemplarity in Western thought, see Alexander Gelley's introd. to id. (ed.), *Unruly Examples: On the Rhetoric of Exemplarity*, (Stanford, Calif.: Stanford University Press, 1995), 1–24.

[2] Marie-Denise Shelton, 'Literature Extracted: A Poetic of Daily Life', *Callaloo*, 15/1 (1992), 167–78.

Détour, and *Relation*. Condé's texts point to ways in which the teleology of *Retour* forces people and places to represent in ways that they may not be able to bear productively. The productive *Détour*-like tensions of exile—from one's home and collectivity—and self-distance make us question the heady valorization of *créolité*, a distinctively Antillean potential for *Relation*, to the extent that it is in danger of becoming a constraining regression.

In this study Condé has become bearer and provoker of a set of Antillean concerns and paradoxes. As we saw in Chapter 4, her Guadeloupean characters' return to Africa becomes an occasion for a reflection on the simultaneous desire for, inevitability, and impossibility of return. In Chapter 5, Tituba's sorcery and allegory suggested, in the relationship between the absence of history and the creative potential of writing, a radical questioning of both the distinction between and the conflation of literature and politics in Antillean writing. Chapter 6 relies on previously problematized notions of return, representation, and the past to read the failed crossing of *Traversée* as the condition of its successful critique of Antillean literary culture. Within the rhythm of repeated return to paradoxes, one sub-paradox can be found in how the shifts of this study engage in a move toward both particularity and paradigm.

The paradoxical pairing of general and particular recalls the way in which the reference to allegory throughout this book has engaged in a dance alternating between two partners. Allegory emerges as both a technical, rhetorical term belonging to an ancient tradition and a topographical notion of crossing specific to the Antilles. Used as an instrument of cognition for real space and time, allegory becomes more than merely a trope among tropes. It becomes a way of understanding the space–time world of a culture. In much the same way, 'in-betweenness' in this book does not merely refer to a neutral, speculative space, but to a space of real journeys, histories, introspection, and retrospection. One of my goals has been to show how allegory can move between its most abstract properties and its literalizing effects in the texts that I discuss, to reliteralize the metaphorical journey while also giving a playful and metaphorizing versatility to the concept of allegory.

The notion that certain literary modes may be locked into material conditions recalls my criticism of Jameson in Chapter 1. Jameson's valorization of Third World 'national allegory' as a form that allows access to the real, literal level of texts, becomes for him a desired alternative to a fragmentary postmodernism. Is my deployment of allegory to illuminate the representational capacities, crises, and impossibilities of the Antilles vulnerable to a version of the criticism to which I subjected Jameson? Does my mapping of discontinuity on to the Antilles resemble the desire to map wholeness onto the third world? I have used allegory to explore a set of problems associated with post-structuralism; at the same time I have taken Antillean culture, history, and literature as my primary points of reference. To the extent that I map the abstractions of allegory onto the topography, history, and conditions of Antillean life and literature, it may appear that I have made the Antilles stand as exemplar of a version of textuality that post-structuralism valorizes. Ironically, it may be charged, it is in this very exploration of the Antillean situation as the embodiment of unencumbered textual play that the abstractions of post-structuralism become concretized, literalized, and made to refer to material reality. Thus, I might be accused of positing the Antilles as a refuge from an endless deferral of meaning in the very process of exploring their productive textual-ities.

This question can also be inserted into the theorizing of the relationship between the postmodern and the postcolonial. On one view, postmodern insights, at their most productive and significant, ought to be articulated as versions of postcolonial modes of critique, cognition, and expression. On another, less sanguine view,

> The 'suspension' of the referent in the literary sign, and the 'crisis of representation' which has followed in its wake, has effected within the dominant forms of Anglo-American post-structuralist theory a wholesale retreat from geography and history into a realm of pure 'textuality' in which the principle of indeterminacy smothers the possibility of social or political significance for literature.[3]

My book has been concerned broadly with the encounter with the 'crisis of representation' in Antillean literature. However, rather than effecting 'a wholesale retreat from geography and history', I have suggested ways in which an emphasis on textuality can provide means of envisioning a connection to geography and the transmission of history. This approach registers both the consequences of the 'suspension' of the literary sign and how those consequences render possible social and political significance even when an easy optimism falters.

[3] Stephen Slemon and Helen Tiffin in eid. (eds.), *After Europe: Critical Theory and Post-Colonial Writing* (Sydney: Dangaroo, 1989), p. x.

To address whether my project enacts its own object of critique, I want to point to the attempts to 'cross' in the texts that I study. One provocative interlocutor asked, 'Kurtz made it up the river; why can't Francis Sancher cross the mangrove?' Admittedly, in the texts that I have read here, attempts to cross generally seem to fail. Francis Sancher dies while trying to cross the mangrove, even as his death leads to other crossings. The triumphant 'chanson de Tituba' is in effect a lament about loss, exile, and heroic failure. The shipwrecks of the *Cahier* shake the anchor of its heroic arrival. The 'expérience du gouffre' ultimately casts into doubt the claim of an identity that is 'one's own'.[4] In what has preceded, I have repeatedly pointed to the ways in which purportedly successful crossing is deeply mingled with failure; texts' claims to cross are subverted within the texts themselves; and impossibility becomes the condition for the possibility of crossing. This paradox has a parallel in my attempt to put into *Relation* the peculiar dynamics of allegory, trauma, and the space–time world of Antillean culture. One by-product of my placing of these concepts into networks of mutual reference, correspondence, and cross-fertilization is my own impossible claim to 'cross', in the ad hoc sense that this book has imparted to the term. That is to say, the connections between crossing and reference, and between the Antilles and the web of problems woven around it, may fail at its most successful points. As Spivak articulates the paradox, 'The impossible "no" to a structure which one critiques, yet inhabits intimately, is the deconstructive philosophical position, and the everyday here and now of "postcoloniality" is a case of it.'[5] Yet, any such 'failure' is by no means disheartening.

Finally, then, the notion of paradox needs revisiting. I have been proceeding on the implicit hope that paradoxes intrigue and inspire thought and curiosity, and bring us further along our paths of enquiry and progress. However, it may be necessary to apply sceptical pressure to that assumption. There may be a point at which paradoxes stop being useful triggers for reflection and start to become obfuscating, forbidding, evasive, and regressive. Disorderliness must be acknowledged; and I have no wish to detract from residual complications and disarray by ending with the conceptual neatness of the paradox. This book has set up a particular and paradigmatic optic for examining the systemic distortions discernible from the contact

[4] Edouard Glissant, *Poétique de la relation*, (Paris: Gallimard, 1990), 19.
[5] *Outside in the Teaching Machine* (London: Routledge, 1993), 280–1.

between French Antillean literature and postcolonial theory. The point of contact is still a site of productivity, and the analytic value of the optic produced at it remains unexhausted. Armed with the model of paradoxical dynamics that can be discerned in the interference patterns, future readers can tackle different literatures and traditions. The above, I hope, serves as a prolegomenon for future readings within a mode that is not monadic, but attentive to improbable recurrences across theories, cultures, and individual talents: 'Nos barques sont ouvertes, pour tous nous les naviguons.'[6]

[6] Glissant, *Poétique de la relation*, 21.

BIBLIOGRAPHY

Abénon, Lucien-René, et al., *Mourir pour les antilles: Indépendance nègre ou esclavage, 1802–1804* (Paris: Éditions caribéennes, 1991).
Ahmad, Aijaz, *In Theory: Classes, Nations, Literatures* (London: Verso, 1992).
—— 'The Politics of Literary Postcoloniality', *Race and Class*, 36/3 (1995), 1–20.
Aidoo, Ama Ata, 'That Capacious Topic: Gender Politics', in Phil Mariani (ed.), *Critical Fictions* (Seattle: Bay Press, 1991), 151–4.
Andrade, Susan Z., 'The Nigger of the Narcissist: History, Sexuality and Intertextuality in Maryse Condé's *Hérémakhonon*', *Callaloo*, 16/1 (1993), 213–26.
André, Jacques, *Caraïbales* (Paris: Éditions caribéennes, 1981).
Antoine, Régis, *La Littérature franco-antillaise* (Paris: Karthala, 1992).
Appiah, Kwame Anthony, 'Identity, Authenticity, Survival: Multicultural Societies and Social Reproduction', in Charles Taylor (ed.), *Multiculturalism: Examining the Politics of Recognition*, expanded edn., ed. Amy Gutmann (Princeton: Princeton University Press, 1994).
—— *In My Father's House: Africa in the Philosophy of Culture* (Oxford: Oxford University Press, 1992).
—— and Gutmann, Amy, *Color Conscious: The Political Morality of Race* (Princeton: Princeton University Press, 1996).
Araujo, Nara (ed.), *L'Œuvre de Maryse Condé: A propos d'une écrivaine politiquement incorrecte* (Paris: Harmattan, 1996).
Armet, Auguste, 'Aimé Césaire, homme politique', *Études littéraires*, 6/1 (1973), 81–96.
Arnold, A. James, 'The Erotics of Colonialism in Contemporary French West Indian Literary Culture', *New West Indian Guide*, 68/1–2 (1994), 5–22.
—— (ed.), *A History of Literature in the Caribbean: Hispanic and Francophone Regions* (Comparative History of Literatures in European Languages Series, 10; Amsterdam: John Benjamins, 1994).
—— *Modernism and Negritude: The Poetry and Poetics of Aimé Césaire* (Cambridge, Mass.: Harvard University Press, 1981).
Ashcroft, Bill, Griffiths, Gareth, and Tiffin, Helen, *The Empire writes back: Theory and Practice in Post-Colonial Literatures* (London: Routledge, 1989).
—— (eds.), *The Post-Colonial Studies Reader* (London: Routledge, 1995).
Bader, Wolfgang, 'Poétique antillaise, poétique de la relation', *Komparatistische Hefte*, 9–10 (1984), 83–100.
Bakhtin, Mikhail, *The Dialogic Imagination*, ed. Michael Holquist, trans. Caryl Emerson and Michael Holquist (Austin, Tex.: University of Texas Press, 1981).
Balbutansky, Kathleen, '*Créolité* in Question: Caliban in Maryse Condé's

BIBLIOGRAPHY

Traversée de la mangrove', in Condé and Cottenet-Hage (eds.), *Penser la créolité*, 101–11.

Bangou, Henri, *La Période révolutionnaire à la Guadeloupe: L'Abolition et le rétablissement de l'esclavage* (Point-à-Pitre: Office municipal de la culture, 1976).

Baudelaire, Charles, *Œuvres complètes*, ed. Claude Pichois, (Bibliothèque de la Pléiade, 1; Paris: Gallimard, 1961).

—— *Les Fleurs du mal*, trans. Richard Howard (Boston: David Godine, 1982).

Baudot, Alain, 'Maryse Condé ou la parole du refus', *Recherche, pédagogie, et culture*, 9/57 (1982), 30–5.

Benjamin, Walter, *Illuminations*, ed. Hannah Arendt, trans. Harry Zohn (London: Fontana, 1992).

—— *The Origin of German Tragic Drama*, trans. John Osborne (London: NLB, 1977).

Bernabé, Jean, Chamoiseau, Patrick, and Confiant, Raphaël, *Éloge de la créolité*, bilingual edn., trans. M. B. Taleb-Kyar (Paris: Gallimard, 1989).

Bhabha, Homi, *The Location of Culture* (London: Routledge, 1994).

Blanchot, Maurice, *L'Écriture du désastre* (Paris: Gallimard, 1980).

Blood, Susan, *Baudelaire and the Aesthetics of Bad Faith* (Stanford, Calif.: Stanford University Press, 1997).

Bloom, Harold, *The Anxiety of Influence: A Theory of Poetry* (New York: Oxford University Press, 1973).

Bongie, Chris, 'Resisting Memories: The Creole Identities of Lafcadio Hearn and Edouard Glissant', *SubStance*, 84 (1997), 153–78.

Brathwaite, Edward, *The Development of Creole Society in Jamaica, 1770–1820* (Oxford: Clarendon, 1971).

—— *Rights of Passage* (London: Oxford University Press, 1967).

Breslaw, Elaine G., *Tituba, Reluctant Witch of Salem: Devilish Indians and Puritan Fantasies* (New York: New York University Press, 1996).

Breton, André, *Légitime Défense* (Paris: Éditions surréalistes, 1926).

—— *Martinique charmeuse de serpents* (Paris: Sagittaire, 1948).

—— 'Martinique, charmeuse de serpents: Un grand poète noir', *Tropiques*, 11 (May 1944), 119–26.

—— *Misère de la poésie: 'L'Affaire Aragon' devant l'opinion publique* (Paris: Éditions surréalistes, 1932).

—— 'Un grand poète noir', Preface to Aimé Césaire, *Cahier d'un retour au pays natal* (Paris: Présence africaine, 1971), 8–27.

Briggs, Robin, *Witches and Neighbours: The Social and Cultural Context of European Witchcraft* (London: Harper Collins, 1996).

Britton, Celia, '*Discours* and *histoire*, Magical and Political Discourse in Édouard Glissant's *Le Quatrième Siècle*', *French Cultural Studies*, 5 (1994), 151–62.

—— 'Eating their Words: The Consumption of French Caribbean Literature', *Association for the Study of African and Caribbean Literature in French Yearbook*, 1 (1996), 15–23.

—— *Édouard Glissant and Postcolonial Theory: Strategies of Language and Resistance* (Charlottesville, Va.: University Press of Virginia, 1999).

—— 'Opacity and Transparence: Conceptions of History and Cultural Difference in the Work of Michel Butor and Édouard Glissant', *French Studies*, 49 (1995), 308–20.

Burton, Richard, 'Between the Particular and the Universal: Dilemmas of the Martinican Intellectual', in Alistair Henessy (ed.) *Intellectuals in the Twentieth-Century Caribbean*, 2 vols. (London: Macmillan, 1992), ii, 186–210.

—— *Le Roman marron: Études sur la littérature martiniquaise contemporaine* (Paris and Montreal: L'Harmattan, 1997).

—— 'Towards 1992: Political-Cultural Assimilation and Opposition in Contemporary Martinique', *French Cultural Studies*, 3 (1992), 61–86.

—— and Reno, Fred, (eds.), *French and West Indian* (Warwick: Macmillan, 1995).

Cailler, Bernadette, *Conquérants de la nuit nue: Édouard Glissant et l'H(h)istoire antillaise* (Tübingen: Gunter Narr Verlag, 1988).

Callaloo 18/3: 'Maryse Condé: A Special Issue' (1995).

Capécia, Mayotte, *Je suis martiniquaise* (Paris: Corréa, 1948).

Caruth, Cathy, *Unclaimed Experience: Trauma, Narrative, and History* (Baltimore: Johns Hopkins University Press, 1996).

Césaire, Aimé, *Cahier d'un retour au pays natal*, bilingual edn., trans. Mireille Rosello with Annie Pritchard (Bloodaxe Contemporary French Poets, 4; Newcastle upon Tyne: Bloodaxe, 1995).

—— *The Collected Poetry*, bilingual edn., trans. Clayton Eshleman and Annette Smith (Berkeley and Los Angeles: University of California Press, 1983).

—— *Discours sur le colonialisme* (Paris: Présence Africaine, 1955).

—— *Et les chiens se taisaient* (Paris: Présence Africaine, 1956).

—— 'Introduction à la poésie nègre américaine', *Tropiques*, 2 (July 1941), 37–42.

—— *moi, laminaire . . .* (Paris: Seuil, 1982).

—— 'Poésie et connaissance', *Tropiques*, 12 (Jan. 1945), 157–70.

—— *Soleil cou coupé* (Paris: Éditions K, 1948).

—— *Une saison au Congo* (Paris: Seuil, 1966).

—— *Une tempête* (Paris: Seuil, 1969).

—— *La Tragédie du roi Christophe* (Paris: Présence africaine, 1963).

Césaire, Suzanne, 'Misère d'une poésie: John Antoine-Nau', *Tropiques*, 4 (Jan. 1942), 48–50.

Chambers, Iain, *Migrancy, Culture, Identity* (London: Routledge, 1993).

Chamoiseau, Patrick, *Antan d'enfance* (Paris: Gallimard, 1990).

—— *Au temps de l'antan: Contes du pays martinique* (Paris: Hatier, 1998).

—— *Chemin-d'école* (Paris: Gallimard, 1994).

—— *Chronique des sept misères* (Paris: Gallimard, 1986).

—— 'En témoignage d'une volupté', *Carbet*, 10 (1990), 143–52.

Chamoiseau, Patrick, 'Reflections on Maryse Condé's *Traversée de la Mangrove*', trans. Kathleen Balbutansky, *Callaloo*, 14/2 (1991), 389–95.
—— *Solibo Magnifique* (Paris: Gallimard, 1988).
—— *Texaco* (Paris: Gallimard, 1992).
—— *Texaco*, trans. Rose-Myriam Rejouis and Val Vinokyurov (New York: Partheon, 1997).
—— and Confiant, Raphaël, *Lettres créoles: Tracées antillaises et continentales de la littérature—Haiti, Guadeloupe, Martinique, Guyane, 1635–1975* (Paris: Hatier, 1991).
Chaudenson, Robert, *Des îles, des hommes, des langues créoles—cultures créoles* (Paris: Harmattan, 1992).
Chow, Rey, *Writing Diaspora: Tactics of Intervention in Contemporary Cultural Studies* (1994).
Cixous, Hélène, and Clément, Catherine, *La Jeune Née* (Paris: Union générale d'éditions, 1975), 9–113.
—— *The Newly Born Woman*, trans. Betsy Wing (Theory and History of Literature, 24; Minneapolis: University of Minnesota Press, 1986).
Clark, Vèvè A., 'Developing Diaspora Literacy: Allusion in Maryse Condé's *Hérémakhonon*', in Davies and Fido (eds.), *Out of the Kumbla*, 315–31.
—— 'Diaspora Literacy and *Marasa* Consciousness', in Hortense Spillers (eds.), *Comparative American Identities: Race, Sex, and Nationality in the Modern Text*, (New York: Routledge, 1991), 40–61.
—— '"Je me suis réconciliée avec mon île": Une interview de Maryse Condé', *Callaloo*, 12/1 (1989), 85–132.
—— 'Pourquoi la Négritude: négritude ou révolution?' in Jeanne-Lydie Gore (ed.), *Négritude africaine, négritude carraibe* (Paris: La Francité, 1973).
Cliff, Michelle, *No Telephone to Heaven* (New York: Vintage, 1989).
Clifford, James, *The Predicament of Culture: Twentieth-Century Ethnography, Literature, and Art* (Cambridge, Mass.: Harvard University Press, 1988).
—— *Routes: Travel and Translation in the Late Twentieth Century* (Cambridge, Mass.: Harvard University Press, 1997).
Condé, Maryse, *Cahier d'un retour au pays natal: Césaire* (Paris: Hatier, 1978).
—— *Le Cœur à rire et à pleurer: Contes vrais de mon enfance* (Paris: Robert Laffont, 1999).
—— *La Colonie du nouveau monde* (Paris: Robert Laffont, 1993).
—— *Les Derniers Rois mages* (Paris: Mercure de France, 1992).
—— *Désirada* (Paris: Robert Laffont, 1997).
—— *En attendant le bonheur (Hérémakhonon)* (Paris: Robert Seghers, 1988; repr. Robert Laffont, 1997).
—— *Hérémakhonon*, trans. Richard Philcox (Washington: Three Continents Press, 1982).
—— *I, Tituba, Black Witch of Salem*, trans. Richard Philcox (Charlottesville, Va.: University Press of Virginia, 1992).
—— *La Migration des cœurs* (Paris: Robert Laffont, 1995).

—— *Moi, Tituba, sorcière... Noire de Salem* (Paris: Mercure de France, 1986).
—— *Mort d'Oluwémi d'Ajumako* (Paris: Pierre-Jean Oswald, 1973).
—— 'Notes sur un retour au pays natal', *Conjonction: Revue franco-haïtienne*, 176, suppl. (1987), 6–23.
—— 'Order, Disorder, Freedom and the West Indian Writer', *Yale French Studies*, 83/2 (1993), 121–35.
—— *La Parole des femmes: Essai sur des romancières des Antilles de langue française* (Paris: Harmattan, 1979; repr. 1993).
—— *Pays mêlé* (Paris: Hatier, 1985).
—— *Pension Les Alizés* (Paris: Mercure de France, 1988).
—— *Une saison à Rihata* (Paris: Robert Laffont, 1981; repr. 1997).
—— *A Season in Rihata*, trans. Richard Philcox (London: Heinemann, 1988).
—— *Ségou: La Terre en miettes* (Paris: Robert Laffont, 1985).
—— *Ségou: Les Murailles de terre* (Paris: Robert Laffont, 1984).
—— *Traversée de la Mangrove* (Paris: Mercure de France, 1989).
—— *Tree of Life*, trans. Victoria Reiter (London: Women's Press, 1994).
—— *La Vie scélérate* (Paris: Seghers, 1987).
—— and Cottenet-Hage, Madeleine (eds.), *Penser la créolité* (Paris: Karthala, 1995).
—— et al. (eds.), *L'Héritage de Caliban* (Guadeloupe: Jasor, 1992).
Confiant, Raphaël, *Aimé Césaire: Une traversée paradoxale du siècle* (Paris: Stock, 1993).
—— *Contes créoles des Amériques* (Paris: Stock, 1995).
—— *Eau de café* (Paris: Grasset, 1991).
—— *Les Maîtres de la parole créole* (Paris: Gallimard, 1995).
—— *Le Nègre et l'amiral* (Paris: Grasset, 1992).
—— *Ravine du devant-jour* (Paris: Gallimard, 1993).
Corzani, Jack, *La Littérature des Antilles-Guyane françaises*, 6 vols. (Paris: Désormeaux, 1978).
—— 'Poetry before Negritude', in Arnold (ed.), *History of Literature in the Caribbean*, 465–77.
Crosta, Suzanne, *Le Marronage créateur: Dynamique textuelle chez Édouard Glissant* (Québec: GRELCA, 1991).
—— 'Narrative and Discursive Strategies in Maryse Condé's *Traversée de la mangrove*', *Callaloo*, 15/1 (1992), 147–55.
Dante Alighieri, *Il Convivio*, ed. G. Busnelli and Giuseppe Vandelli, 2 vols. (Florence: F. Le Monnier, 1934–7).
Dash, J. Michael, *Édouard Glissant* (Cambridge: Cambridge University Press, 1995).
Davies, Carole Boyce, and Fido, Elaine Savory, (eds.), *Out of the Kumbla: Caribbean Women and Literature* (Trenton: African World, 1990).
Davis, Angela, Foreword to Maryse Condé, *I, Tituba, Black Witch of Salem*, trans. Richard Philcox (Charlottesville, Va.: University Press of Virginia, 1992), pp. xi–xiii.

Davis, Gregson, *Aimé Césaire* (Cambridge: Cambridge University Press, 1997).
de Courtivron, Isabelle, and Marks, Elaine, (eds)., *New French Feminisms: An Anthology* (Sussex: Harvester Press, 1981).
de Man, Paul, *Allegories of Reading* (New Haven: Yale University Press, 1979).
—— 'The Rhetoric of Temporality', in Charles Singleton (ed.), *Interpretation: Theory and Practice* (Baltimore: Johns Hopkins University Press, 1969), 173–209.
Deane, Seamus (ed.), *Colonialism and Literature* (Minneapolis: University of Minnesota Press, 1990).
Degras, Priska, 'Maryse Condé: l'écriture de l'Histoire', *L'Esprit Créateur*, 33/2 (1993), 73–81.
Delas, Daniel, *Aimé Césaire* (Paris: Hachette, 1991).
Deleuze, Gilles, and Guattari, Félix, *Kafka: Pour une littérature mineure* (Paris: Minuit, 1975).
—— *Mille plateaux* (Paris: Minuit, 1980).
Depestre, René, *Hadriana dans tous mes rêves* (Paris: Gallimard, 1988).
Derrida, Jacques, *Archive Fever: A Freudian Impression*, trans. Eric Prenowitz (Chicago: University of Chicago Press, 1996).
—— *De la grammatologie* (Paris: Minuit, 1967).
—— *L'Écriture et la différence* (Paris: Seuil, 1967).
—— *Mal d'archive: Une impression freudienne* (Paris: Galilée, 1995).
—— *Marges de la philosophie* (Paris: Minuit, 1972).
—— *Margins of Philosophy*, trans. Alan Bass (Chicago: University of Chicago Press, 1982).
—— *Of Grammatology*, trans. Gayatri Chakravorty Spivak (Baltimore: Johns Hopkins University Press, 1976).
Dirlik, Arif, 'The Postcolonial Aura: Third World Criticism in the Age of Global Capitalism', *Criticial Inquiry*, 20 (1994), 328–56.
Douglass, Frederick, *Narrative of the Life of Frederick Douglass, an American Slave, Written by Himself*, ed. William Andrew and William McFeely (New York: Norton, 1997).
DuBois, W. E. B., *The Souls of Black Folk* (New York: Penguin, 1989).
Dukats, Mara, 'The Hybrid Terrain of Literary Imagination: Maryse Condé's Black Witch of Salem, Nathaniel Hawthorne's Hester Prynne, and Aimé Césaire's Heroic Voice', *College Literature*, 22/1 (1995), 51–61.
—— 'A Narrative of Violated Maternity: *Moi, Tituba, sorcière . . . Noire de Salem*', *World Literature Today*, 67/4 (1993), 745–50.
Edwards, Brent, 'The Ethnics of Surrealism', *Transition*, 78 (1999), 84–135.
Ega, Françoise, *Le Temps des madras* (Paris: Éditions maritimes d'outre-mer, 1966).
Eliade, Mircea, *Le Chamanisme et les techniques archaïques de l'extase* (Paris: Payot, 1951).
Equiano, Olaudah, *The Interesting Narrative of Olaudah Equiano, or Gustavas*

Vassa, the African, Written by Himself, ed. Robert Allison (Boston: St Martins, 1995).
Fanon, Frantz, *Black Skin, White Masks* (New York: Grove Weidenfeld, 1967).
—— *Les Damnés de la terre* (Paris: François Maspéro, 1961).
—— *Peau noires, masques blancs* (Paris: Seuil, 1995).
Felman, Shoshana, and Laub, Dori, *Testimony: Crises of Witnessing in Literature, Psychoanalysis, and History* (New York: Routledge, 1992).
Fineman, Joel, 'The Structure of Allegorical Desire', in Stephen J. Greenblatt (ed.), *Allegory and Representation* (Selected Papers from the English Institute, NS, 5; Baltimore: Johns Hopkins University Press, 1981), 26–60.
Foster, Hal, *Recordings: Art, Spectacle, Cultural Politics* (Seattle: Bay Press, 1985).
Foucault, Michel, 'Of Other Spaces', *Diacritics*, 16 (1986), 22–7.
—— *Surveiller et punir: Naissance de la prison* (Paris: Gallimard, 1975).
—— *La Volonté de savoir* (Paris: Gallimard, 1976).
Freud, Sigmund, *Beyond the Pleasure Principle*, Standard Edition, vol. 1–64 xviii, trans. James Strachey (London: Hogarth, 1920).
—— *Moses and Monotheism*, trans. Katherine Jones (New York: Vintage Books, 1939).
—— 'Mourning and Melancholia', in *Collected Papers*, trans. Joan Rivière, 5 vols. (New York: Basic, 1959), iv, 152–70.
—— and Breuer, Joseph, *Studies on Hysteria*, Standard Edition, vols ii–iii, trans. James Strachey (London: Hogarth, 1893–5).
Frye, Northrop, *Anatomy of Criticism: Four Essays* (Princeton: Princeton University Press, 1971).
Gallagher, Mary, 'Whence and Whither the French Caribbean "Créolité" Movement', *ASCALF Bulletin*, 9 (1994), 3–18.
Gates, Henry Louis (ed.), *'Race', Writing, and Difference* (Chicago and London: University of Chicago Press, 1986).
George, Rosemary Marangoly, *The Politics of Home: Postcolonial Relocations and Twentieth-Century Fiction* (Cambridge: Cambridge University Press, 1996).
Gelley, Alexander (ed.), *Unruly Examples: On the Rhetoric of Exemplarity*, (Stanford, Calif.: Stanford University Press, 1995).
Gellner, Andrew, *Nations and Nationalism* (Ithaca, NY: Cornell University Press, 1983).
Gilroy, Paul, *The Black Atlantic: Modernity and Double Consciousness* (London: Verso, 1993).
Glissant, Édouard, 'Au fond du miroir', *Quinzaine littéraire*, 437 (1–15 Apr., 1985), 7.
—— *Caribbean Discourse*, trans. J. Michael Dash (Charlottesville, Va.: University Press of Virginia, 1989).
—— *La Case du commandeur* (Paris: Seuil, 1981).
—— *Le Discours antillais* (Paris: Seuil, 1981).
—— *La Lézarde* (Paris: Seuil, 1958).

Glissant, Édouard, *Mahagony* (Paris: Seuil, 1987).
—— *Malemort* (Paris: Seuil, 1975).
—— *Poétique de la relation* (Paris: Gallimard, 1990).
—— *Le Quatrième Siècle* (Paris: Seuil, 1964).
Green, Mary Jean, et al (eds.), *Postcolonial Subjects: Francophone Women Writers* (Minneapolis: University of Minnesota Press, 1996).
Guha, Ranajit, and Spivak, Gayatri, *Selected Subaltern Studies* (Oxford: Oxford University Press, 1988).
Hale, Thomas, 'Two Decades, Four Versions: The Evolution of Aimé Césaire's *Cahier d'un retour au pays natal*', in Carolyn Parker and Stephen Arnold (eds.), *When the Drumbeat Changes* (Washington: Three Continents Press, 1981), 186–95.
Hall, Stuart, 'Cultural Identity and Diaspora', in Jonathan Rutherford (eds.), *Identity: Community, Culture, Difference* (London: Lawrence and Wishart, 1990), 225–37.
Haley, Alex, *Roots* (London: Hutchinson, 1977).
Hargreaves, Alec, and McKinney, Mark (eds.), *Post-Colonial Cultures in France* (London: Routledge, 1997).
Harris, Wilson, *The Womb of Space: The Cross-Cultural Imagination* (Westport, Conn.: Greenwood, 1983).
Hartman, Geoffrey H., 'On Traumatic Knowledge and Literary Studies', *New Literary History*, 26 (1995), 537–63.
Hawthorne, Nathanel, *The Scarlet Letter*, ed. Brian Harding (Oxford: OUP, 1990).
Henry-Valmore, Simonne, *Dieux en exil* (Paris: Gallimard, 1988).
Hewitt, Leah, *Autobiographical Tightropes* (Lincoln, Nebr.: University of Nebraska Press, 1990).
—— 'Inventing Antillean Narrative: Maryse Condé and Literary Tradition', *Studies in 20th Century Literature*, 17/1 (1993), 79–96.
Huffer, Lynne, *Maternal Pasts, Feminist Futures: Nostalgia, Ethics, and the Question of Difference* (Stanford, Calif.: Stanford University Press, 1998).
Irele, Abiola, *The African Experience in Literature and Ideology* (Bloomington, Ind.: Indiana University Press, 1981).
—— Introduction to Aimé Césaire *Cahier d'un retour au pays natal* ed. with commentary Abiola Irele (Ibadan: New Horn Press, 1994).
Irigaray, Luce, *Ce sexe qui n'en est pas un* (Paris: Minuit, 1977).
Jack, Belinda, *Francophone Literatures: An Introductory Survey* (New York: Oxford University Press, 1996).
Jacobs, Harriet, *Incidents in the Life of a Slave Girl* (New York: Oxford University Press, 1988).
Jacquey, Marie-Clotilde, and Hugon, Monique, 'L'Afrique, un continent difficile: Entretien avec Maryse Condé', *Notre librairie*, 74 (1984), 21–5.
Jakobson, Roman, 'Closing Statement: Linguistics and Poetics', in Sebeok (ed.), *Style in Language*, (Cambridge, Mass.: MIT Press, 1960), 350–77.

Jameson, Fredric, *Marxism and Form* (Princeton: Princeton University Press, 1971).
—— *The Political Unconscious* (London: Methuen, 1981).
—— *Postmodernism, or The Cultural Logic of Late Capitalism* (London: Verso, 1991).
—— 'Third-World Literature in the Era of Multinational Capitalism', *Social Text*, 15 (1986), 65–88.
JanMohammed, Abdul, and Lloyd, David (eds.), *The Nature and Context of Minority Discourse* (Oxford: Oxford University Press, 1990).
Johnson, Barbara, *Défigurations du langage poétique: La Seconde Révolution baudelarienne* (Paris: Flammarion, 1979).
—— *The Wake of Deconstruction* (Oxford: Blackwell, 1994).
—— *A World of Difference* (Baltimore: Johns Hopkins University Press, 1987).
Kesteloot, Lilyan, *Aimé Césaire* (Poètes d'aujourd'hui, 85; Paris: Seghers, 1962).
—— *Les Écrivains noirs de langue française: Naissance d'une littérature* (7th edn., Brussels: Éditions de l'université de Bruxelles, 1977).
—— and Kotchy, Bartélemy, *Aimé Césaire: L'Homme et l'œuvre* (Paris: Présence africaine, 1973).
King, Adele, 'Two Caribbean Women go to Africa', *College Literature*, 18/3 (1991), 98–105.
Kristeva, Julia, *La Révolution du langage poétique* (Paris: Seuil, 1974).
Kutzinski, Vera, *Sugar's Secrets: Race and the Erotics of Cuban Nationalism* (Charlottesville, Va.: University Press of Virginia, 1993).
Lacan, Jacques, *Écrits* (Paris: Seuil, 1966).
—— *Le Séminaire*, xi. *Les Quatre Concepts fondamentaux de la psychanalyse*, ed. Jacque-Alain Miller (Paris: Seuil, 1973).
Lamiot, Christophe, 'A Question of Questions through a Mangrove Wood', *Callaloo*, 15/1 (1992), 138–46.
Le Brun, Annie, *Pour Aimé Césaire* (Paris: Jean-Michel Place, 1994).
—— *Statue cou coupé* (Paris: Jean-Michel Place, 1996).
Leiner, Jacqueline, 'Entretien avec Aimé Césaire', in *Tropiques*, 2 vols. (Paris: Jean-Michel Place, 1978), vol. i, pp. v-xxxv.
—— *Imaginaire langage, -identité culturelle, négritude* (Paris: Jean-Michel Place, 1980).
Lévi-Strauss, Claude, *Anthropologie structurale I* (Paris: Plon, 1958).
—— 'The Sorcerer and His Magic' in *Structural Anthropology I*, trans. Claire Jackobson and Brooke Grundfest Schoept (Garden City: Anchor, 1967).
Lionnet, Françoise, *Autobiographical Voices: Race Gender, Self-Portraiture* (Ithaca, NY: Cornell University Press, 1989).
—— *Postcolonial Representations: Woman, Literature, Identity* (Ithaca, NY: Cornell University Press, 1995).
Loomba, Ania, and Kaul, Suvir, 'Introduction: Location, Culture, Post-Coloniality', *Oxford Literary Review*, 16/1–2 (1994), 3–30.

Lowe, Lisa, *Critical Terrains: French and British Orientalisms* (Ithaca, NY: Cornell University Press, 1991).
Lucey, Michael, 'Voices accounting for the Past: Maryse Condé's *Traversée de la Mangrove*', in Condé et al. (eds.), *L'Héritage de Caliban*, 123–32.
Ludwig, Ralph, *Écrire la 'Parole de nuit': La Nouvelle Littérature antillaise* (Paris: Gallimard, 1994).
Lyotard, Jean-François, *Le Différend* (Paris: Minuit, 1983).
McClintock, Anne, 'The Angel of Progress: Pitfalls of the Term "Post-Colonialism"', *Social Text*, 31–2 (1992), 84–98.
McGee, Patrick, 'Texts between Worlds: African Fiction as Political Allegory', in Karen Lawrence (ed.), *Decolonising Tradition: New Views of 20th Century 'British' Literary Canons* (Urbana, Ill.: University of Illinois Press, 1992), 239–60.
Macqueen, John, *Allegory* (London: Methuen, 1971).
Mallarmé Stéphane, *Collected Poems*, trans. Henry Weinfeld (Berkeley and Los Angeles: University of California Press, 1994).
—— *Œuvres complètes*, ed. Henri Mondor and G. Jean-Aubry (Bibliothèque de la Pléiade, 65; Paris: Gallimard, 1945).
Manzor-Coats, Lillian, 'Of Witches and Other Things: Maryse Condé's Challenges to Feminist Discourse', *World Literature Today*, 67/4 (1993), 737–44.
Marx, Karl, *The Eighteenth Brumaire of Louis Bonaparte* (1952).
Maximin, Daniel, *L'Isolé Soleil* (Paris: Seuil, 1981).
Memmi, Albert, *Le Portrait du colonisé* (Montréal: Éditions du Bas Canada, 1963).
Mesh-Ferguson, Cynthia, 'Language Conflict and the Francophone Guadeloupean Novel: An Interdisciplinary Inquiry' (unpublished doctoral diss., Yale University, 1994).
Michelet, Jules, *La Sorcière: Nouvelle édition critique avec introduction, variantes et examen du manuscrit*, ed. Walterus Kusters (Nijmegen: Kusters, 1989).
Miller, Arthur, *The Crucible* (New York: Viking, 1953).
Miller, Christopher, *Blank Darkness: Africanist Discourse in French* (Chicago: University of Chicago Press, 1985).
—— *Nationalists and Nomads: Essays on Francophone African Literature and Culture* (Chicago: University of Chicago Press, 1998).
—— *Theories of Africans: Francophone Literature and Anthropology in Africa* (Chicago: University of Chicago Press, 1990).
Monroe, Jonathan, '*Mischling* and *Métis*: Common and Uncommon Languages in Adrienne Rich and Aimé Césaire', in Gustavo Perez Firmat (ed.), *Do the Americas have a Common Literature?*, (Durham, NC: Duke University Press, 1990), 282–315.
Moore-Gilbert, Bart, *Postcolonial Theory: Contexts, Practices, Politics* (London: Verso, 1997).

Morneau, Claude (ed.), *Ulysses Travel Guide to Martinique* (2nd edn., Ulysses Travel Publications, 1996).

Morrison, Toni, *Beloved* (London: Chatto and Windus, 1987).

—— 'Unspeakable Things Unspoken: The Afro-American Presence in American Literature', *Michigan Quarterly Review*, 28/1 (1989), 1–34.

Moudileno, Lydie, *L'Écrivain antillais au miroir de sa littérature* (Paris: Karthala, 1997).

Mouralis, Bernard, 'Césaire et la poésie française', *Revue des sciences humaines*, 48/176 (1979), 125–52.

Mudimbe, V. Y. (ed.), *The Invention of Africa: Gnosis, Philosophy, and the Order of Knowledge* (Bloomington, Ind.: Indiana University Press, 1988).

Mudimbe-Boyi, Elisabeth, 'Giving a Voice to Tituba: The Death of the Author?', *World Literature Today*, 67/4 (1993), 751–6.

Munley, Ellen, 'Du silence de la mort à la parole de la vie: A l'écoute de l'eau et du vent dans *Traversée de la mangrove*', in Yolande Helm (ed.), *L'Eau: Source d'une écriture dans les littératures féminines francophones* (New York: Peter Lang, 1995).

—— 'Mapping the Mangrove: Empathy and Survival in *Traversée de la mangrove*', *Callaloo*, 15/1 (1992), 156–66.

Nandy, Ashis, *The Intimate Enemy: Loss and Recovery of Self under Colonialism* (Oxford: Oxford University Press, 1983).

Nevins, Winfield, *Witchcraft in Salem Village in 1692: Together with Some Accounts of Other Witchcraft Prosecution in New England and Elsewhere* (Boston: Lee and Shepard, 1982).

Ngal, M. a M., *Aimé Césaire: Un homme à la recherche d'une patrie* (Dakar: Nouvelles éditions africaines, 1975).

Ngaté, Jonathan, 'Maryse Condé and Africa: The Making of a Recalcitrant Daughter?', *Current Bibliography on African Affairs*, 19/1 (1986–7), 5–20.

—— '"Mauvais sang" de Rimbaud et *Cahier d'un retour au pays natal* de Césaire: La Poésie au service de la révolution', *Cahiers Césairiens*, 3 (1971), 25–32.

Ngkandu Nkashama, Pius, 'L'Afrique en pointillé dans *Une saison à Rihata* de Maryse Condé', *Notre librairie*, 74 (1984), 31–7.

Ngugi wa Thiong'o, *Decolonising the Mind: The Politics of Language in African Literature* (London: James Currey, 1986).

Niranjana, Tejaswini, *Siting Translation: History, Post-Structuralism, and the Colonial Context* (Berkeley and Los Angeles: University of California Press, 1992).

Nora, Pierre, *Les Lieux de mémoire*, i. *Entre Mémoire et Histoire: La Problématique des lieux* (Paris: Gallimard, 1984).

Owens, Craig, 'The Allegorical Impulse: Toward a Theory of Postmodernism', *October*, 19 (1981), 67–86.

Parry, Benita, 'Current Problems in the Study of Colonial Discourse', *Oxford Literary Review*, 9/1–2 (1987), 27–58.

Peterson, Carla, 'Le Surnaturel dans *Moi, Tituba, Sorcière* . . . *Noire de Salem* de Maryse Condé et *Beloved* de Toni Morrison, in *L'œuvre de Maryse Condé* (Paris: Harmattan: 1996).
Pfaff, Françoise, *Conversations with Maryse Condé* (Lincoln, Nebr.: University of Nebraska Press, 1996).
—— *Entretiens avec Maryse Condé* (Paris: Karthala, 1993).
Phillips, Caryl, *The Nature of Blood* (London: Faber and Faber, 1997).
Pibarot, Annie, 'Césaire lecteur de Mallarmé', in Janos Reisz (ed.), *Frankophone Literaturen Ausserhalb Europas* (Frankfurt on Main: Peter Lang, 1987), 17–27.
Pineau, Gisèle, *La Grande Drive des esprits* (Paris: Le Serpent à plumes, 1993).
Prakash, Gyan, 'Subaltern Studies as Postcolonial Criticism', *American Historical Review*, 99/5 (1994), 1475–90.
Prince, Mary, *The History of Mary Prince, A West Indian Slave, Related by Herself*, ed. Moira Ferguson (Ann Arbor: University of Michigan Press, 1993).
Radford, Danel, *Édouard Glissant* (Poètes d'aujourd'hui, 244; Paris: Seghers, 1982).
Rimbaud, Arthur, *Œuvres complètes*, André Rolland de Renéville and Jules Mouquet (eds.) (Bibliothèque de la Pléiade, 68; Paris: Gallimard, 1946).
Rody, Caroline, *The Daughter's Return: African-American and Caribbean Women's Fictions of History* (Oxford: Oxford University Press, 2000).
Rosello, Mireille, *Littérature et identité créole aux Antilles* (Paris: Karthala, 1992).
Rosenthal, Bernard, *Salem Story: Reading the Witch Trials of 1692* (Cambridge: Cambridge University Press, 1993).
Said, Edward, *Culture and Imperialism* (London: Chatto, 1993).
—— *Orientalism* (London: Routledge, 1978).
Safran, William, 'Diasporas in Modern Societies: Myths of Homeland and Return', *Diaspora*, 1 (1991), 83–99.
Sartre, Jean-Paul, 'Orphée Noir', Preface to Léopold Sédar Senghor, (ed.), *Anthologie de la nouvelle poésie nègre et malgache de langue française* (Paris: Presses universitaires de France, 1948), pp. ix–xliv.
Scarboro, Ann, Afterword to Maryse Condé, *I, Tituba, Black Witch of Salem*, trans. Richard Philcox (Charlottesville, Va.: University Press of Virginia, 1992), 175–225.
Scharfman, Ronnie, '"Créolité" is/as Resistance: Raphaël Confiant's *Le Nègre et l'Amiral*', in Condé and Cottenet-Hage (eds.), *Penser la créolité*, 125–34.
—— 'De grands poètes noirs: Breton rencontre les Césaire', in D. Lefort, P. Rivas, J. Chénieux-Gendron (eds.), *Nouveau monde, autres mondes: Surréalisme & Amériques*, (Collection Pleine Marge, 5; Paris: Lachenal & Ritter, 1995).
—— *Engagement and the Language of the Subject in the Poetry of Aimé Césaire* (Gainesville, Fla.: University Press of Florida, 1980).
Schwarz-Bart, Simone, *Pluie et vent sur Télumée Miracle* (Paris: Seuil, 1972).

—— *Ti-Jean l'Horizon* (Paris: Seuil, 1979).
Seidel, Michael, *Exile and the Narrative Imagination* (New Haven: Yale University Press, 1986).
Senghor, Léopold Sédar, *Poèmes* (Paris: Seuil, 1984).
Shelton, Marie-Denise, 'Literature Extracted: A Poetic of Daily Life', *Callaloo*, 15/1 (1992), 167–78.
Sherzer, Dina (ed.), *Cinema, Colonialism, Postcolonialism: Perspectives from the French and Francophone World* (Austin: University of Texas Press, 1996).
Slemon, Stephen, 'Modernism's Last Post', in Ian Adam and Helen Tiffin (eds.), *Past the Last Post: Theorising Post-Colonialism and Post-Modernism* (Hemel Hempstead: Harvester Wheatsheaf, 1991).
—— 'Post-Colonial Allegory and the Transformation of History', *Journal of Commonwealth Literature*, 23/1 (1988), 157–68.
—— and Tiffin, Helen (eds.), *After Europe: Critical Theory and Post-Colonial Writing* (Sydney: Dangaroo, 1989), pp. ix–xxiii.
Smith, Arlette, 'Maryse Condé's *Hérémakhonon*: A Triangular Structure of Alienation', *CLA Journal*, 32/1 (1988), 45–54.
—— 'The Semiotics of Exile in Maryse Condé's Fictional Works', *Callaloo*, 14/2 (1991), 381–8.
Smith, Michelle, 'Reading in Circles: Sexuality and/as History in *I, Tituba, Black Witch of Salem*', *Callaloo*, 18/3 (1995), 602–7.
Smith, Paul, 'The Will to Allegory in Postmodernism', *Dalhousie Review*, 62/1 (1982), 105–22.
Snitgen, Jeanne, 'History, Identity and the Construction of the Female Subject: Maryse Condé's *Tituba*', *Matatu*, 3/6 (1989), 55–73.
Sourieau, Marie-Agnès, '*Traversée de la Mangrove* de Maryse Condé: Un champ de pulsions communes', *Francofonia*, 24 (1993), 109–22.
Spear, Thomas, 'Jouissances carnavalesques: Représentations de la sexualité', in Condé and Cottenet-Hage (eds.), *Penser la créolité* (Paris: Karthala, 1995), pp. 135–52.
Spivak, Gayatri Chakravorty, 'Can the Subaltern Speak?', in Cary Nelson and Lawrence Grossberg (eds.), *Marxism and the Interpretation of Culture*, (Basingstoke: Macmillan Education, 1988).
—— *In Other Worlds: Essays in Cultural Politics* (London: Methuen, 1987).
—— *Outside in the Teaching Machine* (London: Routledge, 1993).
—— 'Reading *The Satanic Verses*', *Third Text*, 11 (1990), 41–60.
Suk, Julie, 'Poetry of Flesh: Double Consciousness in the Harlem Renaissance and *Négritude*' (unpublished thesis, Harvard University, 1997).
Taleb-Khyar, 'An Interview with Maryse Condé and Rita Dove' *Callaloo*, 14/2 (1991), 347–66.
Tétu, Michel, *La Francophonie: Histoire, problématique et perspectives* (Paris: Hachette, 1988).
Toumson, Roger, *La Transgression des couleurs: Littérature et langage des Antilles, XVIIe, XIXe et XXe siècles* (Paris: Éditions caribéennes, 1989).

Toumson, Roger, and Henry-Valmore, Simonne, *Aimé Césaire: Le Nègre inconsolé* (Fort-de-France: Vent des îles, 1993).
Trinh, T. Minh-ha, *Woman, Native, Other: Writing Postcoloniality and Feminism* (Bloomington, Ind.: Indiana University Press, 1989).
Tropiques, 2 vols. (Paris: Jean-Michel Place, 1978).
Viatte, Auguste, *Histoire littéraire de l'Amérique française* (Paris: Presses universitaires de France, 1954).
Walcott, Derek, *The Antilles: Fragments of Epic Memory: The Nobel Lecture* (London: Faber and Faber, 1993).
Wangari wa Nyatetu-Waigwa, 'From Liminality to a Home of her Own?: The Quest Motif in Maryse Condé's Fiction', *Callaloo*, 18/3 (1995), 551–64.
Warner-Vieyra, Myriam, *Juletane* (Paris: Présence africaine, 1982).
Webb, Barbara, *Myth and History in Caribbean Fiction* (Amherst, Mass.: University of Massachusetts Press, 1992).
Williams, Eric, *Capitalism and Slavery* (New York: Russell & Russell, 1961).
World Literature Today, 67/4: 'Focus on Maryse Condé' (autumn, 1993).
Worton, Michael and Still, Judith (eds.), *Intertextuality: Theories and Practice* (Manchester: Manchester University Press, 1990).
Yale French Studies, 82 and 83: 'Post/Colonial Conditions: Exiles, Migrations, and Nomadisms' (1993).
Yerushalmi, Yosef Hayim, *Freud's Moses: Judaism Terminable and Interminable* (New Haven: Yale University Press, 1991).
Young, Robert, *Colonial Desire: Hybridity in Theory, Culture and Race* (London: Routledge, 1995).
—— *White Mythologies: Writing History and the West* (London: Routledge, 1990).
Zobel, Joseph, *La Rue Cases-Nègres* (Paris: Froissart, 1950).

INDEX

abreaction 144
Africa, return to movement 86n4
  see also Condé, Maryse
Ahmad, Aijaz 5, 20
alienation 103, 162
  black 99; see also identity, quest for
  and colonialism 155
  self 129
  see also détour
allegory 56, 102, 105, 113, 116, 118, 127,
    128, 133, 149, 150, 158–9, 170, 176,
    177, 179, 182–3
  and anteriority 55
  and discontinuity 7–9, 14–16; see also
    nostalgia
  and exemplarity 177
  as fetish 9; see also De Man, Paul;
    Miller, Christopher
  in 1st and 3rd world narratives 13–18;
    see also Jameson, Fredric
  and history 6–7, 117; see also history, and
    allegory
  and identity 17; see also collective, v.
    individual
  national, see Jameson, Fredric
  and nostalgia 7–8, 14
  and opacité 177; see also Glissant,
    Edouard, opacité
  and postcoloniality 5–6, 117
  and poststructuralism 6–7
  power of 54
  and referentiality 52–3; 120–2
  and signification 8–9, 14
  and sorcery 128, 145, 148
  and writing 170
alterity 55
  and anteriority 11
  black 37; see also anteriority, lost; exotic;
    nostalgia
  and gender 39–40
  and intertextuality 29
  and literary production 26–7, 32–4
André, Jacques 61n10
anteriority 110, 111
  and alterity, see alterity, and anteriority
  contamination of 109
  geographical 37
  lost 15, 25, 30–1, 37, 41–3, 55, 57, 60,
    107, 113; see also discontinuity

pure 9, 56, 62, 128
  and retour 62; see also détour; Discours;
    relation
antillanité 57, 69, 82
  see also détour; Discours; Glissant,
    Edouard; relation; retour
Appiah, Anthony:
  'scripted identity' 90
Aragon Affair 27
Aragon, Louis 27
archetype 105–6, 108, 112–3
  and allegory 113–4
  see also identity, quest for
archive 77–8
  see also Derrida, Jacques; history; trauma
Arnold, James 30n28, 151
Ashcroft, Bill 2–3
authenticity 176

Balbutansky, Kathleen 175n59
Baudelaire, Charles 9–11, 12, 37, 39, 135;
  'Parfum exotique' 31–2, 34, 35, 36, 39,
    43
Benjamin, Walter 9–10
Bernabé, Jean 57–8
  see also Éloge
Bhabha, Homi 1, 4, 67n22, 143
  'interstitial perspective' 2, 4
blackness:
  desire for 49
  as lost object 37
Bloom, Harold 34
  anxiety of influence 25, 36
Brathwaite, Edward Kamau 22n62
Breton, André 27, 28, 46–50
  see also Légitime Défense
Britton, Celia 20, 81n53, 82n54, 144n70
Burton, Richard 163n38

Cahier d'un retour au pays natal (Césaire,
  Aimé) 24, 28–31, 35–55 passim 66,
  130, 136, 149, 154, 160, 181, 184
  see also intertextuality
Cailler, Bernadette 58n6
Capécia, Mayotte:
  Je suis martiniquaise 89–91; see also Fanon,
    Frantz; Hérémakhonon
Caruth, Cathy 74–6, 77, 79, 80
  see also Freud, Sigmund; trauma

INDEX

Castro, Fidel 80
Césaire, Aimé 26, 28, 30, 31n31, 56, 65, 66, 67n19, 68, 103n35, 105n37, 124n25, 124n26, 132n45. 135, 137n51, 153, 162
   and exemplarity 50
   influences of 29–30
   political career of 55n48
   see also *Cahier*
Césaire, Suzanne 26, 28, 29
Chamoiseau, Patrick 20–1n57, 72n32, 147, 150, 152n12, 153n19, 156n26, 162–3n38, 171, 175
   see also *Éloge*
Christophe, Henri 105n37
Cixous, Hélène 141
Clark, Vèvè 89n15
Clément, Catherine 141–2, 143–4
collective 70, 176
   v. individual 17, 54, 150
   past 171
   v. personal narratives 171
   representation and masculinity 151
colonialism:
   and emasculation 109
   and history 4–5; see also history, dominant; history, alternative
   neo 3
   and tradition 109–10
Condé, Maryse 18, 20–1, 64–5, 75n37, 93n26, 106n38, 109n40, 151n7, 170n47
   biography of 84–6, 158–9, 163
   and return to Africa movement 87–8
   similarity to protagonists 86–7
   see also *Hérémakhonon*; *Moi, Tituba*; *Saison; Traversée*
Confiant, Raphaël 30n29, 58, 152n12, 153n17, 171n49
   see also *Éloge*
consciousness:
   collective 54, 66, 69; see also *détour*, destination of
   historical 73
conteur 171–2
correspondances 10–11, 42
Corzani, Jack 26n9
créolité 22, 100 n, 32, 149, 150–1, 156n26, 166, 171, 175, 178, 179, 182
   and authenticity 58; see also *Discours*; *relation*
   and castration 153;
   critique of 172; definition of 151–2
   and gender 151, 152–5;
   and Glissant, Edouard 57
   and language, see *détour*
   see also *Éloge*
creolization, process of, see *Discours*
crossing 24, 56, 149
   and alterity 32; see also Baudelaire, 'Parfum exotique'; *Cahier*; Mallarmé, 'Brise marine'
   and anteriority 24; see also *Cahier* and créolité 175
   destination of 41–3
   and displacement 38
   failed 34–5; 45–50, 166; see also literary inheritance; Mallarmé, 'Brise marine'
   impossibility of 184
   and sexuality 129, 130–1, 162, 165
Crosta, Suzanne 156n27

Damas, Léon Gontran 29
Dante Alighieri 6
Davies, Carole Boyce 119n14
Davis, Angela 71, 120
de Man, Paul 6, 7–9
Degras, Priska 178n65
Deleuze, Gilles 149n3
Delgrès, Colonel 76–7
Delphic Oracle 106, 108
departure 160–2
   and alienation 163
   and creativity 163
   and history, see history, and departure
   as precondition for return 42–3
   and return 41–4, 46
   see also crossing; exile; return;
Derrida, Jacques 67
   and archive 77–8
   on incest 114–15
détour 63, 127, 130n42, 134, 138, 167, 182
   and alienation 64–5;
   and *créole* 63–4
   destination of 65–6
   logic of 65
   as metaphor 69
   as political quietism 64, 82
   and *Relation* 67–9
   and return 66–7; see also *Discours*; *relation*; *retour*
détournement 64
diaspora:
   African and Jewish 59n8, 75n36
   black 105, 164

INDEX   203

literacy of 89n15
and neurosis 102; see also *Hérémakhonon*
Dirlik, Arif 21
discontinuity 36, 56, 57, 76, 133, 154
  and history 72–3, 76; see also history,
    periodization of
  and maternity 136, 147
  and mother-child relationship 133, 136
  and nostalgia, see nostalgia, and
    discontinuity
Le Discours antillais (Glissant, Edouard)
  57–74 *passim* 76–7, 79–83
  theory of history in 58–9; see also
    relation
discourse:
  free direct 100
  indirect 100
  displacement 38–9
  and history 74; see also allegory;
    crossing; departure; history,
    continuity of; return; trauma
  tropological 107
double consciousness 95
  see also identity, split
DuBois, W. E. B. 95
Duras, Marguerite 126n32

Edwards, Brent 25n8
Éloge de la créolité (Bernabé, Jean;
  Chamoiseau, Patrick; Confiant,
  Raphaël) 21, 58, 150–5, 152n12, 162,
  163
  see also *créolité*
exemplarity 168–9, 170, 175, 177, 181
  and ambivalence 181
  and history 178
  resistance to 171; see also Césaire, Aimé
  and return 45
  and writing 170
exile 37, 65, 104, 105, 128–34, 160
  and blackness 37
  geographic 58
  and maternity 169
  and sexuality 131
  see also anteriority, black
exotic:
  as trope 11, 25, 28, 34–6; see also
    Baudelaire, 'Parfum Exotique;'
    Cahier; Mallarmé, 'Brise marine'
exoticism 39, 134
  disavowal of 47–8; see also *Cahier*
  inheritance of 24–5, 31, 55
  and *négritude* 50

of 3rd World literature 12; see also
  Jameson, Fredric
Exposition coloniale internationale 98n31

Fanon, Frantz 24n3, 68, 73n33
  on Capécia 89–91
Fido, Elaine Savory 119n14
Fineman, Joel 7, 14
francophone, definition of 18–19
Freud, Sigmund 75–6, 77–8, 79–80

Gauthier, Xavière 126n32
George, Rosemary Marangoly 14n39
Gilroy, Paul 56, 57n2, 59n8, 75n36
Glissant, Edouard 71, 72, 124n25, 124n26,
  137, 149n3, 151, 152, 154n22
  opacité 177;
  transversality 81
  see also *Discours*
Gramsci, Antonio 119n15
Griffiths, Gareth 2–3
Guattari, Felix 149n3
Guevara, Che 156n29

Hall, Stuart 60n9
Hargreaves, Alec 19
Harris, Wilson 22n62
Hawthorne, Nathaniel:
  The Scarlet Letter 130–1
Hérémakhonon (Condé, Maryse) 84, 87,
  88–103 *passim*
  criticisms of 91
  irony in 102
heterogeneity, see identity, split
history 179
  absence of 70–1, 105, 142–3
  alternative 117, 118–9, 143, 73–4
  Caribbean 70
  collective 170
  continuity of 56, 72–3, 154
  dominant 73–4, 82, 117, 127–8, 142
  fragmented 179–80
  and identity 17, 56
  and literature 71
  and materiality 15–16
  periodization of 71–3
  and postcolonialty 56, 71; see also
    postcolonial; postcoloniality;
  and poststructuralism 75
  and referentiality 79–81
  resistance to 171
  and sexuality 129n40

history (cont.)
　and trauma 74–82, 142–3; see also
　　Caruth, Cathy; Freud, Sigmund;
　　trauma
　and writing 115
home:
　acceptance of 62
　as exile 65
　as lost object 25
hybridity, see créolité; identity, split

identification:
　collective 45
　preconditions of 42–3
identity 184
　alienated 35–6
　Antillean 22–3, 102; see also antillanité;
　　créolité; négritude
　black 99
　and difference 65, 69; see also alienation;
　　alterity; Discours
　and history, see history, and identity
　politics of 17
　and politics 166
　and poststructuralism 12, 13–5; see also
　　Jameson, Fredric
　quest for 1, 92–3, 96–100, 102, 106,
　　107–8, 112, 168, 177–8
　and sexual violence 121–2;
　split, 91, 103, 119, 164–5; see also
　　antillianté; collective; créolité; négritude
internal dialogization 100
intertextuality 26–7, 29, 31–7, 50, 100, 107,
　　136, 160
Irele, Abiola 36n36
Irigaray, Luce 154n22

Jack, Belinda 18n48
Jakobson, Roman 68–9
Jameson, Fredric 11–8, 56, 97
　national allegories, 12, 182–3
Johnson, Barbara 17, 29
Joyce, James 170n46

Kesteloot, Lilyan 26n9, 27

Lacan, Jacques 125n27
lack 125
Lamiot, Christophe 156n27
Légitime défense, (Breton, André) 25, 27
Leiner, Jacqueline 27
Léro, Étienne 27
Les Antilles heureuses 25

Lévi-Strauss, Claude 139–41, 142
linguistic wholeness 16
　see also allegory; anteriority
Lionnet, Françoise 149–50, 157
literary inheritance 34–6, 46
　originality, black 27–8; see also,
　　exoticism, inheritance of
　see also, exotic, as trope
literature:
　and collective identity 150; see also
　　créolité
　and politics 138–9, 146, 147–8; see also
　　sorcery, and politics
　political possibilities of 138
loss 124, 133, 147

McClintock, Anne 3n7
McKinney, Mark 19
MacQueen, John 6n15
Mallarmé, Stephane:
　'Brise marine' 32–4, 36
Manzor-Coats, Lillian 119n9
marginality 1–2, 22, 103
Marx, Karl 170n46
Matouba 80
Maximin, Daniel 77n42, 106n38
melancholia 25
memory, failure of 16
Ménil, René 26
metaphor:
　and crossing 31, 52, 51
　doubleness of 39–41
　and exemplarity 51–2
Michelet, Jules:
　La Sorcière 125–6, 141
Miller, Arthur:
　The Crucible 125n29
Miller, Christopher 8–9, 11, 12, 37
　Africanist discourse and allegory 11
Moi, Tituba, sorcière . . . Noire de Salem
　(Condé, Maryse) 71, 117–25, 127–39
　passim, 142–8, 162, 184
　epigraph of 117–22
Moncada 80
Monroe, Jonathan 153n17
Morrison, Toni 70n26
Moudileno, Lydie 23n65, 157n31
Mudimbe-Boyi, Elisabeth 118n8, 119
multiculturalism 16–17
Munley, Ellen 159n36
mythology, feminist, see Moi, Tituba

négresse, see alterity, black

INDEX

négritude 22, 29, 30, 37, 66, 68, 82, 151, 178
  antillanité 57
  and castration 153
  see also Césaire, Aimé
neurosis 143
Ngaté, Jonathan 27n14, 87n6
Ngkandu Nkashama, Pius 87n6
Nkrumah, Kwame 85
nostalgia 9, 14, 15–6, 24–5, 36–7, 95, 134
  and discontinuity 115
  and exotic 135–6
  and motherhood 136
  see also anteriority, lost; exoticism;
    Jameson, Fredric

Philcox, Richard 85
poetic language 55
  and unity 32–4, 42, 54–5
point d'intrication 68, 69, 138
political:
  and personal 108, 112, 114
  v. personal 96–9, 101–2
postcolonial:
  definition of 1–4, 18–9, 22–3
  literature and history 178
postcoloniality
  criticisms of 19–20
  and exemplarity 2
  francophone 30
  and history 79; see also history
  and poststructuralism 2, 183
  and representation 5, 22, 23
  and writing 143
poststructuralism, see identity; Jameson,
  Fredric; postcoloniality

reading, act of 150
realism, and landscape 137
referentiality 79–80
relation 182, 184
  v. assimilation 60
  and impossibility of return 61
  as metonymy 69
  process of 58–9; see also créolité
  and trauma, see also trauma, 60
  see also anteriority, lost; détour; Discours;
    retour
representation 51–2, 120, 149, 151, 178, 183
  problems of 55
  see also exemplarity; signification
retour 63, 102, 130n42, 181
  see also détour; Discours; relation
return 28, 31, 98, 134, 136, 197

to archetypes 108; see also archetypes;
    Saison
  failed 101–3; see also Hérémakhonon
  literary 134–8
  resistance to, see détour; Discours; relation;
    retour
  successful 53–5; see also Cahier;
    consciousness, collective
  see also Cahier; exotic, as trope;
    intertextuality; literary production,
    and difference; négritude
Rimbaud, Arthur 26–7, 103n35
Rody, Caroline 133n46
rupture:
  and origin 114–116
  see also Discours; history, alternative;
    history, and discontinuity; history,
    and trauma

Safran, William 62n12
Said, Edward 71–2
Une saison à Rihata (Condé, Maryse) 84, 87,
    88, 103–16 passim
  archetypes in 106–7
Salem Witch Trials 117, 125, 142
Sartre, Jean-Paul 28, 50
Scharfman, Ronnie 27
Schwarz-Bart, Simone 122n24
self-hatred, racial 89, 93
Senghor, Léopole Sédar 29
shipwreck, see crossing, failed
signification 124–5, 127, 141
slavery 58, 62, 74, 137
  in Antilles 76n41
  middle passage 56, 121
  see also retour
Slemon, Stephen 3, 6–7
sorcery:
  and gender 125–6
  and hysteria 141–4; see also Cixous,
    Hélène; Clément, Catherine
  and maternity 123;
  and performativity 139
  and politics 138–9
  and postcoloniality 127
  as return 142
  and writing 124–5, 127, 139
Sourieau, Marie-Agnès 169n45
Spivak, Gayatri Chakravorty 5, 117, 119,
    120, 184
stereotypes 17, 93–5
  see also identity
Subaltern Studies Group 5

subaltern, *see* Spivak, Gayatri Chakravorty
Suk, Julie 27
supplementarity 2, 67–8
　see also Derrida, Jacques; *détour*; *relation*; *retour*

textuality, performative 54
Tiffin, Helen 2–3
Touré, Sékou 85, 92n23
trauma 61, 67, 68, 74–7, 100, 112, 114, 125n27, 141, 142, 154
　and the Antilles 60–1
　and Glissant 81–3
　and latency 81, 82
　original 131, 169n45
　and repetition 98, 104, 107, 114, 132, 143, 144, 154; *see also* archetypes
　and rupture 114–6
　sexual 122
　see also Caruth, Cathy; Freud, Sigmund; supplementarity
travel, trope of 12, 24, 36, 45, 56
Traversée de la Mangrove 105, 149–50, 155–80 passim 181, 184

imprisonment in 159–63, 166–8; *see also* departure
　as mock epic 173–4
　reception of 171
Tropiques 26

Viatte, August 26n9

Walcott, Derek 22n62
Warner-Vieyra, Myriam 112n41
Williams, Eric 93n25
writing:
　and authenticity 175
　and departure 174
　and failure 177
　role of 157
　and travel 163
　as transgression 127

Yerushalmi, Yosef Hayim 78
Young, Robert 5n12

Zobel, Joseph 153n19